TO FATHOM THE GIST

Volume I

Approaches to the Writings of G. I. Gurdjieff

by Robin Bloor

KARNAK PRESS

To Fathom The Gist: Vol I

To Fathom the Gist

Volume I

Approaches to the Writings of G. I. Gurdjieff

Second Edition: 2025

Copyright © 2019 by Robin Bloor
All Rights Reserved.

Without limiting the rights under copyright reserved above, no part of this publication may be reproduced, stored in or introduced into a retrieval system, or transmitted, in any form or by any means (electronic, mechanical, photocopying, recording or otherwise), without the prior written permission of both the copyright owner and the above publisher of the book. Please do not participate in or encourage piracy of copyrighted materials in violation of the author's rights. Purchase only authorized editions.

The author has made every effort to provide accurate Internet addresses in this work at the time of publication, neither the publisher nor author assumes any responsibility for errors or changes that occur after publication. Further, the publisher and author have no control over and do not assume responsibility for third-party websites or their content.

ISBN 978-0-9789791-4-0

Printed in the United States of America

Karnak Press
Austin, Texas

Dedication

To Rina Hands, a lion of a woman and a teacher of men.

> "I have buried in this book certain bones, so that certain dogs with great curiosity and strong scent may dig down to them and, strange thing, when they have done so, are men."
>
> ~ Gurdjieff

Contents

Chapter 1: The Foreword   1
The aim of this book. Gurdjieff's advice. To fathom the gist. The aim of the first series. The use of the first person plural. The contents of this book - "how to." The various versions of *The Tales*. Gurdjieff's grandchildren. Quotations. The appendices and their purpose.

Chapter 2: A Spectrum of Techniques   7
The uniqueness of *The Tales*. Why did he write in his chosen style? The Introduction to *Meetings with Remarkable Men*,The Arousing of Thought, Form and Sequence. Our role as Hassein. Egoplastikoori and objective art. Work on oneself. The art of fathoming: intellectual postures and processes, background research, objective science, language and style, intentional inexactitudes, etymology and neologisms, the allegorical perspective, the Oskiano of "man in quotation marks." Gurdjieff's comments on the first series.

Chapter 3: Intellectual Postures and Processes   15
Postures. The monkey mind, associative mind, imagination, the value of associative mind. Pattern matching, comparison and conceptual connections. Logical confrontation and common sense. Suggestibility. Analysis and logical thinking. Attention. Representation, imagination, picturing. Materializing thought. Holding the dove, dressing theory up as fact, skepticism. Impartiality. Thinking by analogy. The cosmos as an analog. Questions and learning to formulate them. Keeping questions open. Active mentation. Pondering. Pondering is founded in wonder. Concentration. Constatation. Consistency and completeness. Words. Mentation by thought and mentation by form. Gurdjieff's choice of words. The problem of words. "Love" as an example of the poverty of the English language. Mentation. Egoplastikoori, psychic picturings. The principle of

Itoklanoz. Aim. The analogy of the prison. The development of the intellect.

Chapter 4: background research   **49**
The various English versions of *The Tales*. The 1931 Version. The *1950 Version*. The writing of the 1950 Version. Versions in other languages. The 1992 version – the arch-ludicrous. Practical problems with the 1992 version. Faults with the 1992 version. Researching *The Tales* and research into Gurdjieff, the Man. Our ignorance of context within *The Tales*. The First "Growl" – a criticism of Tolstoy. Tolstoy's excommunication. Prosphora, an unfamiliar word. Karapet of Tiflis. Who is Karapet based on, if anyone? Hypnotism. The misspelling of Braid's name. Mesmer, Pedrini, Ephrosinia and Bambini. Babylon and the era Beelzebub discusses – is it factual? Concerning the opinion of others. Zilnotrago and its possible etymological meaning. The possible etymological meaning of Salzmanino.

Chapter 5: Objective Science   **79**
Galileo and the church as the scientific authority. Modern science as the new scientific authority. Objective Science and subjective science, the fundamental distinction and the difference of approach. Everything is material. The distinction between data and theory. Knowledge bought at the price of labor. Proof in subjective science, proof in Objective Science. The great divide. Our universe as an internal universe. Hydrogen 48 as the dividing line. The crucible. Datum, information, knowledge, understanding and their relationships. Turning information into knowledge. Etymology of the meaning of understanding and the meaning of superstition. Objective Science disagrees with contemporary science. The ether and the view of contemporary science. Etherokrilno. Time. Time as a dimension. Objective Science does not view time as a dimension. Laws of physics. Big Bang. Laws of thermodynamics. The fundamental laws of Physics and the fundamental laws of Objective Science do not at all correspond. Disagreement on the atom. Disagreement on evolution. Disagreement on the nature of suns, planets, moons. The creation myths. Extrapolation. An expanding universe. Quantum mechanics. The crisis in modern Physics.

Occam's Razor and Occam's Corollary. Reasons to think otherwise. The electric universe, a plasma cosmology. Propositions of Objective Science.

Chapter 6: Language and Style   109

Paying attention. Bon ton literary language. Evidence of Gurdjieff's varying writing style. The defects of the reader. How well do we really understand English? Our subjectivity. The use of uncommon English words. The difference between intentional and voluntary. The problem with the verb "feel." Gurdjieff's language skills. Three universal languages. Loan words and foreign words. Ersatz. Solianka. Tzimus. Shachermacher. Milch. Cinque- contra-uno. Gurdjieff's typography. Quotation marks. Capitalization. Full capitalization. Italics. Dashes and hyphens. Footnotes. Meaning by indirect reference. What is called, what they call, something like. Meaning from distinctive variation. Reason. Sun Absolute. CREATOR. Meaning from distinctive qualifications. Being. Essence. Meaning by repetition. Kundabuffer. Lists and their meanings. Gurdjieff's long sentences. An example analyzed. A musical phrase from a symphony. The role of literary analysis as an aid to reading *The Tales*.

Chapter 7: Intentional Inexactitudes   151

Objective art. Intentional inexactitudes as anomalies. Errata. Typographical errors. Anulios. Braid and Brade. Ten books in three series??? The sun neither lights nor heats. The wild scientific goose chase. What Beelzebub actually says. The Ape Question. Darwinian theory? A biological absurdity. Allegory. The New York restaurant. The anomaly of the midget gas stove. The cock cries at midnight. The elevation of Tibet. The anachronism of Buddha in *The Tales*. The size of Atlantis. Beings on other planets of our solar system. The absurd titles of Algamatant and Looisos. When men had tails. Objective time calculation. The mooring of the Occasion. Why at the North Pole? The anomaly of the first transapalnian perturbation. Word choices. Rimk. Shepherds and fishermen. The Gwyniad.

Chapter 8: Etymology and Neologisms   175

Gurdjieff the philologist. The diversity of English and its irregularities. Constructed meaning in different languages. Linguistic word formation. Agglutination. Compounding. Blending. What is the purpose of the neologisms. Gurdjieff explaining and failing to explain meanings. The surprising etymology of Sakaki, Algamatant and Looisos. Classifying the neologisms. Neologisms and morphemes. Word pronunciation. "Aieioiuoa." Hallelujah. The use of information technology to investigate the neologisms. Wikipedia. Etymology. Translation. An exercise for the reader: the word "Pirmaral."

Chapter 9: Allegory 189

Narcissus. Itoklanoz. Egoplastikoori. Familiar allegories: B influence. Snakes and ladders. Shakespeare's psychic dramas. King Lear. The Fool in Lear. The New Testament. The actualization of the Passion. The woman caught in adultery. Hamartia. The Passion as a psychic drama. *The Tales* and The Thousand and One Nights. Scheherazade and Shahryar. The great allegory of *The Tales*. The education of Hassein. Metaphors and symbols. Literal meaning, keva. A list of metaphors. Beelzebub. Ahoon. Hassein. The Captain. Mullah Nassr Eddin as the Fool. Gornahoor Harharkh. Gornahoor Rakhoorkh. The journey and the various planets visited, as an octave. Beelzebub's sojourns to the Planet Earth. The genesis of the Moon. Is Anulios real? The etymology of Anulios. The Italians – an example of a detailed analysis.

Chapter 10: The Oskiano of "Man In Quotation Marks" 227

The treasure hunt. Iransamkeep. Intellectual activity is not one-centered activity. Attention. Pondering. The Oskiano of the intellectual center. The driver of the carriage and his state – our state. Vocabulary. Mentation by words. The Oskiano of the emotional center. Egoplastikoori. The Tower of Babel. The twin princes. Harmony.

Contents

The Appendices   239

Appendix A: Notes on Intellectual Postures And Processes.

Appendix B: Notes on Research.

Appendix C: Notes On Objective Science.

Appendix D: Notes On Language and Style.

Appendix E: Notes on Etymology and Neologisms, List of Neologisms, The Morphemes of the Neologisms.

Appendix F : Notes on Intentional Inexactitudes.

Appendix G: Notes on Allegorical Meaning.

Bibliography   275

Author's Autobiographical Notes   277

To Fathom The Gist: Vol I

Chapter 1: The Foreword

—⁂—

Having thus begun, I can now be quite at ease, and should even, according to the notions of religious morality existing among contemporary people, be beyond all doubt assured that everything further in this new venture of mine will now proceed, as is said, "like a pianola."
Gurdjieff ~ *The Tales*

Although this is the first chapter of this book, it is in reality a foreword rather than an introduction. We provide information here that we believe you, the reader, need to read before starting the book. Forewords to books can sometimes be filled with nothing of value, but hopefully this one is not.

The Aim of This Book

The aim of this book, the first in a short series of such books, is to assist those interested in The Work, or already involved in The Work, in their efforts to try to understand Gurdjieff's writings. It focuses primarily on Gurdjieff's magnum opus, *An Objectively Impartial Criticism of the Life of Man or Beelzebub's Tales to His Grandson*, which constitutes the First Series of *All and Everything*. For the sake of brevity, we refer to it as *The Tales* throughout this volume.

In approaching Gurdjieff's written works, our attention is naturally drawn to his advice on this matter which is declared on the first page of *The Tales*. He writes:

> I find it necessary on the first page of this book, quite ready for publication, to give the following advice:
>
> "Read each of my written expositions thrice:
>
> Firstly-at least as you have already become mechanized to read all your contemporary books and newspapers.
>
> Secondly-as if you were reading aloud to another person.

And only thirdly- try and fathom the gist of my writings."

Only then will you be able to count upon forming your own impartial judgment, proper to yourself alone, on my writings.

And only then can my hope be actualized that according to your understanding you will obtain the specific benefit for yourself which I anticipate, and which I wish for you with all my being.

Anyone who approaches *The Tales* in the manner Gurdjieff advised quickly realizes that these three ways of reading the book are distinctly different. The second and third way are unfamiliar forms of reading to most of us and, as a consequence, we may not perform either of them well. Nevertheless, that is Gurdjieff's unambiguous advice.

It is apparent from experience that it is possible to read Gurdjieff's works "at least as you have already become mechanized to read" quite a few times. The second mode of reading involves more attention. It is not natural for us to read in this way, unless we have experience of reading aloud to others. Neither is it precisely the same as reading to others, since in this mode of reading one is both the reader and the listener. Consequently, we need to divide our attention between reading and listening. This is not the same as listening to a reading from the book or a recording of the book being read, although, in our view, this is also a useful way to experience *The Tales*. Many people have, no doubt, also read *The Tales* more than once in this manner.

The third mode of reading that Gurdjieff recommends requires attempting to "fathom the gist."

We have encountered very few devotees of *The Tales* who have made anything more than a meagre attempt to fathom the gist. We have even witnessed "elders" in The Work obviously deflect questions from others about how to fathom the gist, probably because they themselves simply had no idea of how to do this. We have witnessed poor advice being given and we have witnessed no advice being given. It is one of the reasons this book was written.

Fathoming the gist is not going to be achieved in a single reading or even a few extra readings. *The Tales* is far too long and too deep for that. In our experience, as well as start-to-finish readings, it involves flitting forwards and backwards in the book to follow up references or simply to gather data. The more familiar we become with this book, the more we realize how meticulous Gurdjieff was in his choice of words. So, at the very start, he chooses the metaphorical words "fathom the gist." The word "fathom" implies getting to the bottom of, or at least going

Chapter 1: The Foreword

very deep into. The word "gist" implies the heart of the matter, or the kernel, or the essence. He could have chosen to use the word "understand" but he did not, he chose words that were metaphorical.

At the commencement of *The Tales*, Gurdjieff describes the three series of his writings in the following way:

> All written according to entirely new principles of logical reasoning and strictly directed towards the solution of the following three cardinal problems:
>
> FIRST SERIES: To destroy, mercilessly, without any compromises whatsoever, in the mentation and feelings of the reader, the beliefs and views, by centuries rooted in him, about everything existing in the world.
>
> SECOND SERIES: To acquaint the reader with the material required for a new creation and to prove the soundness and good quality of it.
>
> THIRD SERIES: To assist the arising, in the mentation and in the feelings of the reader, of a veritable, non-fantastic representation not of that illusory world which he now perceives, but of the world existing in reality.

The first series is *The Tales* and his stated intention is to effect a complete and thorough change, both in the mentation and in the feeling of the reader, destroying "the beliefs and views, by centuries rooted in him, about everything existing in the world."

If we take him at his word, then to those of you who have read *The Tales* three times, we can ask: "Has it had Gurdjieff's desired impact on you?" If he did not mean what he wrote, why did he write it?

Use Of The First Person Plural

Throughout this book, the author never uses the word "I" to refer to himself. Instead, he uses the first person plural, "we." Because of the nature of the subject matter – considered suggestions on "How to fathom the gist" – it may help to know that most of what is written, useful or otherwise, is based on the efforts of a single person.

It is not the output of a Beelzebub's Tales Study Group. The author took account of feedback from a few individuals in the Work (mentioned in the acknowledgements on the final page of this book) both prior to publication and in the subsequent revision of this book. Nevertheless, some of the author's ideas are not original. He has read other books that consider the meaning of *The Tales* and he has had many conversations with others about the book. Where he has encountered ideas and insights he considered useful, he has included them. So, the author's use of the word "we" can be taken at times to incorporate, to some degree, other individuals who have struggled with *The Tales*.

In the main, however, the author's use of the first person plural simply reflects the fact that the author does not pretend to unity, either in respect of his inner world or in respect of the ideas and techniques he attempts to convey in this book.

The first person plural, "we," is frequently used in books to try to inveigle the reader into agreeing with what is written, as though the author is not just writing on his own behalf but – in some magical way – knows and represents the interests of the reader. This author hopes his readers do not fall into mindless agreement with what he has written. He hopes instead that the reader will adopt an attitude of healthy skepticism to everything he or she encounters in these pages.

Concerning the Contents

In writing this book, its author has been mindful of the problem of "giving too much." It is an awkward dilemma. Gurdjieff intended his readers to put in a very considerable effort to fathom the gist of his writings. Thus, anyone who produces a book like this one, which attempts to assist readers of *The Tales* to understand more, runs the risk of doing the reader's work for them. There is a balance that needs to be struck.

If the author provides too much, he may steal the reader's opportunity to make useful efforts, and consequently the reader may undervalue what is revealed. If the author provides too little, then the reader will not be assisted in any useful way, and indeed may simply take nothing useful from this book. So, the author is obliged to play the role of Goldilocks and use his judgement to determine what is "just right."

The aim of this book is not to reveal as much as possible of what Gurdjieff may have included in *The Tales*, but to put readers in a position to discover such things themselves. This book is about how to discover meaning in *The Tales* that the reader might otherwise not have found. It is a "how to" book. The author sincerely hopes that the reader will realize that the techniques described and discussed in this

Chapter 1: The Foreword

book are truly practical, and will, as a consequence, apply them – and perhaps even improve on them.

The Various Versions of The Tales

There are many versions of *The Tales*. Aside from the fact that it has been translated into many languages, it was originally translated from Russian to English. An initial English version was published privately by Orage in 1931. The 1950 version, published immediately after Gurdjieff's death, was later revised and that revision was published in 1992. It is distinctly different from the 1950 version. So, for English readers of the book, there are three versions that we are aware of. We discuss this issue in *Chapter 4: Background Research*.

Gurdjieff's Grandchildren

Some writers have suggested that we are Gurdjieff's grandchildren, in the sense that nearly all of the pupils that Gurdjieff taught are no longer living. If we think of such pupils symbolically as Gurdjieff's children, then those of us who were taught by his children can think of ourselves as his grandchildren. If we accept this interpretation of the title of *The Tales*, then this book was specifically aimed at our generation.

Gurdjieff was, by all accounts, a very powerful teacher. As far as we are aware, although many of his immediate pupils were themselves extremely impressive, none of them appears to have attained the extraordinary ability to teach others that Gurdjieff had. Consequently, we may come to the opinion that The Work is a descending octave, that has, as is lawful, begun to descend.

Gurdjieff knew that such a descent was inevitable; he even writes about it several times in *The Tales*. So, we believe, he took measures to also provide an ascending movement to counteract the inevitable descent. We believe that his writings constitute one such ascending movement.

Some have suggested that *The Tales* is a precise and revealing manual of The Work that allows us to distinguish the genuine from the fake. Some have even suggested that *The Tales* is a living teacher that can raise us far above the level of being in which we currently wallow. Perhaps they are right.

Quotations

Each chapter of the book commences with a quotation from Gurdjieff.

The Appendices

This book was written and structured to be a practical guide or manual. Its content consists mainly of explanations, examples, and supporting material. The author's intention is for the reader to read, or even study, each chapter with an eye to practically applying its contents. The hope is that the reader would keep their copy close at hand when trying to fathom the gist of *The Tales*.

We have assumed that most readers will appreciate having a summary of what each chapter explains and will know how to make use of it. We provide such summaries as a series of Appendices rather than inserting them at the end of each chapter.

For many of the chapters, we refer to books we have read with which the reader can, we believe, enrich the ideas presented in the chapter. We mention these books in the summaries but also provide a complete bibliography. The same can be said of Internet resources that we have used in our own efforts to fathom the gist of *The Tales*; we mention them in summaries where appropriate.

Finally, in an effort to assist the work of discovering the meaning of Gurdjieff's many neologisms, we provide a complete list of them and we also provide a list of morphemes along with the words they occur in.

Chapter 2: A Spectrum of Techniques

—⚏—

"Eldest of my grandsons! Listen and always remember my strict injunction to you: In life never do as others do."
Having said this, she gazed at the bridge of my nose and evidently noticing my perplexity and my obscure understanding of what she had said, added somewhat angrily and imposingly:
"Either do nothing–just go to school–or do something nobody else does."

Gurdjieff ~ The Tales

He followed his grandmother's advice. As an author, he wrote a unique book, and wrote it in a way that no book was ever written before. He invented a unique style that owed little or nothing to European literary traditions. He gradually and meticulously edited this book in accord with his observations of the reactions of those who listened to it being read out. This is *The Tales*. It is unique: unique in its scope, unique in its wisdom and unique even in its poetry. However, it is not easy to access. It was deliberately written to be hard to fathom. It presents the reader with a series of challenges that are unfamiliar and somewhat daunting. To discover the jewels hidden beneath the pages of the book, he forces the reader to pay attention, to make considerable effort and to employ all his or her capabilities.

Why?

Gurdjieff makes no secret of why he chose to write in the way that he did. He thought that it was important for the reader to understand why. So he tells us. If you wish to better understand this, then please do the following three things:

Read through *Chapter I of Meetings with Remarkable Men*, up to page 30. Do this several times so you become completely familiar with what Gurdjieff tells us there. This may help you to appreciate one of Gurdjieff's intentional writing techniques. He infuses his books with tales, and these tales are crafted to directly address the emotional rather than the intellectual side of the reader. That section of *Meetings with Remarkable Men* provides a detailed perspective on this mode of writing.

Secondly, reread *Chapter 1, The Arousing of Thought* of *The Tales*. In that introduction, Gurdjieff uses the literary technique he describes so thoroughly in *Meetings with Remarkable Men*. His several tales here include the death of his grandmother, the Transcaucasian Kurd, Karapet of Tiflis, the provincial Russian merchant and more. In our view, these tales constitute Gurdjieff's advice-not-to-the-intellect on how to approach his written works.

Finally, reread *Chapter 46, Beelzebub Explains to His Grandson the Significance of the Form and Sequence Which He Chose for Expounding the Information Concerning Man*. This also contains important information to assimilate.

One needs to keep in mind Gurdjieff's initial statement that his written works are:

> "All written according to entirely new principles of logical reasoning."

This may sound bombastic, but it is probably a simple statement of truth.

Throughout *The Tales*, we are gradually invited into the position of Hassein. Indeed, we fairly quickly become willing to occupy Hassein's position at the feet of Beelzebub, amazed by his many stories. In Chapter 46, we are told by Beelzebub that:

> "When at the beginning of our journey I noticed that you were very interested in the three-brained beings of the planet Earth, I then decided, under the aspect of gratifying that interest of yours, to tell you everything about them in such a way that there should be crystallized in you for your future being-associations the required what are called 'Egoplastikoori, without any admixture of doubt.
>
> "For this, I have in almost all my tales strictly held to the two following principles:
>
> "The first: not to say anything as if it were my own personal opinion, in order that data necessary for your own convictions

should not be crystallized in you in a prepared form according to the opinions of another.

"And in accordance with the second principle: to relate to you in just such an order and in such a premeditated and selected sequence about all the events which proceeded on this planet Earth connected with the arising among these three-brained beings who have taken your fancy, of various gradually progressing inner and outer abnormalities in the process of their ordinary being existence, the total of which has given them their present desolate and almost inescapable state—in order that you should be able to marshal your own subjective reasoning concerning all causes, only on the basis of certain facts which I have told you.

"I decided to do this in order that many diversely essenced 'Egoplastikoori' for your future logical confrontation should be crystallized in corresponding localizations in your common presence, and also in order that from active mentation the proper elaboration in you of the sacred substances of Abrustdonis and Helkdonis for the purpose of coating and perfecting both of your higher being-parts should proceed more intensively."

Gurdjieff, it seems, states that his book is objective and that its form and content are intended to directly crystallize specific Egoplastikoori for our future being-associations. It is important, then, for us to understand what the word "egoplastikoori" means.

Egoplastikoori

In our view, all three series of Gurdjieff's writings are objective works of art. Put simply, an objective work of art is one that has an objective effect upon everyone who experiences it. Gurdjieff expressed this idea to Ouspensky, in *In Search of the Miraculous*, as follows:

"In real art there is nothing accidental. It is mathematics. Everything in it can be calculated, everything can be known beforehand. The artist knows and understands what he wants to convey and his work cannot produce one impression on one man and another impression on another, presuming, of course, people on one level. It will always, and with mathematical certainty, produce one and the same impression."

"At the same time the same work of art will produce different impressions on people of different levels. And people of lower levels will never receive from it what people of higher levels receive.

This is real, objective Art. Imagine some scientific work—a book on astronomy or chemistry. It is impossible that one person should understand it in one way and another in another way. Everyone who is sufficiently prepared and who is able to read this book will understand what the author means, and precisely as the author means it. An objective work of art is just such a book, except that it affects the emotional and not only the intellectual side of man."

If *The Tales* is an objective work of art, the goal of the serious and devoted reader ought to be to receive whatever influence the book is capable of delivering. To do so, he will need to read the book exactly as Gurdjieff advises. He would be foolish not to.

Two things are clear:

1. The reader is instructed directly by the author on how to read the book. The reader will receive far more if he follows Gurdjieff's directions, less or nothing if he does not. In our experience, he will receive little unless he reads it three times as directed. We do not disparage the second mode of reading the book. It is necessary and it is rewarding. Nevertheless, our experience suggests the major part of what can be received from the book emerges when attempting to fathom the gist.

2. Readers of the book will in most cases also be working on themselves. We do not intend to discuss the nature of working on oneself directly in this book, although we will have need to touch on it from time to time. However, we note from our experience that many ideas in The Work are difficult if not impossible to understand unless one works on oneself. In time, if you work on yourself effectively, it will bring results in one way or another; you will change. If that change is productive, then what is called "being" by Gurdjieff will increase. In our experience, this will have an impact on one's ability to comprehend aspects of Gurdjieff's writings. *The Tales* is thus a natural and helpful companion to one's personal work.

In Gurdjieff's above reported talk, he says that "An objective work of art is just such a book, except that it affects the emotional and not only the intellectual side of man." Thus, we should not be expecting the outcome of studying this book simply to be our comprehension of superior intellectual representations of the universe or ourselves. Gurdjieff also says about *The Tales*: "Everyone who is sufficiently

Chapter 2: A Spectrum of Techniques

prepared and who is able to read this book will understand what the author means, and precisely as the author means it."

After Gurdjieff began to teach, he spent far more time on writing than he did composing music with Thomas de Hartmann, or inventing and teaching Movements to Movements classes.

It is our view that Gurdjieff is attempting to provoke two distinct changes in the psyche of the reader. We discuss this in greater detail later, but we think it important to mention it now.

- The first change he wishes to provoke is to provide new words to employ in our "mentation by words." We have few appropriate words in our language for the subjects he covers. So often he uses obscure English words or invented English phrases. At other times he invents whole new words. One such word is "egoplastikoori." It relates to the other change he wishes to provoke.
- Understanding the meaning of the word "egoplastikoori" is important to fathoming the gist. He describes this word as meaning "psychic-picturings" and as determining the mentation of our essence, "mentation by form." We believe that his many tales supply us with "egoplastikoori" that can ultimately change that mentation.

It should be clear from this that fathoming the gist is not just an intellectual exercise. It is a three-centered effort and it walks hand-in-hand with other work on oneself. If pursued with effort, it brings results.

The Art of Fathoming

We have found the following activities productive and, to some degree, within the capability of anyone who is willing to put in the effort. We have thus devoted a chapter of this book to each one of these topics:

- **Intellectual Postures and Processes.** We need to employ the intellect to fathom the gist. There is work for it to do that only it can do. In some ways, those who have strong intellects may have an advantage. Nevertheless, the intellect can also become a barrier to progress and we need to prevent that from happening. Our suggestion is that we create our own intellectual approaches and methods for studying the book. To do so, we need to have a deeper understanding of what the intellect is capable of and how it works, particularly how it works in harmony with the emotional side of us.

- **Background Research.** Background research into the content of *The Tales* is, in our view, necessary. We need to complete our education where it is lacking in respect of the context of some of the topics Beelzebub touches on. Beelzebub speaks of ancient civilizations, including Babylon and Egypt, where there is a partial historical record. He covers Greece and Rome, where the historical record is fairly rich. He covers 20th century Russia, France, Germany, Britain, and America where information abounds, but about which we may be relatively uninformed. Also, many books have now been written that attempt to shed light on *The Tales*. It is even possible that every one of them contains useful information for us. Almost all such books we have read have proven useful in some ways. There are two different study guides – both useful. There are many books about The Work that do not relate directly to *The Tales*, but which can be helpful in understanding Gurdjieff's ideas and Gurdjieff himself. Such books are also, in our view, worth reading.

- **Objective Science.** In many places throughout the book, Beelzebub describes aspects of Objective Science. Consequently it will help if we have a firm grasp of what Objective Science is and how it differs from Subjective Science. This is not such a simple thing. It is not enough just to define differences. It is also necessary to discover the extent of our suggestibility and to master that weakness within us. In particular we need to unhook ourselves from any faith we might have in Subjective Science. Objective Science and Subjective Science are not in agreement.

- **Language and Style.** Gurdjieff does not write as other authors write. He uses the English language in a distinctly different way. He chooses rarely used English words and, at times, adds foreign words and expressions. He makes extensive use of punctuation to emphasize particular words or phrases. He forms sentences that are long and convoluted. In our view, the reader will be better equipped if he is armed with a knowledge of some of the literary techniques that Gurdjieff uses in *The Tales*.

- **Intentional Inexactitudes.** Beelzebub explains the importance of intentional inexactitudes in *Chapter 30, Art*. He deploys inexactitudes throughout all of his written works. When they are encountered they should immediately spark our attention, but in

Chapter 2: A Spectrum of Techniques

our reading of *The Tales* we often skim across them, not even noticing that something very odd has been placed onto the page. We do not stop to ask ourselves: "Why did he write that?" If we are to fathom the gist, we need to ask those questions. In our opinion, the importance of Gurdjieff's many intentional inexactitudes cannot be understated. They can be, and often are, keys that unlock doors.

- **Etymology and Neologisms.** Gurdjieff introduces many neologisms (new words) and unfamiliar names in *The Tales*. This is bewildering to readers, especially as many of the new words are utterly unfamiliar in their construction and difficult to pronounce. The meanings of these words are important, but not obvious. We have to discover their meaning by our own efforts in most cases. Although Gurdjieff sometimes provides an English explanation of the meaning, his neologisms often contain a more precise and revealing meaning than given by his explanations. Some of the keys to *The Tales* are buried in these words.

- **The Allegorical Perspective.** *The Tales* constitute a large and complex set of allegories. Unless you are familiar with allegorical writing, this on its own provides a barrier to fathoming the gist. We need to be able to receive and profit from his extensive use of allegory. The reader will be helped in his work on this aspect of *The Tales* if he quickly grasps the fact that many words that Gurdjieff uses are not to be understood literally, but as metaphorical symbols. Similarly the various tales that Beelzebub tells may have very little value if only the literal meaning of the tale is appreciated.

- **The Oskiano of "Man in Quotation Marks."** We cannot, in our view, presume to understand the mind of Gurdjieff. However we can, in a simplistic way, consider what he is trying to achieve for the reader of *The Tales*. In this chapter we attempt to synthesize the the range of approaches that were discussed, step by step, in the previous chapters of this book.

Gurdjieff is reported to have said:

"...in Beelzebub, I know, there is everything one must know. It is a very interesting book. Everything is there. All that exists, all that has existed, all that can exist. The beginning, the end, all the secrets of the creation of the world; all is there. But one must understand, and to understand depends on one's individuality. The more man has been instructed in a certain way, the more he can see.

Subjectively, everyone is able to understand according to the level he occupies, for it is an objective book, and everyone should understand something in it. One person understands one part, another a thousand times more. Now, find a way to put your attention on understanding all of Beelzebub. This will be your task, and it is a good way to fix a real attention. If you can put real attention on Beelzebub, you can have a real attention in life. You didn't know this secret. In Beelzebub there is everything, I have said it, even how to make an omelet. Among other things, it is explained; and at the same time there isn't a word in Beelzebub about cooking."

We can choose to take his statement seriously. If we do, then why would we not make *The Tales* the focus of our education from this day forward, in the hope that it will eventually become the foundation of our knowledge and being?

We do not for one moment suggest that the techniques and approaches that we try to articulate in this book are the only ones available for fathoming the gist of *The Tales*. There may be other techniques of mentation or even intuition of which we are unaware that can be usefully applied. Some may even be more effective and more powerful. The techniques described here are simply the ones we have used to effect and which we are capable of describing.

Chapter 3: Intellectual Postures and Processes

"A great deal can be found by reading. For instance, take yourself: you might already know a great deal if you knew how to read. I mean that, if you understood everything you have read in your life, you would already know what you are looking for now..."
Gurdjieff to Ouspensky ~ In Search of the Miraculous

We are three-brained. We have a horse, carriage, and driver; an emotional, moving, and intellectual center. If we observe our moving activities we notice that we take up postures and move between postures. To see the truth of this requires self-observation – a detailed knowledge of this is not arrived at without honest work on that. When we observe ourselves we notice that we have characteristic postures that we occupy at different times. If we have done the Movements, then in that activity we find ourselves taking up new unfamiliar postures and making changes between these postures.

It is easy to think of the moving center as adopting postures.

We can also think this way about the emotional center. We have a range of emotions. We can think of each emotion as being a particular emotional posture. We move from affection to anxiety, to hope, to joy, to fear, to boredom, to anger and so on. We can think of the activity of the emotional center as moving between postures.

Thus, it is also easy to think of the emotional center as adopting postures.

The intellectual center also has postures. However, these are more difficult to discern. We can easily list words that describe physical and emotional postures, but it is not so easy to create a list of words that describe thinking postures. Nevertheless, the intellectual center thinks. It has a variety of thinking behaviors.

If we are to succeed in fathoming the gist of *The Tales*, we will require effort from the thinking center. Some of us may be more adept than others in this, but few if any of us have ever actually been instructed how to think, or deliberately developed any capacity in the thinking center. If we are adept in this area it is most likely because we imitated parents, peers or teachers, and successfully managed to copy their good thinking habits.

A disciplined approach to mentation is helpful and possibly necessary for studying *The Tales*. Its study is not just an intellectual task, but significant intellectual effort is required. Some of this effort involves learning new techniques or exercising capabilities that are rarely used. Some of the effort simply involves marshaling one's attention.

The Monkey Mind

The psychological metaphor that symbolizes the workings of the normal mind as a monkey originates in Buddhism. It spread as a depiction of man's normal mind to other Eastern traditions: Zen Buddhism, Taoism and Confucianism. It is depicted in the classical Chinese epic novel *Journey to the West* written by Wu Cheng'en, where the main character is Sun Wukong, the Monkey King.

In general, this idea is of a mind that is restless, whimsical, indecisive and uncontrolled. In Chinese, the term for it is "xinyaun," which literally translates as "heart-mind-monkey." It may be helpful to us if we think of the monkey mind in those terms. It is monkey-like, it involves the intellect and it also involves the emotions.

Most of the time we think by association. We are sitting in an armchair thinking, perhaps, about the play we saw last night, when suddenly the cat jumps into our lap, so now we think of the cat. But our cellphone suddenly rings and we see that a relative is calling and we wonder what it is about. So we answer. And now we are suddenly pitched into a discussion of the upcoming wedding, and so on. This kind of meandering life is described by Gurdjieff in *Views from the Real World* in the following excerpt.

> In the morning you wake up under the influence of an unpleasant dream. The slightly depressed mood disappeared but has left its trace in a kind of lassitude and uncertainty of movement. You go to the mirror to brush your hair and by accident drop your hairbrush. You pick it up and just as you have dusted it off, you drop it again.

Chapter 3: Intellectual Postures And Processes

This time you pick it up with a shade of impatience and because of that you drop it a third time. You try to grab it in midair but instead, it flies at the mirror. In vain you jump to catch it. Smash! . . . a star-shaped cluster of cracks appears in the antique mirror you were so proud of. Hell! The records of discontent begin to turn. You need to vent your annoyance on someone. Finding that your servant has forgotten to put the newspaper beside your morning coffee, your cup of patience overflows and you decide you can no longer stand the wretched man in the house.

Now it is time for you to go out. Taking advantage of the fine day, your destination not being far away, you decide to walk while your car follows slowly behind. The bright sun somewhat mollifies you. Your attention is attracted to a crowd that has gathered around a man lying unconscious on the pavement. With the help of the onlookers the porter puts him into a cab and he is driven off to the hospital. Notice how the strangely familiar face of the driver is connected in your associations and reminds you of the accident you had last year. You were returning home from a gay birthday party. What a delicious cake they had there! This servant of yours who forgot your morning paper ruined your breakfast. Why not make up for it now? After all, cake and coffee are extremely important! Here is the fashionable cafe you sometimes go to with your friends. But why have you remembered about the accident? You had surely almost forgotten about the morning's unpleasantness. . . And now, do your cake and coffee really taste so good?

You see the two ladies at the next table. What a charming blonde! She glances at you and whispers to her companion, "That's the sort of man I like."

Surely none of your troubles are worth wasting time on or getting upset about. Need one point out how your mood changed from the moment you met the blonde and how it lasted while you were with her? You return home humming a gay tune and even the broken mirror only provokes a smile. But what about the business you went out for in the morning? You have only just remembered it . . . that's clever! Still, it does not matter. You can telephone. You lift the receiver and the operator gives you the wrong number. You ring again and get the same number. Some man says sharply that he is sick of you—you say it is not your fault, an altercation follows and you are surprised to learn that you are a fool and an idiot, and that if you call again . . . The rumpled carpet under your foot irritates you, and you should hear the tone of voice in which you reprove the servant who is handing you a letter. The letter is from a man you respect and whose good opinion you value. The contents of the letter are so flattering to you that your irritation gradually dies down and is replaced by the pleasantly embarrassed feeling that flattery arouses. You finish reading it in a most amiable mood.

When we observe ourselves, even if only in a rudimentary fashion, we see that this is how we normally function. Things happen that attract our attention, we attach to them no matter how unimportant they really are and our thoughts proceed accordingly. In this swinging-from-tree-to-tree-like-a-monkey we do not really think about anything, the thinking just happens by association, with our memories furnishing the material to weave into what we think and what we say. The involvement of the emotions is that they seem to provide the energy that attaches us to whatever is happening, and our thoughts proceed accordingly.

If we find nothing in the current moment that we want to attach to, then we may meander off into imagination. This behavior is well described by Lewis Carroll in his satirical poem, *The Aged Aged Man*:

I'll tell thee everything I can:
   There's little to relate.
I saw an aged aged man,
   A-sitting on a gate.
"Who are you, aged man?" I said,
   "And how is it you live?"
And his answer trickled through my head,
   Like water through a sieve.

He said "I look for butterflies
   That sleep among the wheat:
I make them into mutton-pies,
   And sell them in the street.
I sell them unto men," he said,
   "Who sail on stormy seas;
And that's the way I get my bread –
   A trifle, if you please."

Chapter 3: Intellectual Postures And Processes

> *But I was thinking of a plan*
>   *To dye one's whiskers green,*
> *And always use so large a fan*
>   *That they could not be seen.*
> *So, having no reply to give*
>   *To what the old man said,*
> *I cried "Come, tell me how you live!"*
>   *And thumped him on the head.*

We may have observed such behavior in ourselves. Someone is talking to us and we simply stop listening and drift off into imagination. We associate to something else and go with that. And later we stumble back into the conversation making an effort to disguise the fact that we completely lost the thread.

Thinking by association is not without value. We memorize by association. Indeed, techniques we've encountered to strengthen one's memory are mostly techniques for organizing our associative mechanisms for remembering. Associative thinking often leads us to events we have experienced. This becomes clear if we try to answer a "quiz question" such as: "Who won the men's 100 meters in the 2012 Olympics?" We respond by associating to whatever memory we may have of the 2012 Olympics and our mind either produces an answer by association or comes up blank.

In reading *The Tales*, our mind will also associate at times to our memory of some event or other, or perhaps to something we have read on a topic that Beelzebub is describing. This may be a useful association or it may not. If it is not a useful association we need to detach ourselves from it at once so that we do not waste any time on it. This means struggling with our "tendency to attachment" or, as it is more frequently called in The Work, identification.

Pattern Matching

We learn to match patterns that we experience. We take in impressions and in doing so we learn patterns. If you know someone well, then even at a distance you can recognize them. Their appearance or the way that they move identifies them. You recognize their pattern. If someone looks like and moves like someone you know, you may be mistaken. But such situations are rare.

You learned long ago to recognize the words you see on a page. Reading has become a deeply ingrained habit. If you read some words in an unfamiliar typeface, you can still read them. Even handwriting that you have never seen before can usually be read. But if it is Arabic script and you are unfamiliar with that script, you cannot even decipher what the letters are. You have no pattern for that script.

Pattern matching is a capability that everyone has. People use it to do crosswords, to play card games, to play chess, to play backgammon, and many other such games. We use patterns to comprehend the world. For example, you have some inner concept of what a tree is. We go on a nature walk and you can recognize what is and what is not a tree – even if you encounter a species of tree you have never seen before. You are matching the patterns of what you perceive to your inner concept of a tree.

Pattern matching is the main way that we make comparisons and conceptual connections. The horse, for example, is well known to be a symbol for the emotional center. When we witness the behavior of a horse we can get a sense of why it is such an appropriate symbol. And yet there are many things about a horse which are not at all related to emotions. The emotional part of us does not have a specific number of legs, or a tail. It does not feed on grass and hay. There are many dissimilar things. And yet the nature of emotions and the nature of a horse exhibit a common and recognizable pattern.

Pattern matching is particularly important in attempting to access the meaning of allegories.

Logical Confrontation – Common Sense

The word "logic" comes from the Greek "logos," meaning "word or reason." The word "reasoning" is often used to describe the process of deriving proofs of a proposition from a set of principles or premises. Fairly pure examples of this can be found in the proofs of mathematical theorems. In mathematics, the practitioner is usually exploring well defined algebras where the axioms of the algebra are known and unambiguous. Consequently, mathematical variables are well behaved.

Once we attempt to apply the same logical processes to words, we have entered a less certain field, as words are not as well behaved as mathematical variables. Nevertheless, there are impressive examples of the application of logic to be found – in Plato's Dialogues, for example. If we think we need to, we can study such works, and we can also usefully study the common errors in logic that people frequently make.

Chapter 3: Intellectual Postures And Processes

However, for the most part, we know how to think logically and we do so in many situations in life.

If we lose our car keys, for example, we logically deduce the various places they may be. When we plan to do something we have not done before, we use logic to work out the plan and the order of the various steps involved. Scientists use logic in order to design experiments to test various hypotheses. Project managers apply logic to plan everything from building a bridge to flying to the moon.

It is interesting to note that most of the great crusades of destruction by one group of people against another – wars and campaigns of extermination – are actively promoted and justified by logical arguments of one sort or another. Such logical arguments are characterized more by what they exclude from consideration than what they include.

This is amply demonstrated by the following pithy quotation from Joseph Stalin: "Man, problem. No man, no problem."

Logical thinking is thus a stick with two ends. The heartless logic of the dictator is, nevertheless, logic.

Nowhere in *The Tales* does Gurdjieff use the term "logical thinking." He refers instead to "logical confrontation," suggesting that the examination of a set of information to see if any apparent contradictions arise from it is a productive activity. He stresses the importance of this in the following excerpt from Chapter 46 of *The Tales*.

> "In respect of the sequence of my information to you and of the results of your essence-understanding, I must still tell you that if, when I first noticed your interest in the three-brained beings who arise on the planet Earth, I would have given from the very beginning, concerning every event, only my personal conviction and the opinions which had become fixed in me about them during the period of my observations, and only afterwards would have begun to give you the abundant and many-sided 'totality of information' already related by me, then all these facts I related would have been taken in by you without your own being- logical confrontation, and the data which had been crystallized for this information would have settled in your corresponding localizations only simply as information without any genuine being-understanding of them.

Our interpretation of this paragraph is that Gurdjieff is encouraging us to form our own opinions from the information he has provided rather than mirror any opinion he might have arrived at. We are expected to do the work of logical confrontation. He cannot do it for us.

A useful way to think of logical confrontation is to characterize it as "common sense."

One of our difficulties is that we are suggestible. This is an obstacle that Gurdjieff had to confront in all of his teaching. If he just gave us a verbal formulation of an idea, then, to the degree that we accept him as an authority, we would believe it. We would believe it without trying to test the idea ourselves and, in all probability, we would not formulate it accurately or even meaningfully.

We can see this with the simple idea of "man cannot do." If we believe this in a simplistic manner, then logically there can be no point in being a part of The Work. We cannot do and hence any attempt to develop higher capabilities is a complete waste of time. We'd be better spending our spare time playing golf or watching television.

Common sense, or logical confrontation, is of particular use when reading *The Tales*. Time and again we encounter Beelzebub saying something that, on the surface, is absurd. In such situations we must use our common sense. Gurdjieff cannot have written something absurd so that we simply swallow it and move on. Common sense tells us that there must be something else that is meant by his words. So we must try, right then and there, to discover his real meaning.

We need to use our logical faculties time and again in order to fathom the gist of Gurdjieff's writings. Gurdjieff has set us a beguiling problem. He spent a great amount of time writing and refining *The Tales*, and it is his major legacy. The more one reads it, the more one appreciates the extraordinary unprecedented precision of the writing. He clearly wanted it to be widely read. He even declared definitively that "everything is in there." And yet there is scant evidence that many people have penetrated to the heart of the book. Logical confrontation – common sense – suggests that it is possible.

Analysis

Analysis walks hand in hand with logical thinking. We analyze to gather information, we use logical reasoning to make sense of what we discover in our analysis.

Chapter 3: Intellectual Postures And Processes

Note that Gurdjieff never suggested to us that we use any analytical or logical capacity when reading *The Tales* for the first and second time. For the first reading we are requested to read the book as if we were reading a newspaper or a novel. For the second reading we are requested to read it out as if to someone else. There is no suggestion that we should analyze the book until the third reading.

When our approach to the book involves analysis, we quickly begin to notice details of the book that we never noticed before. We pay attention in a different way. We notice, for instance, that with many of his newly invented words he also gives the meaning. Here is an example:

> *"In the common presence of every being existing merely on the basis of Itoklanoz, 'something' similar to the regulator in a mechanical watch is present and is called 'Iransamkeep'; this 'something' means: 'not-to-give-oneself-up-to-those-of-one's-associations-resulting-from-the-functioning-of-only-one-or-another-of-one's-brains.'"*

This is curious. He invents the word "Iransamkeep" and then tells us what it means. And he never uses that word again throughout the whole book or in any of his other books. So why did he choose to invent a new word here? We notice that this happens more than once or twice throughout the book. He invents a new word, explains its meaning and then doesn't use it again. In other places he invents a new word and leaves us with no explanation of what it means. Surely he has a reason for doing this, but what is the reason?

Even fairly superficial analysis yields curious results. The Tales frequently mentions the Sun Absolute, but not always in the same manner. There is: Sun Absolute, Most Holy Sun Absolute, Omni Most Holy Sun Absolute, Most Most Holy Sun Absolute and others. There is no immediately obvious reason why the adjectives vary from none to many in describing the Sun Absolute. Similarly, the names for HIS ENDLESSNESS vary considerably for no immediately obvious reason.

Again, surely he did not take the time to include these variances for no reason whatsoever. We could, of course, propose that he is doing this to confuse and discourage anyone who subjects the book to analysis of this kind. But it does not feel right. Would Gurdjieff play tricks on the reader with the name of God? Probably not.

Gurdjieff rewards readers who subject the book to analysis, as you may appreciate more deeply when you read the later chapters of this book, especially *Chapter 6 on Intentional Inexactitudes*.

Representation

Representation is a posture of the mind. When we represent we create an internal image of a particular situation. We might be playing a game of chess and represent the chess board mentally, moving one piece then another to calculate whether a particular chess move is good or bad. Alternatively, we may be going for a job interview and we represent the conversation that is likely to take place, preparing our responses to questions we expect to be asked.

Representation is an alternative word for imagination, but imagination, as we sometimes use the word, can have the flavor of being divorced from reality. It may involve inattentiveness, self-absorption, or even being lost in an inner fantasy. The word "representation" does not evoke such associations.

We represent on paper, by drawing pictures. There are devices in *The Tales* that we might represent in this way: the transspace system of St. Venoma, the transspace system of Archangel Hariton, the experiments of Gornahoor Harharkh, the Alla-attapan and the Lav-Merz-Nokh. We believe this to be a worthwhile pursuit. How many readers of *The Tales* have ever tried to do that?

Materializing Thought

Representation, in our experience, is more powerful when an attempt is made to materialize the representation, as in the effort to build, say, a Lav-Merz-Nokh. We can think of this as "materializing thought." In using this term we hope the reader will not confuse this with quasi-mystical ideas that are sometimes encountered in New Age literature. We are not suggesting that you, say, concentrate strongly on the idea of a rabbit, in the vain hope that a real live rabbit will suddenly appear before your eyes.

We have thinking processes. In some of us they may be better organized than in others. But even if that is the case, they are not likely to be very well organized. We can prove this to ourselves very quickly by writing down what we think. In our view every serious reader of *The Tales*, a reader that is willing to read the book again and again, should start writing down his or her thoughts about every part of the book that caught their attention. This is likely to be most effective if it is done in such a way as if one were explaining it to someone else.

An important process in this is to take time to edit such writing so that it is clear and concise. This corresponds to crystallization. And, in time, such writing can and should be revisited, to add details or change misconceptions. If we do this we will materialize our thoughts – to our benefit and possibly to the benefit of others.

Holding The Dove

If you hold a dove between two hands, you need to do so with care. Hold it too tightly and you could hurt it, damage it, or even kill it. But if you hold it too loosely it will fly away.

This is a metaphor for how to treat theories. In this modern world we are subjected to theories all the time, usually disguised as information. Most modern advertising equates to inculcating people with theories about some product or service so that it sticks. The advertiser wants you to accept uncritically that some drug or some car or some "something" is a worthwhile purchase. This is theory presented as "verified information."

Modern television stations broadcast many educational programs which are similar to this in nature. They dress theory up as fact, often by means of shameless voice-overs. We hear Darwinian evolution – current scientific dogma – trotted out time and again in a simplistic manner.

In one program we hear: "This male Painted Bunting evolved to acquire such colorful markings so that it could better attract females." In another program on marine life we are told: "The Flounder is a bottom feeder that evolved a cunning camouflage so effective that predators would be unable to see it." So why, we might wonder, did the Painted Bunting not get destroyed by predators that could obviously pick it out, and how come the Flounder didn't die out for the inability of the male and female to attract each other in a colorful way?

If we are going to have any truck at all with the propaganda that is continually pushed out to us by the media, we need to develop a healthy skepticism. This is especially the case when it comes to the prognostications of science. First of all, we need to separate fact from theory:

- Darwinian evolution is not a fact.
- Most ideas of western medicine are not facts.

- The Big Bang is not a fact.
- Black holes are not a fact.
- The model of the atom is not a fact.
- Much of what is written about particle physics and quantum mechanics is not fact, and so on.

We should have no difficulty in being skeptical about such theories, but many of us do. We are suggestible. If some ever-so-clever Nobel Prize winning scientist makes some proclamation we tend to accept it. Consequently, adopting the posture of skepticism may not come easily.

To separate fact from theory, we need to investigate the data on which a theory is based. Only then can we properly state the theory in an honest way. Usually we will discover that there is indeed data which supports the popular scientific ideas of the day. We will also discover that any given theory has detractors within the scientific community and their disagreement with the theory will usually involve the consideration of some other data.

Once we have separated fact from theory, we can hold the theory like a dove. We can try to align the theory with our understanding of Objective Science and gather information of our own to support and oppose the theory. Eventually we can decide whether to open up our hands and let the theory fly away.

It is helpful, by the way, to draw a sharp distinction between skepticism and cynicism; they are not the same, not even brothers. H. L. Mencken defined cynicism succinctly in the following way:

"A cynic is someone who, when he smells flowers, looks around for a coffin."

The Cynics were originally a philosophical school in ancient Greece that rejected the conventional values of the day – the pursuit of wealth, power, sex and fame – and thus they sought to live a simple life. They cultivated indifference. Maybe that wasn't such a bad orientation.

However, the word "cynicism" no longer reflects that origin; it is like the word "sophistry" in that respect. Its meaning has moved. It has come to mean someone who questions the value of almost anything in an indiscriminate way. So cynics are inclined to deride almost any idea or theory, and to enjoy doing so. The cynic has little interest in knowledge. The cynic wishes to raise himself by lowering others.

Chapter 3: Intellectual Postures And Processes

We wish to develop the posture of skepticism, not the derisive posture of cynicism.

Impartiality

The Tales claims to be *An Objectively Impartial Criticism of the Life of Man*. From a fictional perspective it has an impartial setting; an individual who is not from Earth spends many thousands of years observing the behavior of Earth's three-brained beings and relates a good deal of what he has observed to his grandson. He has no axe to grind. He is not human and there is no suggestion that humans have ever wronged him in any way. While he is deeply critical of these three-brained beings, he is careful to separate his criticisms between what is their responsibility and what has been beyond their control. Quite specifically, he says:

> *"You yourself will very well understand that although the fundamental causes of the whole chaos that now reigns on that ill-fated planet Earth were certain 'unforeseeingnesses,' coming from Above on the part of various Sacred Individuals, yet nevertheless the chief causes for the developing of further ills are only those abnormal conditions of ordinary being-existence which they themselves gradually established and which they continue to establish down to the present time.*

The reader of *The Tales* is indisputably one of those three-brained beings who are the object of the criticism. The question is whether we are able to accept the criticism or whether, in the face of what he reports, we calm ourselves and then turn the page. In order to accept his criticism we will have to acknowledge that what he says is not just true of some human beings, but is also true of us.

Consider the following sentence: "Those slugs have dual natures."

He insults us by calling us slugs, but he is just making a joke of Hassein's choice of word.

But do we have dual natures?

We can reject this particular description of us out of hand, or we can pretend to accept it, but secretly reject it. Perhaps we know it to be true, in which case we acknowledge it. But what if we are not so sure of this?

If we are to be impartial, we will have to accept it as a theory. And in our investigation of this theory we will have to ignore our own prejudices if we are to arrive at the truth. If the truth is unpalatable we will have to eat it anyway.

As a reader of *The Tales*, we are required to be as impartial as we are able. We should have no axe to grind.

Thinking By Analogy

Living things are complex. Objects, like a pebble or a knife or a cup, are much less complex. Simple objects have few capabilities and do not have a complicated set of parts. As such, their use and possibilities are easier to understand. In The Work we are presented with the idea of a cosmos, a living thing that consumes three foods, excretes residues, has a psychology and operates via multiple complex inner systems.

Animals, for example, have a digestive system, a blood stream that carries digested food and also absorbs air via a pair of lungs. They have a lymphatic system, an immune system, a nervous system, and so on. Few of us have any idea how any of these systems really work or how all these systems work in harmony for a whole lifetime until one system or another fails. Nevertheless, we know many things about these cosmoses because we ourselves are such cosmoses. We can observe ourselves internally and also we can observe the properties of other cosmoses similar to ourselves.

We do not need to have a perfect knowledge of the human cosmos or any other cosmos to make use of the knowledge we have. We can, for example, consider a city to be a cosmos and then we can begin to make comparisons between it and a human cosmos.

A city "eats" material, from which it grows. It "breathes in" food to serve its population so they can operate its many systems. Parts of it "perceive" information and distribute it to the population. It has circulations of traffic for moving people about and for moving raw materials about. It has communications systems. It is a cosmos of a kind.

Because we have some idea of the nature of a cosmos, we can view a city as a cosmos and this may help us to better understand what a city is. We can even generate theories of how to improve one or another system that is an important part of a city. This is thinking by analogy. The method we use is to compare similar cosmoses and deduce theories as to how a cosmos that we are building (a city) could be improved with reference to a cosmos we understand reasonably well (a human being). In using this mode of thinking we need to be aware both of similarities and differences.

Chapter 3: Intellectual Postures And Processes

For example, an animal or a human being can move. It can move from one moment to another and it can even move its place of residence. A city cannot move. It can grow larger, but it does not move its location. So we need to be careful about any ideas that we may think up with such an analogy. In fact it may be better if we switch analogy. Perhaps we should compare a city with an anthill.

In *Chapter 16 of In Search of the Miraculous*, Peter Ouspensky conducts a very helpful investigation of cosmoses large and small based upon a few simple dimensions of a cosmos: the time of it taking in an impression, the time of it breathing, the time of a day and night for the cosmos, and the length of a lifetime for a cosmos. This allows us to grasp the idea of a planet being alive or an atom being alive. It opens up the whole idea of a living universe rather than a mechanical dead universe in which, by some accident, life has arisen on planet Earth. It is intellectually useful.

Knowing how to think by analogy is, in our view, fundamental to fathoming *The Tales*. It helps us to appreciate the nature of an allegory and *The Tales* are awash with allegories.

The Quest for Questions

Voltaire advised that one should "judge a man by his questions rather than his answers." It is a sensible suggestion, with the rider that in The Work we have little interest in judging others; our attention is focused on observing and impartially judging – or better put – impartially criticizing ourselves.

Questions are magical. They are keys which open doors that we might not even have realized were there. Sadly, most of us are not good at formulating questions. There was that childhood age we all went through when we asked question after question, gradually testing the patience of our parents. At some point, most likely, we were encouraged to be silent – and at some age most of us learned to be so. We quelled our innate curiosity.

There is variety in questions. There are short simple questions, there are long profound questions and there is a whole spectrum of questions that lies between. Short simple questions have answers.

"What is the capital of France?"

"It is Paris."

The question is almost immediately resolved. The answer can be easily checked if need be. After that it has no further value.

We are more interested in profound questions, or what we have come to think of as "long questions." Long questions remain open, almost by definition. They are inevitably subjective to some degree. A long question for one man may be no question at all for another. One sees a beguiling enigma, while another sees nothing at all.

Effort is required to keep some questions open and alive. A struggle between curiosity and despondency – a "yes and no" struggle – can arise. The outcome of such a struggle is not foreordained.

Consider the question "Is there a single supreme deity?" This question has no simple answer. It is a long question. Maybe some individuals have thoroughly answered this question, but if so, we have not encountered them – or if we have, they have been unable to elucidate and demonstrate whatever answer they obtained. This question has occupied the minds of men for thousands of years and it will continue to do so for many more years.

No glib answer will satisfy someone who lives this question. Answers like "yes" and "no" are equally meaningless. We will know the answer when we experience a single supreme deity in an undeniable way or if we demonstrate for ourselves with absolute certainty that no such deity exists.

Another long question is "What am I?" Everyone in The Work has met with this question and stands inside of it. But how long can they sustain such a question? There are thorns that come with this question. *The Tales* provokes many questions.

There is an enigma right at the beginning, where Gurdjieff proclaims that All and Everything consists of ten books in three series. Yet there is scant evidence that ten such books exist. The first series has three books as stated. The second series, as published, has just one book entitled *Meetings with Remarkable Men*, not three as suggested. There is evidence that more were originally intended, since there is an Orage/Heap draft of the book which suggests that at one time the second book in the series was intended to begin with the chapter on *Ekim Bey*. However, no third book is indicated in that draft. The existence of a third book in the series is, however, indicated in *The Herald of Coming Good* which suggests that Gurdjieff's repeated attempt to set up his Institute is described in the third book of the second series. We are not aware of any indication that the third series is anything more than a single book entitled *Life Is Real Only Then, When 'I Am,'* not four, as suggested.

Chapter 3: Intellectual Postures And Processes

So what does he mean? Did he simply change the form of the second series from three books to one, but fail to mention that? Perhaps other books he wrote have been lost, or perhaps he never wrote them? If he never wrote them, why did he confidently proclaim their existence? Or does he mean something else entirely? If so, then what?

There are broad questions that are not easily answered. Gurdjieff was quite capable of writing in a plain and comprehensible style, as he demonstrates with *Meetings with Remarkable Men*. As every reader soon discovers, the literary style of *The Tales* is difficult to penetrate – not "bon ton" at all. So what was the purpose of using such an obtuse style? Was it simply to force the reader to make a great deal of effort, or is there a rhythm in this style of writing that has a direct impact on the reader?

Why did he invent all those 'quotations' from Mullah Nassr Eddin that pepper the text? What does Ahoon represent and what are we to make of it when the narrative suddenly passes to him from Beelzebub? Why did Gurdjieff choose Beelzebub as his hero? Why are *The Tales* told to a grandson rather than simply a young pupil?

At a detailed level, more questions naturally arise. What does a particular section, or page, or paragraph, or sentence actually mean? Why did he choose to invent new and difficult words in certain passages but not in others. It sometimes even comes down to: "Why did he choose to use this word?"

Gurdjieff repeatedly mentions the term "active mentation," at various times throughout *The Tales*, emphasizing the importance of this activity. Towards the end of *The Tales* he explains exactly what he means by active mentation:

> "*I find it necessary to repeat that the 'active mentation' in a being and the useful results of such active mentation are in reality actualized exclusively only with the equal-degree functionings of all his three localizations of the results spiritualized in his presence, called 'thinking-center,' 'feeling-center,' and 'moving-motor-center.'*"

This partly explains why he rarely uses the word "thinking" and instead uses the word "mentation." Mentation involves more than the thinking center.

We will only ask questions if we are motivated to do so. The motivation may arise from the feeling-center, as curiosity. If we do not have the wish to understand *The Tales* we will make no effort to fathom the gist. "Wish" is not born of the intellect. We feel "wish" before we ever formulate it. Nevertheless, the formulation of questions is undeniably a function of the intellect. Active mentation involves formulating questions.

Pondering

A question can only be regarded as long if you return to it again and again. For example, you may have wondered about the existence of Bigfoot ten years ago, but you no longer think of this at all. One day, a news item appears in the newspaper claiming that there has been another sighting of Bigfoot. You read it and again you think "I wonder whether such a creature really exists."

You were never sure, and hence it remained an open question for you, but it was not a long question. You did not visit it many times over ten years, returning to it again and again, trying to get to the truth. You did not ponder on this.

In the years before the remorseless advance of the electronic revolution, when there were no televisions in homes and in bars or radio in the car or muzak in the elevator, pondering was a far more common activity. There was uninterrupted time in which you could consider questions that provoked your curiosity. Nowadays, when we live in such a distracting environment, there may be little opportunity for this. If this is so, we need to make the time.

Our experience suggests that pondering the meaning of various parts, large or small, of *The Tales* is necessary. But perhaps we do not know how to ponder. Gurdjieff explains an approach to pondering in *Views from the Real World*, in the following way:

> Before going any further, it would be useful to learn to think according to a definite order. Let everyone take some object. Let each of you ask himself questions relating to the object and answer these according to his knowledge and material:
>
> 1) *Its origin*
>
> 2) *The cause of its origin*
>
> 3) *Its history*
>
> 4) *Its qualities and attributes*
>
> 5) *Objects connected with it and related to it*
>
> 6) *Its use and application*
>
> 7) *Its results and effects*
>
> 8) *What it explains and proves*

Chapter 3: Intellectual Postures And Processes

9) *Its end or its future*

10) *Your opinion, the cause and motives of this opinion*

This description could be compared to various Yoga practices which involve examining something – a thing, or idea or process – from multiple aspects. In pondering a section of *The Tales* we can prepare a list of ways to look at it. For example:

1. What is the literal meaning?
2. What is the allegorical meaning?
3. How does this relate to the whole book?
4. What do I know of this? Do I know whether what it says is true?
5. How does it apply to my inner world and how can I use it for my personal work?
6. How can I use it in group work?
7. What does it tell me about my past and how I relate to others?
8. What does it tell me about mankind?
9. What does it tell me about the megalocosmos?
10. How do I feel about it?

Different sections of *The Tales* raise different questions. What we have given here is neither a definitive nor an exhaustive list. It is provided simply as an example of questions that can arise.

In our view pondering is an activity in which the Intellect and the Emotions walk hand-in-hand. The intellect is inclined to treat questions as logical challenges and often tries to close them out with a definitive answer. Pondering is founded in "wonder" and often our conscience itself is drawn in to the activity.

With some sections of *The Tales* the process of pondering may begin with few questions or even a single question. That was our experience on reading *Chapter 5, The System of Archangel Hariton*. At first, the only question we could think to ask was: "What on earth is he talking about?"

Concentration

Concentration is a mental activity that few people are naturally good at. It requires strong intention coupled with the ability to ignore or even block out distractions. It is the shepherding of the attention so that it focuses only on what it needs to focus on. We may then be able to accomplish the goal that we have set. If we were capable of real will then maybe we could maintain such a focus without interruption. As we are not, we are obliged to refocus our attention when we realize that it has wandered. This takes practice.

In reading *The Tales*, we need to be mindful of many things that we discuss throughout this book. We need to be aware of Gurdjieff's use of punctuation and how he emphasizes distinct words. We need to be aware of Gurdjieff's style of writing and we have to make efforts to extract what he is trying to convey from his long and involved sentences. We need to take note of the concepts he is wielding and have a sense of their meaning. We need to be on the lookout for intentional inexactitudes and absurdities. We need to ponder the meaning of Gurdjieff's invented words. We need to try to get a sense of the allegorical meaning of the current tale that he is recounting. We need to consider what we ourselves know from our own experience.

To do all of this with any agility demands our concentration. It demands a level of concentration that we are unused to devoting to anything. We have to learn to apply as much concentration as we are able to muster.

Constatation

Although the word "constate" is used over 100 times in *The Tales*, it will have been unfamiliar to most of us before we encountered the book – possibly to the extent that we had to refer to the dictionary to discover what it meant. It is a rarely used verb that has the meaning: to ascertain, to verify, to establish, to prove. Its etymology is from Latin; *con*, meaning 'with' or 'together', and *stare*, the Latin verb 'to stand.'

It may help if we introduce the concepts of "consistency" and "completeness" into the act of constating. For example, we may ponder on the difference between emanations and radiations after reading the following passage:

> ...*yet with the single exception of a certain Chinese man named Choon-Kil-Tez, about whom I shall tell you later in detail, not once has the thought entered the head of a single one of them there that between these two cosmic phenomena which they call 'emanation' and 'radiation' there is any difference whatever.*

After considering many aspects of this question and researching the text for clues, we eventually arrive at a hypothesis of what both of these phenomena are and what the difference between them might be. So we constate; we attempt to verify our hypothesis. In doing so we need to

Chapter 3: Intellectual Postures And Processes

ask whether the theory we have arrived at is consistent with everything we have read and considered. If it has no such consistency then we need to adjust our theory until we have achieved consistency.

We also need to ask whether our research into this matter is complete. Have we identified and considered every line of *The Tales* and Gurdjieff's other writings that mention either emanation or radiation? If not, then we need to do that for the sake of completeness. If our theory still appears valid once we have done that, then our constatation is complete.

This does not necessarily mean that we have arrived at "the truth" but it may mean that we have something that we can now hold between two hands like a dove.

Words

In *Chapter 1, The Arousing of Thought,* Gurdjieff explains that there are two kinds of mentation in Man, mentation by thought and mentation by form. He writes:

> ...on Earth in the past it has been usual in every century that every man, in whom there arises the boldness to attain the right to be considered by others and to consider himself a "conscious thinker," should be informed while still in the early years of his responsible existence that man has in general two kinds of mentation: one kind, mentation by thought, in which words, always possessing a relative sense, are employed; and the other kind, which is proper to all animals as well as to man, which I would call "mentation by form."
>
> The second kind of mentation, that is, "mentation by form" by which, strictly speaking, the exact sense of all writing must be also perceived, and after conscious confrontation with information already possessed, be assimilated, is formed in people in dependence upon the conditions of geographical locality, climate, time, and, in general, upon the whole environment in which the arising of the given man has proceeded and in which his existence has flowed up to manhood.
>
> Accordingly, in the brains of people of different races and conditions dwelling in different geographical localities, there are formed about one and the same thing or even idea, a number of quite independent forms, which during functioning, that is to say, association, evoke in their being some sensation or other which subjectively conditions a definite picturing, and which picturing is

expressed by this, that, or the other word, that serves only for its outer subjective expression.

That is why each word, for the same thing or idea, almost always acquires for people of different geographical locality and race a very definite and entirely different so to say, "inner content."

If we take Gurdjieff at his word, we are faced with a significant problem when reading *The Tales*. We will naturally interpret his words via mentation by form as well as by mentation by words. As Gurdjieff explains, our mentation by form is determined by the context of our upbringing within a specific culture. Because of this it will engender specific associations that are subjective to the culture and geography of our origin and to some extent by our individual experience.

We find a startling example of Gurdjieff's deliberate choice of words when we compare the English version of *The Tales* to the French version. In the English version Gurdjieff uses the words intentional suffering. In the French version this is *souffrance volontaire*, not *souffrance intentionnelle*. Those of us who were not raised in France and are not fluent in French will not be able to understand his word choice for French readers. The concept of intentional suffering is so central to *The Tales* that it is hard to believe his choice of words to be an error or an accident.

We learn many of the words we employ at a very early age, initially by imitation. Perhaps we are playing with a ball and our father says "ball" and points to it. We imitate the sound he makes and associate the object we perceive with that sound. Since this particular object is common to almost all cultures, the immediate possibility of a distinctly different mental picturing, i.e., a different "mentation by form," is not great.

However, when we learn the word "breakfast" a cultural or geographical difference will arise. In some countries sweet foods are normal for breakfast. In others savory foods are the norm. In yet others, there is a mix. In some countries it is a fairly heavy meal and in others it is light. The word "breakfast" quickly acquires a subjective meaning.

There are many differences between cultures, both mundane and profound. Clothing is culturally distinct. Music is culturally distinct. Art is culturally distinct. Literature is culturally distinct. Political ideas are culturally distinct. Religious views, morality, and education are culturally distinct. Most of all, language, including the modes of

Chapter 3: Intellectual Postures And Processes

expression and common metaphors within a given language, is culturally distinct. We also assign meaning to words according to our personal theories and beliefs, or according to theories and beliefs we have borrowed from others.

The associations we attach to any particular word accumulate over time. They are not confined just to one word either, but also to collections of words. Gurdjieff tells us that these associations evoke in our being:

> *"some sensation or other which subjectively conditions a definite picturing, and which picturing is expressed by this, that, or the other word, that serves only for its outer subjective expression."*

This is mentation by form.

We discuss any given topic with someone whom we know and, while the words we use will be recognized, our inner mentation by form may be somewhat different and could be very different indeed. In such a conversation the other person may appear to agree completely with what we say and we may in turn be in apparent agreement with everything they say. Nevertheless, there may be very little true agreement and possibly no agreement at all.

This problem is compounded by the fact that we often use words whose meaning we do not clearly understand. Gurdjieff describes this in *Views from the Real World* as follows:

> *The teaching whose principles we are going to expound here has as one of its tasks the bringing of our thinking nearer to an exact mathematical designation of things and events and the giving to men of the possibility of understanding themselves and each other.*
>
> *If we take any of the most commonly used words and try to see what a varied meaning these words have according to who uses them and in what connection, we shall see why men have no power of expressing their thoughts exactly and why everything men say and think is so unstable and contradictory. Apart from the variety of meanings which every word can have, this confusion and contradiction are caused by the fact that men never render any account to themselves of the sense in which they take this or that word and only wonder why others do not understand it although it is so clear to themselves. For example, if we say the word "world" in front of ten hearers, every one of them will understand the word in his own way. If men knew how to catch and write down their thoughts themselves, they would see that they had no ideas*

connected with the word "world" but that merely a well-known word and an accustomed sound was uttered, the significance of which is supposed to be known. It is as if everybody hearing this word said to himself: "Ah, the 'world' I know what it is." As a matter of fact he does not really know at all. But the word is familiar, and therefore no such question and answer occur to him. It is just accepted. A question comes only in respect of new unknown words and then the man tends to substitute for the unknown word a known one. He calls this "understanding."

If we now ask the man what he understands by the word "world," he will be perplexed by such a question. Usually, when he hears or uses the word "world" in conversation, he does not think at all about what it means, having decided once and for all that he knows and that everybody knows. Now for the first time he sees that he does not know and that he has never thought about it; but he will not be able to and will not know how to rest with the thought of his ignorance. Men are not capable enough of observing and not sufficiently sincere with themselves to do so. He will soon recover himself, that is, he will very quickly deceive himself; and remembering or composing in haste a definition of the word "world" from some familiar source of knowledge or thought, or the first definition of someone else's which enters his head, he will express it as his own understanding of the meaning of the word, though in fact he has never thought about the word "world" in this way and does not know how he has thought.

The word "world" that Gurdjieff has chosen as his example here is a common word with a general meaning. It is surprising that we have a poor grasp of the meaning of such a common word. But more importantly, we have a poor grasp of many words that are important in The Work; words like "will," "consciousness," "intelligence," and "attention." Not only is our mentation by form highly subjective but our mentation by thought is in a dilapidated state.

This may be partly due to the poverty of the English language. When we mentate in words we are inevitably confined by the words we know. Let us take, for example, the word "love." English speakers naturally classify this as an emotion, but in usage the word "love" can apply to several distinct inner states.

This becomes apparent when we consider the Ancient Greek language, which is much richer in words that relate to love. They had four words:

Chapter 3: Intellectual Postures And Processes

- *Storge.* This word conveys familial love, the kind of love that one experiences for family and that one observes in the love of parents for their children.
- *Eros.* This is sexual or passionate love, the kind of love that may accompany sexual desire.
- *Philos.* This is brotherly love, the love or affection that one might experience for comrades.
- *Agape.* This is the highest form of love. This word was chosen by writers of *The New Testament* to denote, for example, the unconditional love of God.

In English translations of *The New Testament*, "agape" is generally translated as "charity." That might have been an appropriate equivalence when The *New Testament* was first translated into English, but now the word "charity" tends to denote financial generosity to a "good cause," which may indeed be provoked by a love of some kind for a disadvantaged individual or for the goals of a charitable organization. But it may also be the consequence of guilt, or the desire to avoid paying taxes or even to have one's name become attached to the new wing of a hospital. Whatever it might be in reality, it is probably not "agape." So by virtue of our many associations, the word "charity" does not evoke the concept of pure love.

In our view, Shakespeare unambiguously describes "agape" in his famous *Sonnet 116*:

> Let me not to the marriage of true minds
> Admit impediments. Love is not love
> Which alters when it alteration finds,
> Or bends with the remover to remove:
> O no! it is an ever-fixed mark
> That looks on tempests and is never shaken;
> It is the star to every wandering bark,
> Whose worth's unknown, although his height be taken.
> Love's not Time's fool, though rosy lips and cheeks
> Within his bending sickle's compass come:
> Love alters not with his brief hours and weeks,
> But bears it out even to the edge of doom.
> If this be error and upon me proved,
> I never writ, nor no man ever loved.

To Fathom The Gist: Vol I

In *The Tales*, Beelzebub reports the contents of the Legominism of the Very Saintly Ashiata Shiemash concerning our subjective concepts of the word "love."

"In the presences of the beings of contemporary times, there also arises and is present in them as much as you please of that strange impulse which they call love; but this love of theirs is firstly also the result of certain crystallized consequences of the properties of the same Kundabuffer; and secondly this impulse of theirs arises and manifests itself in the process of every one of them entirely subjectively; so subjectively and so differently that if ten of them were asked to explain how they sensed this inner impulse of theirs, then all ten of them—if, of course, they for once replied sincerely, and frankly confessed their genuine sensations and not those they had read about somewhere or had obtained from somebody else—all ten would reply differently and describe ten different sensations.

"One would explain this sensation in the sexual sense; another in the sense of pity; a third in the sense of desire for submission; a fourth, in a common craze for outer things, and so on and so forth; but not one of the ten could describe even remotely, the sensation of genuine Love.

"And none of them would, because in none of the ordinary beings-men here has there ever been, for a long time, any sensation of the sacred being-impulse of genuine Love. And without this "taste" they cannot even vaguely describe that most beatific sacred being-impulse in the presence of every three-centered being of the whole Universe, which, in accordance with the divine foresight of Great Nature, forms those data in us, from the result of the experiencing of which we can blissfully rest from the meritorious labors actualized by us for the purpose of self-perfection.

"Here, in these times, if one of those three-brained beings "loves" somebody or other, then he loves him either because the latter always encourages and undeservingly flatters him; or because his nose is much like the nose of that female or male, with whom thanks to the cosmic law of "polarity" or "type" a relation has been established which has not yet been broken; or finally, he loves him only because the latter's uncle is in a big way of business and may one day give him a boost, and so on and so forth.

"But never do beings-men here love with genuine, impartial and non-egoistic love.

Chapter 3: Intellectual Postures And Processes

Thanks to this kind of love in the contemporary beings here, their hereditary predispositions to the crystallizations of the consequences of the properties of the organ Kundabuffer are crystallized at the present time without hindrance, and finally become fixed in their nature as a lawful part of them.

In the light of this we might like to ponder long and deep on what our comprehension of "love" actually is. How much experiential data do we actually have about this emotion?

When we read *The Tales* with attention and with an appreciation of our subjective associations, we can begin to recognize how Gurdjieff attempts to improve our mentation and circumvent its weaknesses. We may notice, for example, that he chooses many unfamiliar words and combinations of words.

Consider here just the word "mentation." It is referred to time and again in *The Tales* and in most cases where it is used it is qualified in a different way. Sometimes hyphens are used, sometimes quote marks and often different adjectives. As readers we are not given the chance to fix on a single view of the meaning of this word, because he keeps serving up slightly different perspectives. Indeed, the list of different ways in which he uses this important word may engender bewilderment. Here is that long list, in the order in which they occur:

Mentation and feelings, the process of the mentation, human mentation, mentation by thought, mentation by form, the form of my mentation, your mentation, conscious mentation, the mentation of most of my readers, the mentation of the contemporary reader, impetuous mentation, active being mentation, being-associative-mentation, logical-mentation, the kind of mentation which is considered among your favorites as the 'highest manifestation of Reason,' sane logical mentation, the form of mentation and the verbal exposition, being-logical-mentation, my logical mentation, being-sane-mentation, sane-logical-mentation, being-mentation, logical mentation, normal being-mentation, data for their being-mentation, more or less normal logical being-mentation, comparative mentation, reasonable deliberation by his being-mentation, active mentation, form-of-their-being-mentation, logical-confrontative-mentation, associations flowing in his mentation, being-confrontative-logical-mentation, active mentation, logical-being-mentation, sane mentation, being-mentation, being-mentation according to the law of sane logic, normal mentation, this mentation of theirs, the mentation of beings,

Aimnophnian mentation, their strange shortsighted mentation, being-Aimnophnian-mentation or perceptible logic, superpeculiar being-Aimnophnian-mentation, exceptionally distorted being-Aimnophnian mentation, intensive active mentations, the intensive tension of my 'active mentation, 'relatively sane being-mentation, sane being-mentation, healthy being-mentation, 'bobtailed' logical mentation, the mentation proper to three-brained beings, the form of mentation of our dear teacher, the future normal mentation of their children, the full possibility of normal mentation, this particularity of their mentation-very complicated for any 'logical analysis, strange mentation, the strangeness of the mentation, degenerated mentation, this new tempo of my mentation, mentation by association, that form of mentation which is called 'sane-mentation, your future active mentation, conscious mentation, the process of active mentation, impartial mentation, logical mentation, continuously tense mentation, human mentation, the laws of association of human mentation, "mentation," which people call consciousness, ordinary mentation, and already feeble mentation.

Reading this list should provide an appreciation of Gurdjieff's precision as an author. If you do a word-by-word and phrase-by-phrase analysis of most books (this book you are reading included, no doubt) you will quickly identify areas of repetition, where the author has chosen his words by habit, and used a given word or phrase repeatedly in the same way. Such writing is comfortable for readers, as they become familiar with the author's style – but it inevitably lacks precision.

Gurdjieff provides a complete contrast to such "bon ton" style. The reader is at times obliged to make efforts just to determine the sense of one of his sentences. It can be necessary for the reader to reread paragraphs, or even whole pages, simply because he was unable to maintain his concentration throughout. And yet, while the text may be complex, it is not incomprehensible at all.

The Tales would still be remarkable if Gurdjieff had done nothing more than introduce such a literary style. But he goes further, introducing hundreds of new words – undoubtedly because our language is inadequate to the subject matter.

Chapter 3: Intellectual Postures And Processes

Egoplastikoori

The following excerpt comes from *Chapter 46, Beelzebub Explains to His Grandson the Significance of the Form and Sequence Which He Chose for Expounding the Information Concerning Man*:

> "When at the beginning of our journey I noticed that you were very interested in the three-brained beings of the planet Earth, I then decided, under the aspect of gratifying that interest of yours, to tell you everything about them in such a way that there should be crystallized in you for your future being-associations the required what are called 'Egoplastikoori,' without any admixture of doubt."

Here, Beelzebub describes what he has been attempting to do for Hassein by relating his many tales about those strange three-brained beings of planet Earth. His intention was to crystallize the required Egoplastikoori for Hassein's future being-associations. So Gurdjieff wishes to change the functioning of our 'mentation by form.' His stated goal is:

> To destroy, mercilessly, without any compromises whatsoever, in the mentation and feelings of the reader, the beliefs and views, by centuries rooted in him, about everything existing in the world.

His method for doing this is, either in whole or in part, to crystallize Egoplastikoori within us. He proceeds to say:

> "I decided to do this in order that many diversely essenced 'Egoplastikoori' for your future logical confrontation should be crystallized in corresponding localizations in your common presence, and also in order that from active mentation the proper elaboration in you of the sacred substances of Abrustdonis and Helkdonis for the purpose of coating and perfecting both of your higher being-parts should proceed more intensively.

We take this to mean that we need these Egoplastikoori so that in future our logical confrontation (logical evaluations) should more closely approach sane logical mentation. In order to change our mentation by thought, he has chosen to change our mentation by form.

It is important, then, that we understand the meaning of Egoplastikoori. Gurdjieff first uses this word in *Chapter 24, Beelzebub's Flight to the Planet Earth for the Fifth Time*. The text reads:

"Now I wish to explain to you about the expression I just used, namely, the 'Building-of-the-Tower-of-Babel.' This expression is very often used on your planet by the contemporary three-brained beings there also. "

I wish to touch upon this expression frequently used there and to elucidate it to you chiefly because firstly I chanced to be a witness at that time of all the events which gave rise to it, and secondly because the history of the arising of this expression and its transubstantiation in the understanding of your contemporary favorites can very clearly and instructively elucidate to you that, thanks as always to the same abnormally established conditions of ordinary being-existence, no precise information of events there which have indeed occurred to beings of former epochs ever reaches beings of later generations. And if, by chance, something like this expression does reach them, then the fantastic Reason of your favorites constructs a whole theory on the basis of just one expression such as this, with the result that those illusory being-egoplastikoori, or what they call 'psychic-picturings' increase and multiply in their presences owing to which there has arisen in the Universe the strange 'unique-psyche of three brained beings which every one of your favorites has.

This is a fairly brutal criticism of our ability to reason, not leveled at humanity in some general sense, but leveled at each one of us individually by the phrase "the strange 'unique-psyche' of three-brained beings which every one of your favorites has." He levels this at me.

In this paragraph he defines the term "being-egoplastikoori," saying that we would call these phenomena "psychic-picturings" and he also states that we are inculcated with illusory psychic picturings that derive from baseless theories. From this point forward in *The Tales* he never again uses the term *psychic-picturings*. In *Chapter 28, The Chief Culprit in the Destruction of All the Very Saintly Labors of Ashiata Shiemash*, we read:

"Already by the time this terrestrial what is called 'Papa's-and-Mama's-darling' was approaching the age of a responsible being, he was, as it is said there, very well 'instructed' and 'educated, that is, he had in his presence a great deal of data for all kinds of being 'egoplastikoori, consisting, as it is usual there according to the abnormally established conditions of their existence, of various fantastic and dubious information; and later, when he became a

Chapter 3: Intellectual Postures And Processes

responsible being he manifested himself automatically through all kinds of corresponding accidental shocks.

This is a description of Lentrohamsanin, which makes clear that the subsequent behavior of this individual was, to some degree, caused by egoplastikoori formed from fantastic and dubious information, as a consequence of which his later manifestations were automatic. In Chapter 29, *The Fruits of Former Civilizations and the Blossoms of the Contemporary*, we read:

"And hence it is that almost a half of what are called the 'egoplastikoori' arising in the Reason of the contemporary beings of that ill-fated planet, from which what is called a 'being-world-outlook' is in general formed in beings, are crystallized just from the 'truths' invented there by those bored fishermen and their subsequent generations.

Gurdjieff attributes half of our egoplastikoori to the influence upon us of the Ancient Greeks and their wiseacring. Finally, also in *Chapter 29*, in Gurdjieff's description of the principle Itoklanoz, the principle by which three-brained-beings of the planet Earth evolve, we read:

"According to this principle, the duration of being-existence and also the whole of the contents of their common presences are in general acquired from the results arising from the following seven actualizations surrounding them, namely, from:

(1) Heredity in general

(2) Conditions and environment at the moment of conception

(3) The combination of the radiations of all the planets of their solar system during their formation in the womb of their productress

(4) The degree of being-manifestation of their producers during the period they are attaining the age of responsible being

(5) The quality of being-existence of beings similar to themselves around them

(6) The quality of what are called the "Teleokrimalnichnian' thought-waves formed in the atmosphere surrounding them also during their period of attaining the age of majority–that is, the sincerely manifested good wishes and actions on the part of what are called the 'beings-of-the-same-blood', and finally,

(7) The quality of what are called the being-egoplastikoori of the given being himself, that is his being-efforts for the

transubstantiation in himself of all the data for obtaining objective Reason.

We can immediately realize that the first six of these actualizations are already part of our past. There is very little, if anything, we can do to change any of these things. As a consequence, the seventh actualization of the principle of Itoklanoz is overwhelmingly important, because this we can change, and it is precisely in this that *The Tales* can bring about a change.

Aim

In The Work, "Aim" is not a simple concept. In life, it can be simple. We need to buy a new toaster so we have the aim to do that. We go out to some retail establishment, to examine what they offer. If we find something appropriate we buy it. If not, we go to another retailer until we find what we want. Then we buy. Our aim has been achieved.

In The Work it is possible, in fact it is likely, that we are not even able to form a clear aim. Most likely we were attracted to The Work because we were searchers for some kind of knowledge, or we wished to change ourselves in some way. We were dissatisfied and we believed that we had exhausted the possibilities of "normal life," so we sought something outside of that. If we had something we thought of as an aim it was probably vague.

Nevertheless, once we met The Work and became familiar with many of its propositions and concepts, we stayed with it. Why did we do that?

Our view of this is best explained by analogy:

We are in a kind of prison. The walls of this prison, the locked doors and barred windows, go by the name of waking sleep. We in The Work have come to understand that almost all of our life is passed in waking sleep; we live in a dream. We yearn for the rare moments of awakening – the moments of consciousness – we have experienced. But those moments of consciousness did not provide an escape from our prison.

At one time or another we stood on a chair and looked out through a window of this prison, or we walked along the top of the prison walls and saw the world beyond the prison. Maybe we were even visited by someone who was not in this prison that we occupy and we noticed that they were not burdened in the way that we are.

So, as we are, we can have but one real aim: to escape from the prison. Should we be able to make such an escape, we have no real idea of what

Chapter 3: Intellectual Postures And Processes

we will do in the world outside that we yearn so strongly to live in. We may dream of how we would live in such a world, but these dreams are based upon all sorts of suppositions which may not be true at all. They are not meaningful goals.

If we accept this analogy as corresponding to the truth, then our general aim in reading Gurdjieff's writings is to discover the keys that will help us unlock the sturdy doors of our prison. Gurdjieff, a man who we can easily believe escaped from this prison, challenges us to "fathom the gist." We can either accept that challenge or turn away and hope that our efforts along a different line of the Work will free us from this oppressive prison.

In Summary

Our opinion, drawn from Gurdjieff's words, is that to fathom the gist requires both the development of the intellect – even for those who are relatively strong in this center – and an increase in being. Both are required. Gurdjieff said "the brain is a muscle." We can exercise that muscle in the ways described in this chapter – not just by reading about the various intellectual postures and muscles described here, but by practicing them. *The Tales* is the gymnasium in which such exercises can be carried out.

TO FATHOM THE GIST: VOL I

Chapter 4: Background Research

—∞—

It's all the same. Our thoughts work day and night. Instead of allowing them to think about caps of invisibility or the riches of Aladdin, rather let them be occupied with something useful. In giving direction to thought, of course a certain amount of energy is spent, but no more is needed for this purpose in a whole day than for the digestion of one meal.

Gurdjieff ~ *Meetings with Remarkable Men*

The *Tales* was made available to the public in 1950, a few months after Gurdjieff's death, the galley proofs having been shown to him on his deathbed. A German version was also published in 1950 and a French version was published in 1955. Since then versions have been produced in many languages, including Armenian, Dutch, Greek, Hebrew, Hungarian, Italian, Japanese, Spanish, Portuguese and Russian.

The Various Versions of The Tales

There are currently four English versions of *The Tales*:

- The Toomer version of *The Tales*. This version, the earliest known version, emerged only recently (in 2024). It was initially in the possession of Jean Toomer.
- The 1931 version of *The Tales*. This privately published and circulated among Orage's American group
- The 1950 version published shortly after Gurdjieff's death
- A 1992 version, a revision of a kind, published by Penguin

We discuss each of these versions below, partly because any serious English-speaking reader of *The Tales* should, in our view, be interested in why more than one version of *The Tales* exists and will probably wish to spend time on only the most useful text.

The Toomer Version

This is the earliest known draft of *Beelzebub's Tales to His Grandson* – far earlier, as is clear from the text, than the 1931 version. Its exact date of origin is difficult to estimate. It is clearly an incomplete draft of the book, with many chapters missing and other chapters significantly reduced.

The draft, contained in a binder titled "Jean Toomer's Copy of All and Everything" was given to Mr Robert Fertman sometime around 2008 or 2009. It was passed to him by a member of his Gurdjieff group who in turn had been passed it by someone who was connected to the family of Jean Toomer. It was in poor condition, damp and browned by what appeared to be fire and smoke damage.

To his credit, Fertman worked on it carefully and diligently separating pages and putting it into a readable state. He created a PDF of the book and shared it with the Gurdjieff Heritage Society, which has it available on their website (gurdjieff-heritage-society.org).

In our view, studying this version can prove valuable. The manuscript appears to be a draft that (most likely) Jean Toomer was in the process of editing.

The text begins with an outline of the book and then proceeds with most f the chapters of the first book, although the early chapters are lumped together in a chapter entitled, *Why Beelzebub Was On Our Solar System*. Most of the second book in the series is missing, as is most of the third.

In some parts the text is close to the later versions of *The Tales*, but in many parts it is distinctly different, and in general easier to understand as, in this draft, Gurdjieff had not added many of the details that make the 1950 version challenging. This version will prove very useful to those who take the time to study it.

The 1931 Version

The 1931 version of *The Tales* is the version that Arthur Orage initially edited, at times with the help of Jean Toomer, from 1924 to 1931. This brought the text to a readable state. Orage privately published the book, chapter by chapter, for members of his American group. It probably had to be paid for by most of those who acquired a copy, since Orage used the book to raise funds for Gurdjieff. It was thus a series of individual chapter drafts of the book. It clearly comprises a significantly later version than the Toomer version.

Chapter 4: Background Research

In many parts of the 1931 version, the text is very close to the 1950 version. In other parts it differs significantly, particularly in *Chapter 39, The Holy Planet Purgatory*. It is both significantly different from the Toomer version and the 1950 version. The differences are instructive.

One particularly useful characteristic of both the Toomer version and the 1931 version is that quite a number of Gurdjieff's neologisms are spelled differently than in the 1950 version. This can be helpful.

Considering this logically, Gurdjieff obviously refined his newly minted words gradually rather than getting them "right first time." Consequently reading through the Toomer version and the 1931 version can give us a small insight into how he evolved some of his words. Two glaring examples of differences in both books are:

- "Triamonia," which later became "Triamazikamno."
- "Eftologodiksis," which later became "Heptaparaparshinokh."

Most other examples are minor. An "Eternal-Hasnamuss-individual" who was named "Kharnakhoomoo" in the 1931 version, eventually became "Harnhoom," "Altoozori" became "Alstoozori, "Ethernokrilno" became "Etherokrilno," and so on.

There are some minor typographical differences. Some words that were not wrapped in quotes or capitalized in the 1931 version are wrapped in quotes or capitalized in the 1950 version. There is also the distraction, for American readers, that the manuscript was typed with English punctuation and English spelling.

The 1950 Version

Our opinion is: The 1950 version of *The Tales* is the version Gurdjieff created for us.

It and the German version of 1950, are the only versions that Gurdjieff saw and approved before he died. The 1950 version was published in New York by Harcourt Brace, and in London by Routledge & Kegan Paul. It was republished by E. P. Dutton & Co. in the U.S. in 1964, and again in 1973, as a three-volume paperback. It was republished again in the U.S. by Two Rivers Press.

And finally it was republished by Penguin Arkana in 1999 in paperback. This 1999 edition of the 1950 version manuscript included corrections of all known errata, including the insertion of two paragraphs previously omitted from page 568 of *Chapter 32, Hypnotism*.

We have noticed just one strange anomaly in this 1999 Penguin Arkana edition. It relates to a change in typography. In the original 1950 version, the typographical feature of fully capitalizing the first word or two of the first sentence of each chapter had been adopted. That typographical feature was removed from this 1999 edition of the 1950 version, which neither adds nor detracts, in our opinion. However, for *Chapter 30, Art*, we find an unexpected exception – most likely an error.

The Writing of the 1950 Version

Orage's explanation of Gurdjieff's initial creative process (to C. S. Nott) was as follows:

> "... he had a revelation of the book from beginning to end. In two or three hours he dictated a sort of synopsis and sent it to me. I said that it was utterly unintelligible and could not be shown to anyone."

We do not know whether this critical feedback caused Gurdjieff any pause. Work on the book proceeded from that point on, anyway.

Gurdjieff's writing process was unique. Much of the time, he wrote *The Tales* in note form in cafes and restaurants. It is believed that those original notes were thrown away when no longer needed. He dictated from the notes in Russian to Olga de Hartmann, or at times in Armenian to Lilly Galumnian. This is reflected by the words that Gurdjieff wrote to appear under the copyright notice of each edition of the 1950 version:

> Originally written in Russian and Armenian. Translations into other languages have been made under the personal direction of the author, by a group of translators chosen by him and specially trained according to their defined individualities, in conformity with the text to be translated and in relation to the philological particularities of each language.

Further detail of Gurdjieff's writing process is described in Teachings of Gurdjieff, by C. S. Nott, where Orage is quoted as saying:

> As you may know, he writes in pencil in Armenian; this is translated into Russian and then into literal English by Russians; it is then gone over by one or two English and American pupils at the Prieuré, who have only a rough knowledge of the use of words. All I can do at present is to revise the English when it obscures the sense.

Chapter 4: Background Research

Orage also adds:

> "Although I've talked over the chapters with Gurdjieff and discussed the sense of them, he will never explain the meaning of anything."

In any event the "polishing" of the English 1931 version of *The Tales* was completed by Orage with the assistance of Jean Toomer. It is hard to imagine Gurdjieff finding better writers and translators for the English language. Orage was once described by George Bernard Shaw as "the finest literary mind of his generation," and Jean Toomer, author of *Cain*, was no literary lightweight.

Sadly, Orage died in 1934 and probably never worked on *The Tales* again after the distribution of the 1931 manuscript. Subsequently, the book was repeatedly revised by Gurdjieff and other designated assistants; changes were often made after Gurdjieff had listened to a chapter being read out and observed the reaction of the listeners.

Versions of *The Tales* in other languages have also been produced. The only other complete version of *The Tales* that can be claimed to be approved by Gurdjieff is the German version. This was overseen by Louise March and published in 1950. In *The Gurdjieff Years 1929-1949: Recollections of Louise March* by B. McCorkle, Louise March describes the precision of that effort. She is reported as saying that Gurdjieff:

> ...considered a single word or the flow of a sentence so very important . . . we translators knew Gurdjieff as 'the teacher of exactness.' With Gurdjieff we came to use words exactly. He stated clearly that philology was a better route to Truth than philosophy.

We looked at roots of words. There were many philological rows.

In some ways this may be the most important comment made about the writing of *The Tales*. The French version, under the aegis of Jeanne de Salzmann, was first published in 1956. Reportedly, the English version of *The Tales* was used as the basis for both the German and French versions.

The Tales has also been translated from the English 1950 version into Dutch, Japanese, Spanish, Italian, Hebrew and other languages.

There is a question mark over the Russian version of *The Tales*, which need not concern English readers, but we mention it in passing. In 1927, Gurdjieff, reportedly, decided not to have a Russian text for *The*

Tales. Nevertheless, a Russian version of *The Tales* appeared. This purports to be an "original Russian manuscript," created from the "original Russian basis for the English version." It was published by Traditional Studies Press in the year 2001.

This version was written in pre-Bolshevik Russian, but published using the modern Russian alphabet, so it may be compromised in a minor way, phonetically. In our view, it cannot be taken as a genuine source document. However, it may be useful as a reference for determining the pronunciation of Gurdjieff's neologisms. There are also two unauthorized Russian versions of Beelzebub that are believed to have been translated from the English 1950 version.

The 1992 Version – The Arch-Ludicrous

In 1992, much to the immediate surprise of many people in The Work, a "revised version" of *The Tales* was published. This revision was, reportedly, begun on the initiative of Jeanne de Salzmann and overseen by her. The translation team was reported to include members of the Gurdjieff Foundation of New York, assisted by members of the Gurdjieff Society (London) and the Institut Gurdjieff (Paris).

If you compare the 1992 version with the French version of *The Tales* it soon becomes clear that it is very definitely an edited translation of the French version. It is flawed in many ways.

When it appeared, this "revised version" provoked an outcry from many in The Work. A. L. Staveley, who ran a well regarded group based in Aurora, Oregon, wrote an open letter to Dr. Michel de Salzmann in protest. In summary, that letter says, or implies in various ways, that the "revised version" is a damaging translation and it should not have been published.

In our view, the revision misses the critically important fact that Gurdjieff's writing has a definite rhythm, just as poetry has a rhythm, and in many areas the 1992 version revisions destroy or damage that rhythm. In our opinion, the 1992 version is indeed a damaged version of *The Tales*. We do not recommend reading it and can think of no reason to own a copy of it. We are not simply "taking sides" in some dispute; our opinion is born of experience. One of our correspondents sent an extract from *The Tales* to us and asked our assistance in gleaning an allegorical perspective. We initially spent an hour on this task, as it was not a section we had previously examined in depth.

Chapter 4: Background Research

Then, quite by accident, because we referred to one of our indexes of *The Tales*, we discovered that the extract had been taken from the damaged 1992 version. We replaced that text with the correct text from the 1950 version. It was clear to us that the meaning of the section was easier to divine in the 1950 version. Prior to that we had avoided this "revised version" simply because we found criticisms of it by others convincing. We avoid it now because of experience.

In *Chapter 21, The First Visit to India*, Beelzebub says:

> "But to the grief of every Individual with Pure Reason of any gradation whatsoever and to the misfortune of the three-brained beings of all succeeding generations who arise on that planet, the first succeeding generation of the contemporaries of this genuine Messenger from Above, Saint Buddha, also began, owing once again to that same particularity of their psyche, namely, of wiseacring–which until now is one of the chief results of the conditions of the ordinary being-existence abnormally established there—to wiseacre with all His indications and counsels, and this time to superwiseacre so thoroughly that there reached the beings of the third and fourth generations nothing else but what our Honorable Mullah Nassr Eddin defines by the words:
>
> " 'Only-information-about-its-specific-smell'

It is comic, indeed ludicrous, that Gurdjieff could write the above words and that, nevertheless, forty years after his death, the same wiseacring that he condemns in the above extract, and again and again throughout the pages of *The Tales*, should be carried out on his extraordinary work of genius. Revising *The Tales* is such a ludicrous act that it causes one to ponder on why it was done.

It is an enigma.

Since Jeanne de Salzmann was entrusted with Gurdjieff's publications following his death, and since the evidence suggests that she oversaw the revision, it is not beyond the bounds of possibility that Gurdjieff told her to do it. Consequently, we are loath to criticize Jeanne de Salzmann directly for the existence of the revised version. We do not know what her motive was. As far as we can tell, the publishing of the revised edition has merely engendered legitimate concern for the preservation of the 1950 version. If that was the purpose of the revision, then it has had the desired effect.

Faults With The 1992 Version

For those who care, here is a list of categories of faults that can be found in many places in the revised 1992 version:

- In various places the typography has been changed for no good reason at all. The impact is that the important emphasis and meaning that Gurdjieff's use of quotes and capitalization confer are diminished or lost.
- In many places one word has been switched for another quite similar word from English. Gurdjieff needed no help in choosing words.
- The rhythm of the words in many sentences has been mangled. Imagine taking, say, T. S. Eliot's *Little Gidding,* and altering the words a bit to "improve the meaning." It is a ludicrous suggestion. To do the same to Gurdjieff's writings is arch-ludicrous.

Combine all of these abuses together, as they are combined at times in the 1992 version, and the meaning of the text easily becomes obscured or lost. The revised 1992 version came with the declared "justification" that it was an attempt to make the text more accessible by "clarifying the verbal surface while respecting the author's thought and style."

This statement is perhaps as difficult to fathom as some parts of *The Tales*.

- What is a "verbal surface?"
- How is it possible to clarify such a thing?
- In revising a text, how is it possible to respect the author's thought unless you actually know what it is?
- How is it possible to respect an author's style and yet change it?

This "justification" is rich in nonsense.

We chose to research the various versions of *The Tales* for our own benefit, so that we would be able to clear up the confusion in our own mind about which version to use.

Researching The Tales Itself

We do background research to enrich our knowledge of the subject being described, or to better appreciate the context in which it is being described. As regards *The Tales*, there are two strands to this:

- Background research into Gurdjieff himself

Chapter 4: Background Research

- Background research into the various tales Gurdjieff tells.

We think it is probably unnecessary to advise readers of *The Tales* to find out as much as they can about Gurdjieff: how he taught, what is known of his history and cultural origins, and what he did to establish The Work. There is a rich literature on this.

Gurdjieff was born and raised in the Caucasus, a large geographical area peppered with many different cultures and religions. As far as we know the first languages he spoke were Armenian, Greek and Russian. Very few readers of *The Tales* will have any knowledge or raw information that corresponds to what Gurdjieff may have gathered in his early years–both incidental knowledge and knowledge he deliberately sought. We know that he was well read in respect of the scientific theories of his day and had an extensive knowledge of medicine and that he spoke many languages and was skilled in many trades, but we do not know the full extent of his general knowledge. Thus, when he engages in telling some tale in respect of some custom adopted in some culture, we have no idea how well he knows what he's writing about.

This brings us to the second strand: research into *The Tales* Gurdjieff tells. By virtue of our own ignorance, we have no option but to do research into some of the information he includes in *The Tales* and some of the topics he writes about.

This can be a fairly onerous and time consuming task, but it can also be rewarding. The first few pages of this chapter, for example, involved considerable research effort. We consulted four different books and several Internet sources to discover as much as we could about the background to *The Tales*, and it took time.

There are many parts of *The Tales* where it is, in our view, wise to do background research. Sometimes we may want to be better informed about a complex historical event such as the British expedition to Tibet in 1903-1904, led by Lieutenant Colonel Younghusband. In other situations we may simply want to have a better appreciation of a single word that Gurdjieff uses.

Research is something that we may not be skilled in, but it is an activity we cannot avoid if we wish to fathom the gist. For the next few pages of this chapter, we will provide a few examples of research that we have done on various parts of *The Tales*, in the hope that it encourages other readers to do the same or something similar.

We begin with research into *Chapter 12, The First "Growl."*

Tolstoy

In *The First "Growl,"* Beelzebub relates the tale of a "writer" who decided to write his own "Gospel" and, as a consequence of this, was anathematized by the church authorities of the day. Many readers will not recognize who Gurdjieff is referring to here. However, Orage, in his notes on *The Tales*, reveals that the "writer" Gurdjieff is referring to is Tolstoy.

If we had not encountered Orage's note, those of us who are not well versed in Russian history and Russian literature simply would not know what this chapter referred to. We would have no context, and to understand the literal meaning of this chapter we need that context.

If we research Tolstoy's life we discover that he did indeed produce his own version of the Gospel. In 1896, Tolstoy wrote a book entitled *The Four Gospels Harmonized and Translated*. Prior to that, Tolstoy wrote a series of essays criticizing the authority of the Russian Orthodox Church, including *Criticism of Dogmatic Theology* and *Confession*. In 1901, the Church, possibly with the blessing of some Russian politicians of the day, responded by excommunicating him and posting a notice on the door of every church. The notice read:

> *"God has permitted a new false prophet to appear in our midst today, Count Leo Tolstoy. A world-famous author, Russian by birth, Orthodox by baptism and education, Count Tolstoy, led astray by pride, has boldly and insolently dared to oppose God, Christ and his holy heirs. Openly and in sight of all, he has denied the mother who nurtured him and brought him up: the Orthodox church; and he has devoted his literary efforts and God-given talent to spreading doctrines which are contrary to Christ and the Church, and to undermining their fathers' faith in the minds and hearts of the people – the Orthodox faith. . . In his works and letters . . . he preaches the abolition of all the dogma of the Orthodox Church and of the very essence of the Christian faith with fanatical frenzy; he denies the living and personal God glorified in the Holy Trinity, Creator and Providence of the universe; he refutes our Lord Jesus Christ, God made Man, Redeemer and Savior of the world, who suffered for us and for our salvation, and who has been raised from the dead; he refutes the Immaculate Conception of the human manifestation of Christ the Lord, and the virginity, before and after the Nativity, of Mary, Mother of God, most pure and eternally virgin; he does not believe in the life hereafter or in judgement after death; he refutes all the Mysteries of the Church*

Chapter 4: Background Research

and their beneficial effect; and, flaunting the most sacred articles of faith of the Orthodox community, he has not feared to mock the greatest of all mysteries: the Holy Eucharist . . . therefore the Church no longer recognizes him among her children and cannot do so until he has repented and restored himself to communion with her."

Tolstoy was already a well-known and highly regarded novelist at the time, having written *The Cossacks, War and Peace* and *Anna Karenina* in the years between 1860 and 1877. Nevertheless, his excommunication simply expanded his reputation internationally. His home-grown religious ideas and writings influenced, among others, Mahatma Gandhi and Martin Luther King, Jr.

It is possible that Gurdjieff actually met Tolstoy, although there is no hard evidence of that. However, there can be no doubt that Gurdjieff had a low opinion of Tolstoy's religious ideas of "new formation."

Prosphora

"Prosphora" is a word from *The Tales* that we skipped over many times before we actually decided to discover its meaning. In *Chapter 42, Beelzebub in America*, Beelzebub discusses American bread, saying:

"The case is still worse on that continent with that product which, for them as well as for almost all the three-brained beings of the Universe, is the most important product for first being-food and, namely, that product called 'prosphora, which they themselves name 'bread.'

So the immediate question presents itself: "Why does he use the word "prosphora?"

This question can be answered very quickly by looking up the meaning of this word. "Prosphora" is the plural of the Greek prosphoron, which actually means "offering." The word is used specifically for the small loaves of leavened bread that are used both in Orthodox Christian and Greek Catholic (Byzantine) liturgies.

How does that information alter ones appreciation of that part of *The Tales*?

Karapet of Tiflis

Gurdjieff tells the tale of Karapet of Tiflis in *Chapter 1, The Arousing of Thought*. He refers to Karapet as "that precious jewel, Karapet of

Tiflis." Since the tale refers to a man whose job was to release steam into the whistle at the railway station in Tiflis in order to wake up the railway workers and station hands, it seems a little odd to think of him as a "precious jewel."

According to Gurdjieff's tale, Karapet, having learned that a feeling of unease would come upon him after blowing the whistle, because perhaps of the feelings of annoyance directed towards him by those whom he had disturbed from slumber, enacted the following ritual:

> *So when he would come in the morning to the rope with which he released the steam for the whistle, he would, before taking hold of the rope and pulling it, wave his hand in all directions and solemnly, like a Mohammedan mullah from a minaret, loudly cry:*
>
> *"Your mother is a — —, your father is a — —, your grandfather is more than a — — ; may your eyes, ears, nose, spleen, liver, corns . . ." and so on; in short, he pronounced in various keys all the curses he knew, and not until he had done so would he pull the rope.*

This seems easy enough to understand in a literal way. Perhaps there is some genuine psychological impact from the citizens of the town whom Karapet awakens. But why did Gurdjieff choose the name Karapet for this character? It is possible, of course, that Gurdjieff is describing a true event and that the individual involved actually had that name. Karapetyan (also written Garabedian) is a reasonably common Armenian surname. But this explanation is, in our view, improbable.

If we try to find the etymological roots of the word Karapet, we discover that "Kara" can mean "black." Gurdjieff gives this meaning for Kara in *The Tales* when explaining the meaning of Karakoom. The Greek "chara" means joy. The morpheme "pet" may stand for "heart." The word "parapet" consists of the morphemes "para" and "pet," meaning a defensive construction on a fort or castle at the height of the chest. So perhaps this name Karapet means "joy of the heart."

However, a little direct research into the name Karapet reveals the existence of the Saint Karapet Monastery, one of the oldest monasteries in "Greater Armenia," currently located in the Kurdish village of Chengeli in eastern Turkey. In Armenian, the monastery is named the Monastery of St. John Karapet, which is taken to mean the Monastery of St. John The Baptist. This possible meaning throws a completely different light on the tale of Karapet.

Chapter 4: Background Research

Which explanation is correct?
The reader decides.

Hypnotism

In Chapter 32, Hypnotism, Beelzebub discusses the origin of this science.

He states:

> "This 'abnormal' particular property of their psyche was first constated by the learned beings of the city Gob of the country Maralpleicie; and even then they made it a serious and detailed branch of science which spread over the whole of the planet under the name of 'non-responsible-manifestations-of-personality.'
>
> "But later, when the turn of their 'regular-process-of-reciprocal-destruction' came round again, this detailed branch of their science, which was then still comparatively normal, began like all their good attainments to be gradually forgotten and finally also entirely disappeared
>
> "And only many centuries later did this branch of their science again show signs of reviving.

He then describes how Franz Mesmer (1734-1815) almost succeeded in reviving this science, but was "pecked to death" by contemporary learned beings of new formation.

> "Although contemporary learned beings there affirm that the beginning of this branch of their science was made by a certain English professor named Brade and that it was developed by the French professor Charcot, yet in reality, this was not so at all.
>
> "From my detailed investigations of this said question, by the way, it became also clear that the former, Brade, had unmistakable signs of the properties of a Hasnamuss, and the latter, Charcot, had the typical properties of a mama's darling.
>
> "And terrestrial types of this kind, particularly the contemporary ones, can never discover anything quite new.

Note here that Gurdjieff deliberately misspells Braid's surname. We explain the reason for that later in this book. There is no mystery about how James Braid (1795 – 1860) came into contact with hypnotism. It is recorded that he personally attended demonstrations given by a traveling Swiss mesmerist, Charles Lafontaine, and examined the physical condition of Lafontaine's mesmerized subjects. He quickly concluded that they were in quite a different physical state, and then invented a theory as to how the phenomenon occurred. In doing so, he invented the word "hypnotism."

However, Beelzebub then goes on to explain that hypnotism was actually discovered by an Italian abbot called Pedrini who investigated the behavior of a nun called Ephrosinia. This is strange indeed, because as far as we are able to determine, there is no record of such an abbot or nun in writings about hypnosis. Neither is there any record we can find of Mesmer encountering such an abbot and, as Mesmer is credited with reviving hypnotism, this is strange indeed.

The only notable Pedrini we have unearthed through research is Teodorico Pedrini, an Italian Catholic missionary who is credited to some degree with introducing western music to China. We doubt if Gurdjieff is referring to him.

Ephrosinia is not a common Italian name – it would most likely be spelled Efrosinia in Italian. The name derives from Euphrosyne, who was one of the Graces in Greek myth. She represents "mirth" or "joy," which might at a stretch – be Gurdjieff's intended meaning, but in our view it doesn't seem likely.

There was a notable nun Euphrosynia, born in Alexandria, who dates back to the 5th century and who later became a saint. There is also a Saint Euphrosyne of Moscow, a Saint Evfrosinia of Polotsk, a Saint Febronia-Evfrosinia of Murom and a Saint Evfrosinia of Suzdal, all of whom led exemplary devoted lives according to what was written of them.

The other character mentioned in this section is an acquaintance of Pedrini's named "Doctor Bambini." We can find no references anywhere to a notable Doctor Bambini. "Bambini" is the Italian for "children."

In this example, research has, so far, only deepened the mystery.

Babylon

Beelzebub visits Babylon on his fifth descent, described in *Chapter 24, Beelzebub's Flight to the Planet Earth for the Fifth Time.*

If we accept what is written literally, the description of Babylon seems a little confused when compared to the official historical record. Since Gurdjieff does not name the peculiar Persian King, it is difficult to know for sure which historical period he is describing and which "Persian King" he might mean. Here is an extract from that chapter:

Chapter 4: Background Research

"When the peculiar Persian king I mentioned began, thanks to the hordes in subjection to him, to conquer beings of other communities and to seize by force the learned among them, he assigned as a place for their congregation and existence the said city of Babylon, to which they were taken in order that this lord of half the then continent of Asia could thereafter freely examine them in the hope that one of them might perhaps happen to know the secret of turning cheap metal into the metal gold.

"With the same aim he even made at that time a special what is called 'campaign' into the country Egypt.

If we think only of successful Babylonian kings then Hammurabi (1792-1750 BCE) or Nebuchadnezzar (605-562 BCE) might fit the picture. But neither of them were actually Persian. Cyrus the Great, (576 BC-530) who took control of Babylon after the death of Nebuchadnezzar qualifies, but sadly he never invaded Egypt as the "Persian King" is supposed to have done. We have not been able to find any reference to any Babylonian or Persian king collecting "learned beings." We also read of Hamolinadir, who was in Babylon at the time:

"Some of his phrases reached even contemporary beings of the planet Earth, and among them there is also the phrase "The-Building-of-the-Tower-of-Babel'

The biblical stories of the Tower of Babel date back well before the time of Nebuchadnezzar and Cyrus the Great.

Our research suggests that Gurdjieff was not attempting to report historical fact at that point in *The Tales*, but simply wanted to weave a meaningful tale for the reader.

The Opinions Of Others

Quite a few books have now been published that seek to shine some light on *The Tales*. It has been our habit to buy a copy of every one of them and read it, keeping it for later reference. We tend to value the opinions expressed by others, even when we do not agree with them.

There are several books which are direct records of the notes taken by people who attended meetings of Orage's American group, where the text of *The Tales* was discussed. One such book is A. R. Orage's *Commentaries on G. I. Gurdjieff's All and Everything: Beelzebub's Tales to His Grandson*, edited by C. S. Nott. Another is *Orage's Commentary on Gurdjieff's "Beelzebub's Tales to His Grandson": New York Talks 1926-1930*, by A. R. Orage, Lawrence Morris and Sherman Manchester.

Additionally, *The Teachings of Gurdjieff*, a delightfully written book by C. S. Nott, includes the full transcript of Orage's commentaries published in the first book mentioned above.

Just reading the pages of these books, one gets a sense of the brilliance of Orage. Importantly, though, these notes are of great practical use. One experiences Orage's immediate recognition of allegorical themes and his tendency to relate themes in *The Tales* to the world in which we live. He provides us with a model we can imitate.

Salzmanino

In *The Tales* in Chapter 35, *A Change in the Appointed Course of the Falling of the Transspace Ship Karnak*, Beelzebub requests of the Captain of the Karnak that, after visiting the Holy Planet Purgatory, they then visit the planet Deskaldino where the Great Saroonoor-ishan, Beelzebub's first educator, has "the place of his permanent existence." We read:

> To this request of Beelzebub's, the captain of the ship Karnak answered:
>
> "Very good, your Reverence, I will think out how it may be possible to carry out your desire. I do not know just what obstacles there were then for the captain of the ship Omnipresent, but in the present case, on the direct route between the holy planet Purgatory and the planet Deskaldino, there lies the solar system called Salzmanino, in which there are many of those cosmic concentrations which, for purposes of the general cosmic Trogoautoegocratic process, are predetermined for the transformation and radiation of the substances Zilnotrago; and therefore the direct falling of our ship Karnak, unhindered, through this system, will scarcely be possible. In any case, I will try in one way or another to satisfy the desire expressed by your Reverence."

In a footnote in *The Tales*, Gurdjieff provides the following information about Zilnotrago:

> * The word "Zilnotrago" is the name of a special gas similar to what we call "cyanic acid."

Curiously cyanic acid, aside from being a poison, has the chemical formula HOCN: exactly one atom each of Hydrogen, Oxygen,

Chapter 4: Background Research

Carbon and Nitrogen. It is a volatile chemical that, in contact with water, resolves into ammonia and carbon dioxide.

We first encounter Zilnotrago in *Chapter 3, The Cause of the Delay in the Falling of the Ship Karnak*, where it is in fact the cause of the delay referred to in the title of the chapter. The text reads:

> "But just through where our ship must pass, there must also pass, about a 'Kilpreno' before, the great comet belonging to that solar system and named 'Sakoor' or, as it is sometimes called, the 'Madcap.'
>
> "So if we keep to our proposed course, we must inevitably traverse the space through which this comet will have to pass.
>
> "Your Right Reverence of course knows that this 'Madcap' comet always leaves in its track a great deal of 'Zilnotrago,' which on entering the planetary body of a being disorganizes most of its functions until all the 'Zilnotrago' is volatilized out of it.

Cyanic acid would indeed disorganize most of the functions of one's planetary body and in sufficient quantity would cause death. We note here, by the way, that Gurdjieff's "spaceships" actually absorb the atmospheres through which they pass, distinctly unlike the spaceships one encounters in science fiction or in reality.

We also note a difference in these two encounters with Zilnotrago. In the first a comet "Madcap" leaves Zilnotrago in its wake. In the second the system Salzmanino has many cosmic concentrations which, for purposes of the general cosmic Trogoautoegocratic process, are predetermined for the transformation and radiation of the substances Zilnotrago.

This is a different situation. The problem is not Zilnotrago from the passage of a single comet, where one can simply wait it out, but that the whole system of Salzmanino is to be avoided completely because of the cosmic concentrations in it that radiate Zilnotrago – and do so naturally, as part of the Trogoautoegocratic process.

Zilnotrago is a curious substance then, as it is something that is radiated rather than something formed by chemical combination. It is disruptive. What does the Zilnotrago mean?

Its etymology is uncertain. In Slovenian *zilno* means "vascular," i.e., relating to the blood system and vessels. In Slovak, the meaning of *zilno* is almost the same; it means "venous." *Tragos* is Greek for "goat." The English word "tragedy" comes from the Greek *tragos* and *oide*, which means song. "Tragedy" thus originally meant "goat song." It is presumed, by some, but not known for sure, that the word refers to a song that a chorus would sing prior to the ritual sacrifice of a goat.

Zilnotrago suggests to us the sacrifice of a two-brained being, or, to be more precise, the radiations that accompany the sacrifice of a two-brained being.

So what then of Salzmanino?

Salzmanino has an easy to discover etymology. The word breaks down into *Salz, man, ino*. *Salz* is German for "salt." *Man* is English for man. *Ino* is a common Italian suffix denoting "little." For example, in Italian *buffone* is a clown, and *buffalino* is a little clown. Putting this together we can take Salzmanino to mean "man of little salt."

We suspect that Gurdjieff is not referring to Madame de Salzmann or any other de Salzmann. Her surname has a double 'n.'

Chapter 5: Objective Science

—ɷ—

"Not a single one of those sorry-scientists' has ever thought that the difference between these two cosmic processes is just about the same as that which the highly esteemed Mullah Nassr Eddin once expressed in the following words:
"They are as much alike as the beard of the famous English Shakespeare and the no less famous French Armagnac.
Gurdjieff ~ The Tales

In the Middle Ages in Europe, it was generally thought that the Bible and various Greek writings, particularly the works of Plato and Aristotle, constituted all the knowledge available to man. A variety of now discarded theories were accepted as true. The authority that presided over this "knowledge" was the Roman Catholic Church; it assumed the role of "arbiter of truth." Its behavior in this role is revealed by studying its famous dispute with Galileo, which ultimately undermined its authority.

Galileo and the Inquisition

The Church was not anti-scientific per se. In Galileo's time the Jesuits had become an intellectual force, with a group of astronomers and scientists located in Rome. The Roman Church funded various scientists from its own coffers; many important scientific ideas of the day stemmed from clerics.

In proposing a heliocentric model of the solar system, Galileo was not proposing an original idea. The theory of heliocentricity was also known in Ancient Greece, but Aristotle himself rejected it. Following Nicolas Copernicus' death, his detailed account of the heliocentric model was published. Without provoking the Vatican, Johannes Kepler published a book that expanded on Copernicus' work about ten years before Galileo joined the argument. In fact, Kepler's book was criticized more by the rapidly growing Protestant movement than by the Roman Church.

Nevertheless, neither the Roman Church nor the Protestant movement found the idea palatable and neither did most scientists of that era. The religious objection stemmed from various passages in *The Bible*, in particular Psalms 104:5, which states, *"The Earth is firmly fixed; it shall not be moved."* Additionally, there was also Aristotle's scientific objection which pointed out that if the solar system were heliocentric then there would be observable parallax shifts in the stars' positions as the earth moved in its orbit. Galileo had not observed any parallax shifts with his famous telescope.

Galileo sparked the attention of the Inquisition, not by advocating the theory of heliocentrism, but because he, already a scientist with a considerable reputation, insisted it was the truth rather than just a theory. His stance was theological. As such, he could be accused of heresy, since he directly opposed the stated view of the Roman Church and, additionally, he had no evidence to dispute Aristotle's scientific objection. A confrontation with The Inquisition was sufficient to silence Galileo. He recanted, perhaps for fear that he would be burned at the stake as Giordano Bruno had been not so long before.

In modern times the behavior of the Roman Church towards Galileo is regarded as supremely arrogant behavior in defense of superstition. It can certainly be viewed that way. There is ample evidence to support it. Cardinal Bellarmine, the foremost Vatican theologian of Galileo's time wrote, "Freedom of belief is pernicious. It is nothing but the freedom to be wrong."

The arrogance of this declaration is somewhat reminiscent of a nineteenth century satirical verse that lampooned Benjamin Jowett, theologian, translator of Plato and Master of Balliol College Oxford.

> *First come I, my name is Jowett*
> *There's no knowledge but I know it*
> *I am the Master of this college*
> *And what I don't know is not knowledge.*

New Lamps for Old

The scientific authority of the Roman Church collapsed with the onset of the "Age of Enlightenment." From the 17th century onwards the halls of academia, the Universities and scientific societies, became the new "authority of scientific truth."

Chapter 5: Objective Science

Their mode of operation was not identical, since no individual scientist was given the authority of a Pope. What was and was not considered scientifically credible was arrived at by consensus and peer review. Nevertheless, the scientific establishment has behaved in a similar way to the Roman Church in its heyday, blessing some ideas (Darwinism, The Laws of Thermodynamics, Einsteinian Physics, etc.) and rejecting other ideas as heresy.

The manner in which the learned beings of contemporary science can sometimes treat heretics is described in *The Tales* in Chapter 32, *Hypnotism,* where the response to Mesmer's theories about hypnotism is described. Mesmer and his theories were 'pecked to death':

> "As this honest Austro-Hungarian learned being then began making his elucidating experiments not as all the learned beings of the Earth of new formation had in general become mechanized to do, he was, according to the custom there, very meticulously 'pecked to death.'
>
> "And this process of the pecking to death of this poor Mesmer was then so effective that it has already passed by its own momentum to the learned beings of the Earth from generation to generation.
>
> "For instance, all the books now existing there on the question of this hypnotism-and of such books there are thousands there—always begin by saying that this Mesmer was nothing more nor less than a rogue with an itching palm and a charlatan of the first water, but that our 'honest' and 'great' learned beings very soon saw through him and prevented his doing any kind of mischief.
>
> "The more the learned beings of recent times of this peculiar planet are themselves personally, in the sense of 'idiotism, squared, the more they criticize Mesmer and say or write concerning him every possible kind of absurdity to bring him into contempt.
>
> "And in doing this, they criticize exactly that humble and honest learned being of their planet, who, if he had not been pecked to death would have revived that science, which alone is absolutely necessary to them and by means of which alone, perhaps, they might be saved from the consequences of the properties of the organ Kundabuffer."

When some of the "accepted" theories of modern science are subjected to sincere scrutiny we encounter many areas where we ought to have legitimate doubt as to whether they accord with reality.

Despite this, and despite the fact that *The Tales* seeks to destroy our suggestibility, and despite our personal work, many in The Work appear to give credence to the cherished theories of modern science. Indeed, it is frequently our experience that many people in The Work accept many of the concepts of contemporary science without question. This is a terrible, terrible, error.

There are excellent reasons why we should not do so. In this respect it is worth devoting time and effort to studying what Gurdjieff wrote and taught. We will then be better able to appreciate the differences between Gurdjieff's Objective Science and contemporary science which usurped Catholicism to become the new religion of the modern age. (It is incidentally, an atheistic religion.)

Objective Science and Subjective Science

Both Subjective and Objective Science demand an intellectual posture of skepticism, which assumes that the scientist does not know, but seeks to know.

Subjective Science operates roughly as follows: The scientist begins with a hypothesis that is most likely based on some already existing "accepted truths." He proceeds by formulating experiments, analyzes the results of those experiments and then either proclaims that the hypothesis has been wholly or partly confirmed, or if that is not the case, alters the hypothesis to conform with the experimental results. Results and theories are subjected to peer review. Thus the scientific community decides what is accepted as proven and what is accepted as a credible theory. This process is repeated time and again. This is how contemporary science evolves or involves.

Modern science can thus be described as "bottom up." It starts from some basic assumptions about reality and, via "provably repeatable" experimentation, it builds a "tower of knowledge." Occasionally some of the basic assumptions of this science are challenged and proven to be wrong. As a consequence the "tower of knowledge" is periodically remodeled.

In Objective Science, we are given formulations of fundamental laws and information about them. It is suggested to us that these laws come from "higher mind" and can only be thoroughly understood by higher mind. Our goal, as Objective Scientists, is to attempt to comprehend these laws and how they operate. We are expected to adopt an attitude of skepticism as we investigate them. We do not formulate original

Chapter 5: Objective Science

hypotheses and investigate them, but we do formulate personal hypotheses about what these laws may mean or imply in our attempts to understand them. We carry out experiments to gather information. As such we confirm or refute the formulations we have been given.

Objective Science can thus be characterized as "top-down," coming from (in theory) higher mind, with the possibility that by our efforts we may ascend step by step to that level. If the formulations of Objective Science that we have been given are wrong, then we will never get anywhere close to the truth by our activity.

As individuals in The Work, we give credence to the formulations of Objective Science mainly because we have personally verified some of the formulations and information passed to us. Most, if not all of us, have done this through internally testing the psychological formulations of The Work, such as inner considering, identification, keeping accounts, formatory thinking and so on. We have personally proven the description of these activities to be accurate.

Objective Science and Subjective Science share the attitude of skepticism and the activity of experimentation. They are also both completely materialistic. Aside from that, they have little in common. Subjective Science is atheistic in its behavior, assuming no higher intelligence than that of man has any influence on the universe. Objective Science is theistic.

The First Skirmish

In *In Search of the Miraculous*, Ouspensky reports Gurdjieff as saying that everything is material (even God is material) and thus knowledge is material. This is a primary point of differentiation between Objective Science and Subjective Science.

Subjective Science exhibits very little appreciation of the difference between knowledge and information, whereas Objective Science insists that there is a very important distinction.

To take a simple example, a husband comes into his home and tells his wife, "The car is in the drive." This is knowledge that he has and that he passes to his wife as information. As she has no reason to doubt her husband she now believes that the car is in the drive, but she does not know that. In order to turn that information into knowledge she will have to investigate – she will have to make a small effort and take a look. If she does so that information becomes knowledge, but if she does not it remains as information.

Information can be true or untrue, but knowledge is always true – not necessarily because you know it to be true, but because someone does. In general, when information is passed from academia to the populace about scientific ideas, rarely is any distinction made between data and theory. For example, we have the common recent reports that black holes have been identified at the center of many galaxies – and it is generally now held that all galaxies have black holes at their centers.

This is not knowledge, even in respect of the astronomers who have analyzed data gathered from observatories, for the simple reason that a black hole is a theoretical construct derived from mathematical formulae. There is no proof that black holes exist at all, although astrophysicists believe in them. As a consequence they suspect that such objects exist and they interpret data that they have gathered in a way that seems to confirm the possibility of black holes at galactic centers.

The astrophysicists who have gathered and analyzed such data can claim to have "knowledge" of black holes, but their belief that black holes exist is nothing more than an interpretation of data. It is not knowledge. The people who read the writings of such scientists may claim to know that black holes exist, but as they have done no investigation of the matter at all this cannot be knowledge – in fact it is hearsay.

In Objective Science, knowledge is always bought at the price of labor. One can tell someone about the idea of, say, "inner considering." If they have never heard of this concept before, they can, using their mind and their memory, come to the conclusion that maybe they inner consider on certain occasions. No matter how long they cogitate on this and how firmly they come to accept the idea, they still do not know that they inner consider. They have simply accepted a theory.

However, if they just once observe themselves impartially in an interaction with someone, when the mechanism of inner considering actually occurs, they will know for sure. They have to work in a specific way to turn the information (the theory) they received into knowledge. And the more that they observe themselves inner consider in this way, the more firmly will the whole area of inner considering become an area of knowledge for them. They will know increasingly more about this human characteristic.

Objective Science calls for careful personal verification, carried out impartially, in a posture of honest skepticism.

Chapter 5: Objective Science

The Second Skirmish

Let us now imagine a conversation between someone who has genuinely observed inner considering in themselves and a subjective scientist (a psychologist, let us say). Imagine that the psychologist disputes that inner considering occurs in the way that is described to him by the one who has observed it.

In terms of Subjective Science there is nothing more to be said. There is no possibility of the one who has seen it in himself demonstrating the knowledge that he has established to someone else. To acquire that knowledge the psychologist will have to do the work of finding out. However, if he holds a cherished theory that represents the inner psychology of man in a different way, he will most likely prefer to stay attached to his theory than to investigate at all.

"Proof" in Subjective Science is established by repeated experiment and peer review. Proof in Objective Science takes place in the inner world by the transformation of a theory into personal knowledge and understanding. No one else can establish the truth but oneself and once a truth is established the opinion of others has no importance at all.

Nevertheless, the position of the psychologist in our example is not devoid of merit. There are very good reasons not to simply believe another person's convictions, even if they appear quite sincere and intelligent. Anyone who has been in The Work for long quickly discovers that we are quite capable of deluding ourselves, and we must learn not to do so. We strive to adopt the inner postures that prevent such delusion.

In The Work, we gradually acquire certainty about any given psychological theory. Knowledge does not come with a single observation, it comes with many.

The Great Divide

There is very little common ground between Objective Science and Subjective Science. There can be data which both scientific approaches agree upon and accept as true information. However, beyond that there is no meeting point.

Objective Science is anchored in the inner world. We can characterize its foundation by considering the question: "What do you know for sure?" This is a beguilingly simple question which, when returned to again and again, establishes a genuine foundation for determining what we know and how we know it. To take a simple example, it has been suggested to us, as part of our education, that the universe is composed of atoms. There is a complex set of theories and deductions that Subjective Science has built up around this idea. For example, there are said to be many different kinds of atoms: hydrogen, helium, lithium, beryllium, boron and so on.

Do we personally know that any of this is true?

If we are honest we have to admit that we do not. Few of us have actually carried out the experiments that might indicate the existence of such chemical elements. It is all hearsay. Few of us have even witnessed an experiment that demonstrates the existence of atoms as conceived by modern science.

We are not suggesting here that there is no validity to this fundamental view of matter, only that for us it is information and not knowledge.

Nevertheless there are some genuine facts that we can establish as knowledge. While we cannot be absolutely certain of the past, since memory is not, for us at our level, a perfect mechanism, we can be certain of the present moment. If we bring attention to the present moment we can ascertain some very definite facts, such as:

- I have a body.
- I have an awareness, an attention.
- I experience sensations.
- I experience thoughts.
- I experience emotions.

Once we establish these facts, we have knowledge.

And if we now ponder the universe from this foundation, we are very likely to conclude that the universe is within us. Everything external to our individual core of existence is experienced through the six senses. Our experience of the universe beyond our body consists entirely of our interpretations and formulations of information received through these six senses.

It is clear that there is an external universe beyond our personal cosmos, as it impacts us. Events occur in that universe and we experience them and digest them to some degree. We respond to events in this external universe and that is how we exist from day to day.

Chapter 5: Objective Science

This is the great divide between Objective Science and Subjective Science. In Objective Science the foundation of reality is in our personal cosmos. In Subjective Science the foundation of reality is in the external cosmos – the megalocosmos.

There is a kind of paradox in this. Objective Science begins from a subjective position. It proceeds with our investigation of our subjective world as we attempt to establish an objective reality. Subjective Science begins from an objective foundation, the megalocosmos in which we all exist, but it inevitably becomes subjective as it seeks out consensus. These two distinct approaches to science come into conflict nowadays at the level of thought (Hydrogen 48).

Modern science has nothing credible to suggest about processes at this level or any level higher – because it has no means of experimentation that can examine these psychological levels. In Objective Science we attempt to gather data, at that level and above, through impartial observation of our inner universe. Such data is rejected by modern science as "inadmissible" within their scientific method.

The great divide is characterized by this:

Subjective Science has little interest in "being." It is concerned with mechanism and various theories that seek to elucidate the nature of mechanisms. Its achievements – and it is not without its achievements – are manifested in external physical phenomena. However, many of the things that are represented as scientific achievement, such as the Moon landing and the atom bomb are achieved with significant participation from engineers. Engineers, to their credit, tend to be pragmatic and not to be wedded to specific scientific theories.

Objective Science is concerned with knowledge and being. It regards the external universe as corresponding to the inner universe in many ways. The Objective Scientist is a genuine Alchemist. His inner world is the apparatus in which various substances are brought together and he observes the outcome of their combination. In doing so he is able to formulate credible theories about the nature of the megalocosmos and to test them.

He is the crucible in which chemicals are mixed, not the paper on which formulae are written.

Datum, Information, Knowledge, Understanding

The data and information that Subjective Science gathers together and about which it generates theories can be very useful to us. While there may be some examples of contemporary scientists fixing the data, scientific discipline forbids such behavior and any scientist discovered doing this would discredit themselves completely. However there is a tendency for contemporary scientists, and particularly reporters who work in this field, to mix fact and theory. For that reason, if we intend to use the information of contemporary science, we need to develop a habit of separating fact from theory.

We can define the terms "datum," "information," "knowledge," and "understanding" as follows:

A *datum* is a bare molecule of information without context.

Here is an example: Brazil 0, France 1. This single datum tells us very little. It appears to be the score from a sports match of some kind. But we do not know whether this is so, and even if we did, we do not know whether it is the final score, or a score from part way through the game. We do not even know when the game was played or where.

If we now add some more contextual data, it can acquire the status of information, as we have chosen to define it here:

Let us say, that this was the final score in a football match on July 1st, 2006, during the World Cup. The goal was scored by Thierry Henry, a superb volley that was enough to eliminate Brazil from the competition.

So we now have information, but these two sentences do not just contain more data. They also contain some opinion (theory) that the volley was superb and that it was enough to defeat Brazil. If we are to separate fact from theory we will have to categorize those opinions as theory.

The effort to separate fact from theory is always necessary. In the modern world we are inundated with so much information that is riddled with theory, some of it unintentional. But a great deal of it is clearly biased to some end or other and some of it is pure propaganda.

Even with the information provided in our example, we do not have knowledge of the football match it reports on. In order to claim knowledge, we would have had to watch the football match. If we had, then we might be able to provide an opinion on the theories we have

Chapter 5: Objective Science

encountered. Even if we have such knowledge, we cannot claim any understanding of that game of football. In order to do so, we would have to have played football, maybe even played at an international level.

In order to understand, we have to do.

We are taught many things in school. Gurdjieff depicts our process of education as learning by rote. This may conjure up memories of repeating the multiplication tables, or learning some poem or other by heart, which we may have been obliged to do. But the learning by rote that he refers to goes much deeper than that. In general, our education most likely consisted of being provided a great deal of information about various areas of study. We very rarely had the opportunity to turn that information into knowledge.

We cannot even be sure that our teachers actually had such knowledge. They too might just have been repeating by rote what they had learned. They made suggestions and we were suggestible. Much of what we may believe we know is not known by us at all.

Even if we attain some genuine knowledge as part of our education, it is unlikely that we will have acquired much understanding. Knowledge is expensive and understanding is more expensive still.

The word "understanding" clearly means "standing under," as perhaps the foundations stand under a building. Although it may not appear so, the words "superstition" and "understanding" are distant relatives of each other. The etymology of superstition is from the Latin verb *superstare* which contains the prefix *super* meaning "above," and *stare*, which is the Latin verb "to stand." So understanding and superstition can be considered opposites, one having the sense of "to stand under" and the other "to stand above."

Alfred Orage defined superstition fairly precisely when he said, "Superstition is an emotional attitude towards a lie."

Important Distinctions

Objective Science, as articulated by Gurdjieff in *The Tales* and as reported by Ouspensky in *In Search of the Miraculous*, disagrees with contemporary science in many fundamental ways. To fully appreciate how far apart they are in their conceptions of reality we need to compare and contrast.

Etherokrilno and the Ether

Until 1887 physicists were reasonably convinced that all space throughout the universe was permeated by a medium called the ether. This was believed to be necessary as a transmission medium that enabled the propagation of electromagnetic radiation and gravitational forces. This assumption was abandoned after the famous Michelson-Morley experiment.

This experiment tried to detect the relative motion of the Earth through the ether, which was believed to be stationary. It was presumed by the experimenters that light would travel at different speeds according to whether it was moving forward with the motion of the Earth through space, or at right angles to the motion of the Earth. However, the experimenters found no difference whatsoever in the speed of light no matter what direction they pointed their equipment in.

It is important to note here that there were detractors who questioned the Michelson-Morley hypothesis and experimental result, but the idea of "no ether" prevailed despite the fundamental problem of electromagnetic radiation (EMR). EMR travels in waves, and does so in a vacuum. So the question is: if they are waves, then waves in what?

Nevertheless physicists began to assume that there was no ether whatsoever and, when Einstein proposed his Special and then his General theories of Relativity, which were agnostic about the existence of ether, the world of Astrophysics began to line up behind Einstein. This theory is now dominant in the world of astrophysics.

The world of Quantum Mechanics, however, is not in agreement with the Einsteinian view of the universe. While it does not propose an ether, it proposes something that sounds suspiciously similar. It proposes that there is an invisible field of energy that permeates the entire universe, called the Higgs Field (named for Peter Higgs who proposed this theory in 1964). The field is home to a fundamental particle, called the Higgs Boson, which allows this energy field to interact with other subatomic particles. Particles acquire mass when they pass through this field. If this field did not exist then, in theory, particles would be embarrassed by having no mass at all. This is why there was a great deal of joy among quantum physicists when an experiment carried out by CERN, using the Large Hadron Collider, appeared to confirm the existence of the Higgs Boson.

Chapter 5: Objective Science

In summary then, most astrophysicists have no truck whatsoever with the idea of an ether, whereas quantum physicists support the existence of a field that permeates all of space.

If it seems from this that physics is suffering from a split personality, that's because it is.

Objective Science proposes the existence of an ether, referred to in *The Tales* by the word "etherokrilno." In *Chapter 17, The Arch-absurd: According to the Assertion of Beelzebub, Our Sun Neither Lights nor Heats*, it is described unambiguously, as follows:

> *"Etherokrilno is that prime-source substance with which the whole Universe is filled, and which is the basis for the arising and maintenance of everything existing.*
>
> *"Not only is this Etherokrilno the basis for the arising of all cosmic concentrations without exception, both large and small, but also all cosmic phenomena in general proceed during some transformation in this same fundamental cosmic substance as well as during the processes of the involution and evolution of various crystallizations-or, as your favorites say, of those active elements- which have obtained and still continue to obtain their prime arising from this same fundamental prime-source cosmic substance.*
>
> *"Bear in mind, here, that it is just because of this that the mentioned objective Science says that 'everything without exception in the Universe is material.'*

In *Chapter 39, The Holy Planet 'Purgatory,'* we read:

> *"In the beginning, when nothing yet existed and when the whole of our Universe was empty endless space with the presence of only the prime-source cosmic substance 'Etherokrilno,...*

Thus *The Tales* insists that not only does etherokrilno exist now, but it existed prior to the creation. This is in stark contrast to astrophysics which currently holds to the idea that space itself did not exist prior to the Big Bang.

The Heropass, Time

Contemporary science, by virtue of the General Theory of Relativity, currently regards time as a dimension that combines with length, breadth and height to describe four dimensional space-time within which the universe is believed to exist. This mathematical framework enables accurate calculations of gravitational effects at the level of our solar system.

The two theories of Relativity led to a particularly important discovery about time keeping with accurate mechanical clocks in different locations. The speed of clocks varies according to the gravitational force that acts upon them. This is referred to as time dilation. Time moves slightly more slowly as the force of gravity increases. Thus at the top of a mountain (i.e., further from the center of the Earth), time passes just a little faster.

From a practical perspective, this became important in the building of the GPS system that, via communication with satellites, allows us to know precisely (within a few meters) our geographical location on the surface of the Earth. Because of time dilation effects, it is necessary for the satellites that are used for GPS to have clocks that run slightly faster than clocks at ground level. The difference in speed of these orbiting clocks is just 38 microseconds (millionths of a second) per day. Nevertheless, they need to be set at that rate so that geographical locations are calculated accurately. *The Tales* is not in disagreement with this difference in the speed of clocks. In *Chapter 16, The Relative Understanding of Time,* it says:

> "*Time in itself does not exist; there is only the totality of the results ensuing from all the cosmic phenomena present in a given place.*
>
> "*Time itself, no being can either understand by reason or sense by any outer or inner being-function. It cannot even be sensed by any gradation of instinct which arises and is present in every more or less independent cosmic concentration.*
>
> "*It is possible to judge Time only if one compares real cosmic phenomena which proceed in the same place and under the same conditions, where Time is being constated and considered.*"

This does not specifically refer to or point out the proven time dilation effect of Relativity but it insists that time can only be judged by comparing phenomena that occur in the same place. A satellite in orbit is not in the same place as something on the surface of the Earth. Nevertheless, *The Tales* does not depict time as a dimension in the way that Relativity does. It describes it as the only phenomenon in the exterior world that is subjective.

Chapter 5: Objective Science

"Only Time alone has no sense of objectivity because it is not the result of the fractioning of any definite cosmic phenomena. And it does not issue from anything, but blends always with everything and becomes self-sufficiently independent; therefore, in the whole of the Universe, it alone can be called and extolled as the 'IdeallyUnique-Subjective-Phenomenon.

"Thus, my boy, uniquely Time alone, or, as it is sometimes called, the 'Heropass, has no source from which its arising should depend, but like 'Divine-Love' flows always, as I have already told you, independently by itself, and blends proportionately with all the phenomena present in the given place and in the given arisings of our Great Universe."

Initially it might seem from this excerpt that Objective Science has no specific means of measuring time. However, it has. *The Tales* goes on to say that:

"Meanwhile, remember this also, that since Time has no source of its arising and cannot like all other cosmic phenomena in every cosmic sphere establish its exact presence, the already mentioned objective Science therefore has, for its examination of Time, a standard unit, similar to that used for an exact definition of the density and quality-in the sense of the vivifyingness of their vibrations-of all cosmic substances in general present in every place and in every sphere of our Great Universe.

"And for the definition of Time this standard unit has from long ago been the moment of what is called the sacred 'Egokoolnats-narnian-sensation' which always appears in the Most Holy Cosmic Individuals dwelling on the Most Holy Sun Absolute whenever the vision of our UNIBEING ENDLESSNESS is directed into space and directly touches their presences.

"This standard unit has been established in objective Science for the possibility of exactly defining and comparing the differences between the gradations of the processes of the subjective sensations of separate conscious Individuals, and also of what are called diverse-tempos among various objective cosmic phenomena which are manifested in various spheres of our Great Universe and which actualize all cosmic arisings both large and small.

The subjectivity of time is explained by reference to microcosmic creatures that live in a drop of water, whose lifetime maybe no more than a day or even hours or minutes. Such creatures experience their whole lifetime subjectively as being roughly the same length as we experience our whole lifetime. Ouspensky pursued this idea in *In Search of the Miraculous*, when he compared the lifetimes of suns, planets, nature, human beings and individual cells.

Gurdjieff would probably have known Einstein's theories when he wrote *The Tales*, but if so he made no obvious attempt to align with them.

Fundamental Laws

Physics has proposed a number of fundamental laws which are believed to apply throughout the universe. The most fundamental of these is the law of conservation of mass-energy. This states that: The total mass-energy in a closed or isolated system is constant.

This was originally two propositions, that mass within a closed system was constant and that energy within a closed system was constant. It was altered in the wake of Einstein's discovery and the later proof of the mass-energy equivalence formula: $E = mc^2$.

This law of conservation of mass-energy gave rise to the three laws of thermodynamics. The first law of thermodynamics states that:

> *The change in the internal energy of a closed system is equal to the amount of heat supplied to the system, minus the amount of work done by the system on its surroundings.*

This is a variation of the law of conservation of mass-energy with the added nuance of covering situations where heat is added to a closed system.

The second law of thermodynamics states that:

> *The entropy of any closed system not in thermal equilibrium always increases.*

Entropy is the measure of a system's thermal energy per unit temperature that is not available for doing useful work. This says, in effect, that temperature in a closed system eventually evens out.

The third law of thermodynamics states that:

> *The entropy of a system approaches a constant value as the temperature approaches zero.*

This means that, at the limit, where temperature is absolute zero, the entropy of the system is zero.

Chapter 5: Objective Science

These three laws deal with closed systems, which are an idealization. It is impossible to create a completely closed environment where no energy enters or leaves.

Nevertheless, when these laws are applied to the dispersion of heat in less than perfect situations, they prove accurate.

Also if you choose to view the universe as a complex organization of a finite amount of mass and energy, and you attempt to propose theories about it, then science will usually insist that your theory abides by these fairly simple laws, because the universe is regarded as a closed system.

Objective Science proposes a creation where both mass and energy are brought into existence and thus its creation theory must be viewed as violating the first of these laws. However, contemporary physics also poses a creation theory, the Big Bang, where mass and energy are created from nowhere.

In order to permit the possibility of the Big Bang, which posits that the whole universe was once condensed into a volume smaller than a proton, physicists are obliged to violate their First Law of Thermodynamics for a fraction of a second after creation, just to get the show on the road. Other laws of physics include Newton's famous laws of motion, electrostatic laws, the law of gravity, laws of quantum behavior, and laws that are a consequence of Einstein's relativity theories, which include the proposition that nothing can travel faster than light and that the speed of light in a vacuum is a constant.

Objective Science proposes two overriding laws, the Law of Seven and the Law of Three. From its perspective these are the laws that created our universe through the will of our ENDLESSNESS and which govern it and everything that arises within it. In *The Tales* many other laws are mentioned but all of them can be assumed to be consequences of these two primordial laws. There is nothing we are aware of within contemporary physics or any of modern science that offers any parallel to these two laws.

Atoms and Elements

Contemporary science views matter as being composed of atoms. The atoms are categorized into elements which are arranged according to the number of protons in their nuclei in Mendeleev's Table of Elements. Objective Science does not categorize matter in that way. Its approach is explained by Gurdjieff, as reported by Ouspensky, in *In Search of the Miraculous*, as follows:

> *"The special chemistry of which I speak looks upon every substance having a separate function, even the most complex, as an element. In this way only is it possible to study the cosmic properties of matter, because all complex compounds have their own cosmic purpose and significance. From this point of view an atom of a given substance is the smallest amount of the given substance which retains all its chemical, physical, and cosmic properties. Consequently the size of the 'atom' of different substances is not the same. And in some cases an 'atom' may be a particle even visible to the naked eye."*

In contemporary chemistry there are compounds that are formed from combinations of elements. Objective Science doesn't have an equivalent concept. Every substance that has separate properties is an element. For that reason, water would be viewed as an element and both steam and ice would be viewed as different elements, even though they are composed of the same molecules as water. Objective Science's atom is determined not just by physical properties but also by cosmic properties. As such Objective Science allows for everything to be regarded as alive or part of something that is alive.

Evolution

Contemporary science is strongly in alignment with Darwin's Theory of Evolution, which holds that all life is related and has descended from a common ancestry via an evolutionary process. Nowadays, this theory posits that complex life forms evolve from simpler forms via random mutations to an organism's genetic code. Useful mutations are preserved because they aid survival via a process of "natural selection." Some life forms die out over time because they fail to compete effectively. Eventually, through a process of cumulative mutation, new species form.

Darwin's theory was not entirely new. The Greek philosopher, Anaximander, postulated the development of life from inanimate matter, with man being an evolutionary development from animal life. Darwin went much further by gradually assembling a "tree of life" which tried to map the descent of different life forms one from another, leaning to some extent on the fossil record. He also introduced the idea of "survival of the fittest."

Chapter 5: Objective Science

There are many rational objections to this Darwinian idea which make it difficult to accept. Sadly, in this situation, contemporary science finds itself in a bind. As it has no good theories to explain life and its evolution on this planet, science homes in on and champions the least bad theory. Contemporary science abhors a theoretical vacuum.

There is a particular problem surrounding the genesis of life itself on this planet which arises from the simple question "How did it start?" There is no evidence to consult here and vague models of a primeval chemical soup being struck by lightning, lack credibility, because nobody has been able to mix such a soup and apply the requisite thunderbolt successfully. This led English astronomer Fred Hoyle to compare the chance evolution of cellular life to the probability of a tornado "sweeping through a junkyard" and assembling a jet airplane.

Recent deep sea discoveries cast an interesting light on this particular problem. Life exists deep in the ocean around deep sea thermal vents that boil up through fissures in the Earth's crust at depths where no light whatsoever penetrates. The pressure is massive in those locations and the water emerges from the fissures at 360 °C. and yet a variety of life forms seem to evolve around these vents (e.g. tube worms and crabs), utterly unaware of sunlight. The life forms in such locations form a complete independent ecosystem, with bacteria feeding by a process of chemosynthesis on noxious chemicals from the vent, smaller life forms feeding on the bacteria and larger life forms feeding on the smaller ones. All other life on Earth could be extinguished without such an ecosystem even knowing.

It seems possible, then, that life will appear wherever it can find a process to profit from. In any event Darwinian evolution would need to pull a rabbit out of a hat to invent an explanation for such deep sea ecosystems. Objective Science presents an entirely different perspective to Darwinian evolution. In *In Search of the Miraculous*, Gurdjieff describes the lateral octave from the Sun as engendering organic life on Earth, as follows:

> "In the present instance sol begins to sound as do. Descending to the level of the planets this new octave passes into si; descending still lower it produces three notes, la, sol, fa, which create and constitute organic life on earth in the form that we know it; mi of this octave blends with mi of the cosmic octave, that is, with the

earth, and re with the re of the cosmic octave, that is, with the moon."

Ouspensky expands on this by saying:

> "The role of organic life in the structure of the earth's surface was indisputable. There was the growth of coral islands and limestone mountains, the formation of coal seams and accumulations of petroleum; the alteration of the soil under the influence of vegetation, the growth of vegetation in lakes, the "formation of rich arable lands by worms," change of climate due to the draining of swamps and the destruction of forests, and many other things that we know of and do not know of."

Organic life thus helps in the formation of the surface of the Earth. Shellfish create shells which by the action of waves at the sea shore are worn down over time to become sand, which later, through geological activity, is compressed into sandstone. The same is true to some degree of Earth's atmosphere. Contemporary science theorizes that the early atmosphere of Earth was formed by volcanic action releasing gases, particularly carbon dioxide, but also nitrogen, water vapor, carbon monoxide, sulfur gases and methane. In time, with the development of bacterial life and later plant life, the atmosphere was gradually transformed to one that had a far higher content of free oxygen, which in turn enabled animal life as we know it.

Objective Science depicts life on Earth partly as absorbing the influences of the planets in our solar system and transmitting them to Earth. As such Nature could be regarded as the Earth's digestive process. If this is the case, then evolution of life on Earth must be driven by the influence of the planets, with Nature deliberately designing the biosphere to carry out its function in serving the Earth, as well as its function in serving the Moon.

Objective Science also states that there is a planetary influence on individual lives, rather than just an influence on species. This is mentioned several times in *Views from the Real World*. The following are two excerpts from this book:

> ...the planets exert a very great influence on the life of the earth and on all existing and living organisms—a far greater influence than our science imagines. The life of individual men, of collective groups, of humanity, depends upon planetary influences in very many things.

And:

Chapter 5: Objective Science

Generally speaking, planetary influences on the earth alternate: now one planet acts, now another, now a third, and so on. Some day we shall examine the influence of each planet separately, but at present, in order to give you a general idea, we shall take them in their totality.

Schematically we can picture these influences in the following way. Imagine a big wheel, hanging upright above the earth, with seven or nine enormous colored spotlights fixed round the rim.

The wheel revolves, and the light of now one and now another projector is directed toward the earth-thus the earth is always colored by the light of the particular projector which illuminates it at a given moment.

All beings born on earth are colored by the light prevailing at the moment of birth, and keep this color throughout life. Just as no effect can be without cause, so no cause can be without effect.

And indeed planets have a tremendous influence both on the life of mankind in general and on the life of every individual man. It is a great mistake of modern science not to recognize this influence.

On the other hand this influence is not so great as modern "astrologers" would have us believe.

Man is a product of the interaction of three kinds of matter: positive (atmosphere of the earth), negative (minerals, metals) and a third combination, planetary influences, which comes from outside and meets these two matters. This neutralizing force is the planetary influence which colors each newly born life. This coloring remains for the whole of its existence. If the color was red, then when this life meets with red it feels in correspondence with it.

We may also recall that two of the seven actualizations of the principle of Itoklanoz, as stated in *The Tales* involve the planets: the conditions and environment at the moment of conception and the combination of the radiations of all the planets during formation in the womb. The principle of Itoklanoz applies to all one-brained, two-brained and three-brained beings on Earth.

Gurdjieff derides Darwin in *The Tales* with the following mention:

"The stimulus for the revival there of this Ape question was this time also a 'learned' being, and of course also 'great, but now a learned' being of quite a 'new formation' named Darwin.

"And this 'great' learned being, basing his theory on that same logic of theirs, began to 'prove' exactly the opposite of what Menitkel had said, namely, that it was they themselves who were descended from these Mister Apes."

Nevertheless *The Tales* also paints a comparable picture to that painted by modern biology about the arising of life on Earth:

"So, my boy, owing to all the aforesaid, there first arose on this planet Earth also, as there should, what are called 'Similitudes-of-the-Whole, or as they are also called 'Microcosmoses, and further, there were formed from these 'Microcosmoses, what are called 'Oduristelnian' and 'Polormedekhtic' vegetations.

"Still further, as also usually occurs, from the same 'Microcosmoses' there also began to be grouped various forms of what are called 'Tetartocosmoses' of all three brain-systems.

"And among these latter there then first arose just those biped "Tetartocosmoses whom you a while ago called 'slugs.'

The Solar System

Contemporary science estimates the solar system to be about 4.5 billion years old, having been formed from the gravitational collapse of part of a very large molecular cloud. In theory, most of the mass collapsed to form the Sun, while the rest formed a disk that circled the Sun, consisting of rocks and gases that formed various planets and moons, by gradual accretion. This is known as the Nebula Hypothesis.

The original nebula is presumed to have formed from one or more supernova explosions. This is deemed to have been the case because modern astrophysicists believe that only light elements, such as hydrogen and helium, were formed by the Big Bang itself, other heavier elements being formed by nuclear fusion within stars and then being ejected during supernovae.

It is believed that the death of the solar system will occur in about 5 billion years. The Sun, having expended much of its hydrogen fuel, will cool and expand outward to become a red giant, before it casts off its outer layers as a planetary nebula and shrinks back to become a white dwarf smaller in size than the Earth. As the Sun's gravitational pull diminishes, passing stars may tow away the planets that were not destroyed by its growth into a red giant, and thus it may languish forever, gradually losing heat and utterly alone.

Chapter 5: Objective Science

Objective Science begs to differ, as articulated by Gurdjieff to Ouspensky in *In Search of the Miraculous*:

> What interested me in this talk was that G. spoke of the planets and the moon as living beings, having definite ages, a definite period of life and possibilities of development and transition to other planes of being. From what he said it appeared that the moon was not a "dead planet," as is usually accepted, but, on the contrary, a "planet in birth"; a planet at the very initial stages of its development which had not yet reached "the degree of intelligence possessed by the earth," as he expressed it.
>
> "But the moon is growing and developing, said G., "and some time, it will, possibly, attain the same level as the earth. Then, near it, a new moon will appear and the earth will become their sun. At one time the sun was like the earth and the earth like the moon.
>
> And earlier still the sun was like the moon."

Ouspensky then poses a question:

> "In what relation does the intelligence of the earth stand to the intelligence of the sun?" I asked.
>
> "The intelligence of the sun is divine," said G. "But the earth can become the same; only, of course, it is not guaranteed and the earth may die having attained nothing."
>
> "Upon what does this depend?" I asked.
>
> G.'s answer was very vague.
>
> "There is a definite period," he said, "for a certain thing to be done. If, by a certain time, what ought to be done has not been done, the earth may perish without having attained what it could have attained."

These two views of the solar system contrast irreconcilably. Objective Science views the Solar System as a being, a cosmos. Cosmoses, whether small like a single bacterium, or large like a huge galaxy, are the same system. The way they work is corresponding. As such, we reflect within ourselves the operation of the whole megalocosmos. As *The Tales* describes:

> At this very place in the process of the first outer cycle of the fundamental sacred Heptaparaparshinokh, namely, after the formation of the Third-order-Suns or planets, just here, owing to the changed fifth deflection of the sacred Heptaparaparshinokh, which as I have already said is now called Harnel-Aoot, the initially

given momentum for the fundamental completing process, having lost half the force of its vivifyingness, began in its further functioning to have only half of the manifestation of its action outside itself, and the other half for itself, i.e., for its very own functioning, the consequences of which were that on these last big results, i.e., on these said Third-order-Suns or planets, there began to arise what are called, 'similarities-to-the-already-arisen.'

Two Creation Myths

Contemporary science is currently wedded to the Big Bang theory. According to this creation myth, the universe emerged from a mathematical singularity. This means that the whole of its matter and energy was compressed into a point smaller than a proton, which suddenly expanded rapidly and dramatically, eventually resulting in its present continuously expanding state. The Big Bang is estimated to have occurred approximately 13.75 billion years ago. After the initial expansion the universe was entirely a plasma, but it cooled sufficiently to allow energy to be converted into various subatomic particles, which in turn formed hydrogen, helium and the odd smidgeon of lithium.

Thus, giant clouds of these elements formed and gradually coalesced, via the force of gravity, to form stars and clusters of stars. Once stars had formed, nuclear fusion could occur and heavier elements, such as carbon, oxygen, nitrogen and sulfur could form, and then be scattered about by supernovae. Once that had occurred it was possible for life to eventually arise on planets that would themselves eventually form.

While, in our view, future generations of humanity will laugh until their sides split that intelligent human beings once believed this theory; at this point in time it is held as the best explanation available for explaining a range of observed phenomena, including the abundance of light elements, the cosmic microwave background radiation and the redshift of light coming from distant galaxies.

The Big Bang is not based on any particular cosmological model. It is based entirely upon extrapolation from observations. The redshift of light from distant galaxies and galaxy clusters is presumed to be caused by those galaxies moving away from us. Therefore if we model their movement back into the past we eventually arrive at a point when those galaxies formed, and before that time our model suggests that all the matter and energy must have emerged from a single point.

Chapter 5: Objective Science

Overextrapolation

The scientific belief in the Big Bang theory can be assigned to over-enthusiastic extrapolation. In scientific terms if we observe a phenomenon happening again and again in roughly the same way, we are likely to propose that there is some regular law involved. If we can represent that behavior mathematically, we have a neat mechanism for predicting behavior directly from the math. Our mathematical formula will doubtless involve the variable of time and thus, using that formula, we can project behavior both forwards and backwards in time.

Imagine then that we observe a car a mile away from us traveling towards us at 30 mph, but gradually increasing its speed so that as it passes us its speed is 35 mph. We observe it for another mile along this straight road and after a further mile its speed has increased to 40 mph. Imagine now that we repeatedly observe this phenomenon and the observed measurements are always the same. It is reasonable for us to extrapolate forward a little and posit that the car will, after a further mile, be traveling at 45 mph, but it is not reasonable for us to suggest that after a further 100 miles it will be traveling at 540 mph. The extrapolation has been taken too far. Similarly, it is not reasonable for us to extrapolate backwards and conclude that 7 miles prior to the car coming into view it was traveling backwards.

However, if you observe the universe to be in a particular state, and you also believe it to be a collection of inanimate matter interacting via forces that you presume to understand, then – even though you may only have been gathering observations for 100 years at the most – extrapolating its presumed motion backwards in time for 13.7 billion years may seem reasonable. It isn't. Not at all. It's an extrapolation too far.

If we accept the Law of Seven, then we expect that at certain times there will be deflections to the established momentum of any system. As such, we should regard mathematical extrapolation as only applying for a time, after which we should expect a deflection to occur unless there is some 'help from outside. A straight line extrapolation that goes all the way back to the moment of creation is deeply suspect.

In *The Tales*, the creation is explained as a consequence of our COMMON FATHER OMNI-BEING ENDLESSNESS deciding to change the sacred laws of Heptaparaparshinokh and Triamazikamno:

"And so, my dear boy, our COMMON FATHER CREATOR ALMIGHTY, having then in the beginning changed the functioning of both these primordial sacred laws, directed the action of their forces from within the Most Holy Sun Absolute into the space of the Universe, whereupon there was obtained the what is called 'Emanation-of-the-Sun-Absolute' and now called, 'Theomertmalogos' or 'Word-God.'

"For the clarity of certain of my future explanations it must here be remarked that, in the process of the creation of the now existing World, the Divine Will Power' of our ENDLESSNESS participated only at the beginning.

"The subsequent creation went on automatically, of its own accord, entirely without the participation of His Own Divine Will Power, thanks only to these two changed fundamental primordial cosmic laws.

"And the process itself of creation proceeded then in the following successiveness:

"Thanks to the new particularity of the fifth Stopinder of the sacred Heptaparaparshinokh, these emanations issuing from the Sun Absolute began to act at certain definite points of the space of the Universe upon the prime-source cosmic substance Etherokrilno from which, owing to the totality of the former and the new particularities of the sacred primordial laws, certain definite concentrations began to be concentrated.

"Further, thanks to these factors and also to their own laws of Heptaparaparshinokh and Triamazikamno which had already begun to arise in these definite concentrations with their action upon each other, everything which had to be gradually began to be crystallized in these concentrations, and as a result of all this, those large concentrations were obtained which exist also until now and which we now call 'Second-order-Suns.'

"When these newly arisen Suns had been completely actualized and their own functionings of both the fundamental laws had been finally established in them, then in them also, similarly to the Most Most Holy Sun Absolute, their own results began to be transformed and to be radiated, which, together with the emanations issuing from the Most Most Holy Sun Absolute into the space of the Universe, became the factors for the actualization of the common-cosmic fundamental process of the sacred law of Triamazikamno, and that is to say:

Chapter 5: Objective Science

"The Most Most Holy Theomertmalogos began to manifest itself in the quality of the third holy force of the sacred Triamazikamno; the results of any one of the newly arisen Second-order-Suns began to serve as the first holy force; and the results of all the other newly arisen Second-order-Suns in relation to this mentioned one newly arisen Sun, as the second holy force of this sacred law.

"Thanks to the process of the common-cosmic sacred Triamazikamno thus established in the space of the Universe, crystallizations of different what is called 'density' gradually began to be formed around each of the Second-order-Suns out of that same prime-source Etherokrilno, and grouping themselves around these newly arisen Suns, new concentrations began to take form, as a result of which more new Suns were obtained, but this time 'Third-order-Suns.'

"These third-order concentrations are just those cosmic concentrations which at the present time are called planets.

Our interpretation of this excerpt from *The Tales* is that the emanations from the Sun Absolute interacted with the ether bringing energy into being, which gave rise to Second-order-Suns, which we would think of as stars like our own Sun. And then, in the neighborhood of each of these Suns, planets were formed by virtue of the Law of Three, with the Sun as active force, the emanations of other suns acting as passive force and Theomertmalogos as neutralizing force. These planets also emerged from the ether, but having lower density than the Suns.

In this explanation of creation, planets are not formed by the action of supernovae spraying heavier elements into space which then condense; planets form directly from the ether, just as whole human beings form directly from a fertilized egg. This is likely a very slow process viewed from our subjective experience of time.

As regards the motivation for the creation, *The Tales* states that:

"From the third most sacred canticle of our cherubim and seraphim, we were worthy of learning that our CREATOR OMNIPOTENT once ascertained that this same Sun Absolute, on which HE dwelt with HIS cherubim and seraphim was, although almost imperceptibly yet nevertheless gradually, diminishing in volume.

"As the fact ascertained by HIM appeared to HIM very serious, HE then decided immediately to review all the laws which maintained the existence of that, then still sole, cosmic concentration.

"During this review our OMNIPOTENT CREATOR for the first time made it clear that the cause of this gradual diminishing of the volume of the Sun Absolute was merely the Heropass, that is, the flow of Time itself.

We could ask the question "How big was the Sun Absolute prior to the creation?" Given this description, we can be reasonably certain that we are not expected to believe that it was smaller than a proton.

We might also wonder whether the Megalocosmos is expanding as modern astrophysics seems to believe. We find this difficult to be sure of, but we suspect that once the emanations from the Sun Absolute commenced, they began to have their impact in every direction, taking time to do so. Nevertheless, there is no reason to suspect that this impact ever ceased. In all probability it continues to do so.

Quantum Mechanics

Of all the disciplines of contemporary science, subatomic physics or quantum mechanics is the most mysterious. This is perhaps because it includes a number of experiments that have bewildering results and which are very difficult to rationalize.

The primary mathematical models of astrophysics involves four dimensional space-time as proposed by Einstein. The mathematics of pre-Einsteinian classical physics was Newtonian mechanics applied within a three-dimensional Euclidian space. The mathematics that models the events of quantum mechanics is based on the abstract structures of multidimensional Hilbert spaces and operators on these spaces.

As such quantum mechanics is modeled in an entirely different way to astrophysics at the mathematical level. And that comes as no surprise when we realize that quantum mechanics and Einstein's physics have not been reconciled and, in all likelihood, will never be reconciled. If both of these theories of physics are true, then we are obliged to conclude that the universe applies one set of laws right down to the level of the atom, but below that employs an entirely different set of laws.

At the subatomic level we find a world that is driven by probabilities rather than certainties and includes apparent paradoxes, such as the ability for a particle to go from one place to another without passing

Chapter 5: Objective Science

through the space in-between. This is referred to as tunneling, implying perhaps that the particle vanished into another dimension before reappearing in this one. Another strange behavior is known as quantum entanglement. Two "entangled" particles can affect the behavior of each other instantaneously at very great distances – apparently violating the theory that the speed of light represents an upper bound for passing information.

The problems of Quantum Mechanics partly stem from the fact that it is very difficult to measure anything smaller than an atom, because our measuring devices are built of atoms. Nowadays, remarkably, we are even able to pick up a single atom and move it to a new location using a scanning tunneling microscope. But we cannot isolate and directly examine any particle smaller than that. We can fire individual photons at a surface and examine the effect upon that surface. We can isolate individual subatomic particles (hadrons), accelerate them, then smash them into one another in a hadron collider and examine photographic traces of that event. In fact, all scientific measurements of the subatomic world are indirect, so quantum scientists find themselves in a similar position to the prisoners in Plato's cave, able only to see the shadows of reality rather than reality itself. Objective Science doesn't suppose there to be any difference between any level of existence within the megalocosmos. The laws of Heptaparaparshinokh and Triamazikamno apply at every level from the ether to the megalocosmos as a whole.

The Crisis in Modern Physics

Occam's Razor states that among competing hypotheses, the one that makes the fewest assumptions should be preferred–given that the competing hypotheses are equally tenable in the face of existing evidence. In other words, the simpler hypothesis is probably the right one. Bertrand Russell expressed this idea with the following advice: "Whenever possible, substitute constructions out of known entities for inferences to unknown entities." We can reverse this principle and propose the concept of "Occam's Corollary." When scientists keep having to introduce wholly new assumptions and concepts to support their cherished theory of a given phenomenon, we should seriously consider the possibility that they are barking up the wrong lamppost.

In our view, Occam's Corollary applies to most of the current theories of astrophysics.

Let us consider the body of scientific data that has been assembled and continues to be assembled. The information we have about the universe has been gathered mainly by recording electromagnetic radiation (radio waves, infrared radiation, visible light, ultraviolet light, X-rays and gamma rays). We can also detect subatomic particles (including some neutrinos) coming from space. A recent innovation has been to use satellites that gather sound waves. This information has been used to get a view of the behavior of matter beneath the surface of the Sun.

We also have a few examples of moon rocks retrieved after visits to the Moon and we have a body of information gleaned from the analysis of meteors that have fallen to Earth. To add to that we have placed robots on Mars to carry out scientific examination of the surface of that planet. There are also experiments done on Earth with nuclear fission and fusion which provide us with information about atomic behavior that may occur within stars and on other planets.

In total, this constitutes all of contemporary science's data about the universe – and most of this data is very recent. At best we have about 100 years of data – which means that, in the grand scheme of things, we have not been gathering information for very long. The Big Bang, black holes, pulsars, red giants, white dwarfs, red dwarfs, brown dwarfs and neutron stars are all theoretical ideas of what might exist out there in space, based on gathered information and extrapolations made primarily from Einstein's theories of Relativity.

Scientists have detected a background cosmic microwave radiation coming from every part of the distant universe, but they only have theories as to what causes it. Every model modern science has of the universe is theoretical and founded primarily on mathematical extrapolation.

The popular theories of modern science are arrived at by a complex process of consensus. The individuals that make up the scientific community are mostly dependent upon financial grants to fund the research they wish to carry out. Those who go against the prevailing 'accepted theories' are thus less likely to receive these grants – although to be fair, they are not necessarily starved of support or suppressed or even pecked to death in the way that Mesmer was. The dissemination of any given theory is also controlled to some degree by scientific magazines which select what is published and hence what is generally available as information to interested individuals. Thus the phenom-

Chapter 5: Objective Science

enon of fashion occurs within science. Some theories are adhered to primarily because they are established views rather than because they have the best fit to known data.

There are some scientists who adhere to the idea that an ether exists – they just happen to be few in number.

A Crisis of Evidence

Black holes are theoretical constructs for which there is no evidence at all, despite the fact that science fiction movies are deeply in love with such fantasies. Having gone "all-in" with black holes, astrophysicists doubled down on the ludicrous idea of the Big Bang, as the kick-start event of the whole Universe.

As British author Sir Terry Pratchett commented, "In the beginning there was nothing, and it exploded." In recent years astrophysicists have tried to justify this laughable idea by producing mathematical models that seek to prove that it happened. Sadly, a mathematical model can never prove anything. It's a model.

Now, the enthusiasm for Big Bang came from the the redshift observation, that light from some distant stars is redshifted along the light spectrum, which can be interpreted to mean that such objects are moving away. The lie was given to this by Halton Arp who studied photographs of various galaxies that had quasars, which were clearly situated in front of the galaxy, but had redshifts much greater than the galaxy itself. Another explanation for redshift was required, but that was, of course ignored. Big Bang had a hypnotic hold on the world of astrophysics.

More recently astrophysicists have dreamed up the ideas of dark matter and dark energy. Both these phenomena are, of course, undetectable.

The theory is that electromagnetic forces play no part at all in the movement of stars in spiral galaxies orbit. Based on visible matter, the expectation would be that stars further from the galactic center should obit much slower than those closer in. But they don't. So rather than examine any alternative hypothesis, they invented the idea of invisible matter existing to explain the motion.

By contrast the dark energy idea was introduced to explain the expansion of the universe. It's a child of Big Bang. Anyway the rough theoretical score at the moment is that matter we cannot detect (the dark stuff) makes up 25% of the universe, while energy we cannot detect (the dark stuff) makes up roughly 70% of the universe. So only something in the region of 5% of the universe can be explained by observation.

You would think that such a conclusion would cause astrophysicists to think again, but no. They double down.

The Electromagnetic Force and the Gravitational Force

The ratio of the strength of the electromagnetic force to the gravitational force is approximately 10^{36}. This is a vast almost unimaginable difference.

The gravitational attraction between the Sun and its nearest neighbor 4.3 light-years away is roughly equivalent to the gravitational attraction between two specks of dust that are 4 miles apart. Yes, 4 miles. Even dust particles an inch from each other show no indication of mutual attraction.

Astrophysicists ignore the electromagnetic force completely, offering the opinion that, because it can both attract and repel it simply cancels out. They offer no proof for this assertion.

This is perhaps as ridiculous as their dark matter/dark energy assertion.

A New Cosmology, An Electric Universe

A battle of ideas has begun in the sphere of the intellect. The last such conflict destroyed the Catholic Church's intellectual hegemony and appointed a distinctively different priesthood in its place. Its church was academia, its creed was the scientific method and its priests went by the name of "scientist."

The creed that governs man's worldview and intellectual life is important because of the illusions it fosters. Mankind has a collective intellectual personality—an alliance of many "I"s. The intelligentsia naturally adopt its fashionable opinions and champion its "sainted" concepts. The priesthood of the day claims to profess a cast iron loyalty to the truth, hiding their hypocrisy as best they can when they betray it. Seekers of the truth inevitably see through the false facade of "knowledge" it erects, and turn away.

The priesthood that defends the dominant Standard Lambda CDM Model of astrophysics is no different in spirit to the priesthood that forced Galileo to his knees. It is against their interests to give air time to any theory or intellectual movement that challenges their precious

Chapter 5: Objective Science

dogma. They will happily promote almost any absurdity—gravitational lenses, neutron stars, dark matter, any academic fantasy you please—to conceal their intellectual bankruptcy.

Nevertheless, their empire is crumbling and, in the coming decades, a newly-minted priesthood will eventually replace them.

However, Objective Science is unlikely to become the creed of this refreshingly new scientific establishment. Even so, it will serve mankind and objective science well if a theory that approaches closer to reality replaces modern science's current bizarre dogma.

A cosmology based on the concept of an electric universe is such a theory. It is a body of knowledge that a small group of talented fringe scientists has gradually assembled from research, some of it quite old and generally ignored by mainstream science. Chief among them was Wal Thornhill (now deceased). It includes Michael Clarage, Donald E. Scott, Stewart Talbot and many others.

If you currently have little knowledge of what a cosmology based on an electric universe comprises, the following will serve as an introduction.

Birkeland Currents

Kristian Birkeland (1867–1917) was a Norwegian scientist who studied the aurora, gathering magnetic field data in the far North. Identifying a global pattern of electric currents associated with the aurora, he concluded that the Sun was the cause. He theorized that the Earth's geomagnetic field guided energetic particles ejected by the Sun from sunspots towards Earth, to the poles, where they produced the visible aurora. He was correct.

Because of his pioneering work, such field-aligned currents are known today as Birkeland currents. The importance of these currents was ignored for decades – the general assumption was that nothing "electrical" happened in space. It wasn't until 1967, 50 years after Birkeland's death, that a US space probe proved that sunspot emissions indeed caused the aurora. But even then, the phenomenon provoked little interest.

The Sun-Earth interaction is just a small part of a very big picture; Birkeland currents pervade the whole universe. They are the highways and byways of plasma – the fourth state of matter which is matter in ionic or electrically charged form. Happily, such currents are easy to

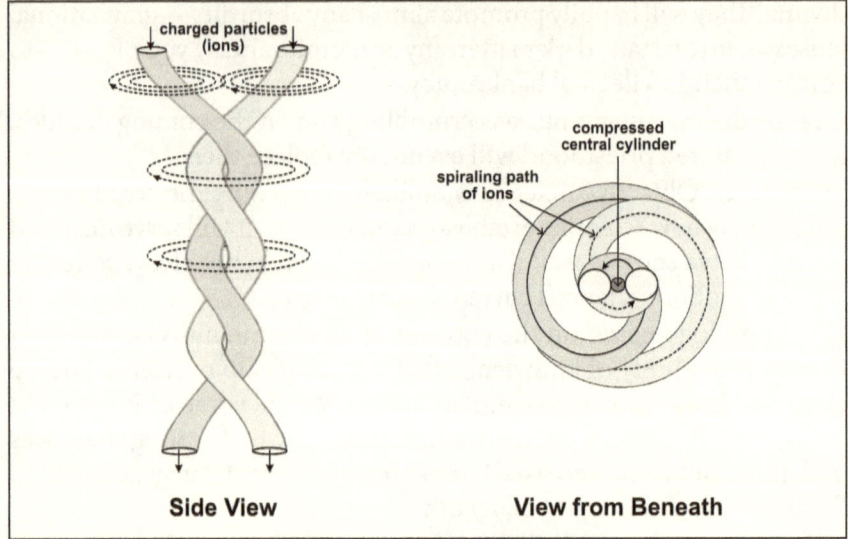

Figure 1. Birkeland Currents

create and test in the laboratory at a much smaller scale, so their behavior is no secret.

Figure 1 illustrates the twisted spiral form that Birkeland currents take. A spiral, like the one on the left side of the illustration, lines up with the direction of the Earth's magnetic field. The charged particles from the Sun create the aurora in alignment with the Earth's magnetic field at the North or South poles.

The mechanism is this. When a charged particle encounters a magnetic field at any angle other than 90^0, it moves in a spiral (a helical path) that follows the magnetic field's direction. This behavior tends to create not one, but two twisting plasma flows (i.e. electric currents) as illustrated on the left side of Figure 1. Any new charged particle which turns up falls into one of those two plasma flows.

Initially, these two plasma flows attract each other so that the radius of the spiral diminishes. The cross-section view from beneath, on the right side of *Figure 1*, represents this tightening of the two spirals. However, when a certain level of proximity occurs, a balancing force of repulsion is generated that holds the twin streams apart. The configuration is thus extremely stable, with a centrifugal and centripetal force balancing each other. These tightly wound pairs are Birkeland currents.

Chapter 5: Objective Science

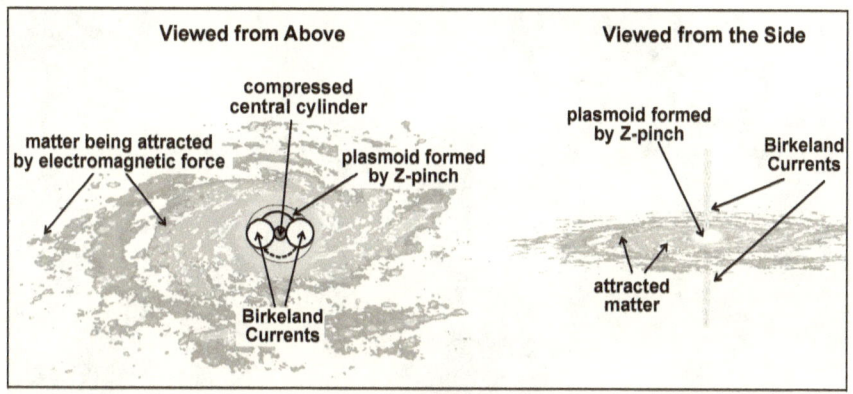

Figure 2. Z-pinch Plasmoid

The Z-pinch

Figure 2 illustrates what is called a "z-pinch." Electric currents flowing within a plasma tend to form Birkeland currents, creating a magnetic field that compresses the plasma between the twin currents into a central cylinder as illustrated. It is called a z-pinch for the simple reason that if you mathematically represent the spiraling motion in respect of an x and y-axis, then the cylinder forms along the z-axis.

You can think of this as an elaboration of the situation where two parallel wires carrying current in the same direction attract each other. Replace the wires with plasma, which can naturally carry a current, and you get spiraling Birkeland currents, which attract each other and compress the space between them.

In extremis, when the density of the current is very high in a Z-pinch, a specific kind of plasma structure (a plasmoid) will form. In a Z-pinch, a spinning plasma torus forms, which produces a very strong attractive electromagnetic force in the plane perpendicular to the Birkeland currents. The Z-pinch attracts charged matter in its vicinity.

Looking down from above, as in the illustration, it looks like a whirlpool of charged matter being attracted to the center by the electromagnetic force. The right side of the diagram shows the side view.

Galaxies

Birkeland currents occur at every scale, and as far as we know, function in the same way at every scale. They can be created and observed in a laboratory at a small scale; they occur at planetary scale

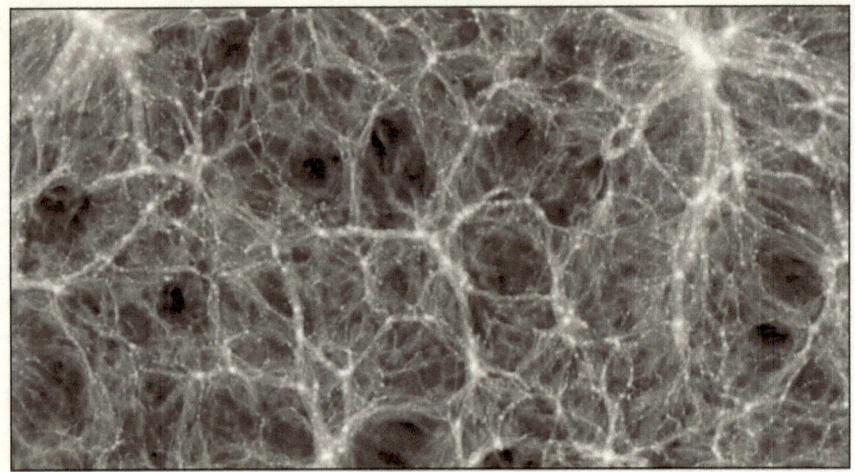

Figure 3. Birkeland Currents Connecting Galaxies

with the aurora borealis, they occur on the scale of the Sun. Astronomical observations demonstrate that they occur on the vast scale of galaxies. Plasma cosmology proposes that the Z-pinch within Birkeland currents is the mechanism by which galaxies form—solar systems too.

Circumstantial evidence for this is provided by *Figure 3* above, which shows galaxies chained together by Birkeland currents. It is a fragment taken from a map assembled by scientists and published by the journal *Nature*. They created a map of over 8000 galaxies to provide a picture of our local part of the universe.

Our Milky Way lies in the borderlands of a galaxy supercluster that scientists named Laniakea, from the Hawaiian words for "immense heaven." Galaxies fill the universe irregularly, clustering in some areas and avoiding others. (Nature also provides a Youtube video on this topic*).

A universe formed and maintained by plasma and plasma flows, rather than gravity, is far more credible than one supposed formed by gravity. Before 1967 there was little evidence that space was permeated with plasma and that electromagnetic forces played any part in the solar system or beyond. Astrophysicists assumed that space was filled with widely dispersed uncharged atoms and molecules. Thus gravity was believed to be the only force responsible for the motion of galaxies, suns and so on.

* *https://phys.org/news/2018-03-astronomers-galaxies-clockwork.html*
The title of this Nature video is Laniakea: Our Home Supercluster

Chapter 5: Objective Science

Although plasmoids and the Z-pinch effect do not on their own fully explain galaxy formation and evolution, it's almost certain they are part of the picture.

The Solar System

The fabric of the universe is almost all plasma. It's not just the shiny suns and galaxies. Nowadays, space probes seem to find plasma wherever they go. Our solar system is teeming with it. Everywhere we point telescopes, we find evidence of plasma and little else. Matter in the form of air, water, or earth makes up only a minuscule proportion of the whole.

The scale of the universe is immense. Estimates suggest that there are several trillion (observable) galaxies. The estimate for the number of stars in the average galaxy is currently 100 billion—a vast number. In all likelihood, each of those stars supports a family of planets, moons, and comets too. All of these bodies exist within apparently endless space that appears to be overflowing with plasma.

To add to the complexity of the situation, none of this is static. The galaxies move relative to each other; the suns move within their galaxies in ways not yet well understood. The planets revolve around suns and the moons around their planets. Our solar system is the only one we can examine in detail. A plasma-oriented illustration of it is shown in *Figure 4* on the next page. Just as all suns within a galaxy gather in a single plane perpendicular to the Birkeland currents, so do all the planets, moons, and other condensed matter in a solar system. It is called the plane of the ecliptic. The heliosphere, a vast atmosphere that surrounds the Sun and determines the extent of its local influence, is almost spherical—in fact it is "apple-shaped."

The region referred to as the Kuiper belt is a kind of asteroid belt which lies beyond Neptune. It may contain as yet undiscovered "planets," and comets are believed to originate there. Some astronomers suspect that comets can also originate beyond the heliopause. They suggest a theoretical region called the Oort cloud as their origin. We show it in the diagram in the plane of the ecliptic, but it could as easily be a spherical shell that surrounds the whole heliosphere, and it may not exist at all.

The solar system is maintained by two electric circuits: an interstellar current and a local current. The interstellar Birkeland currents enter the Sun at its north and south poles and stimulate its activity. Protons

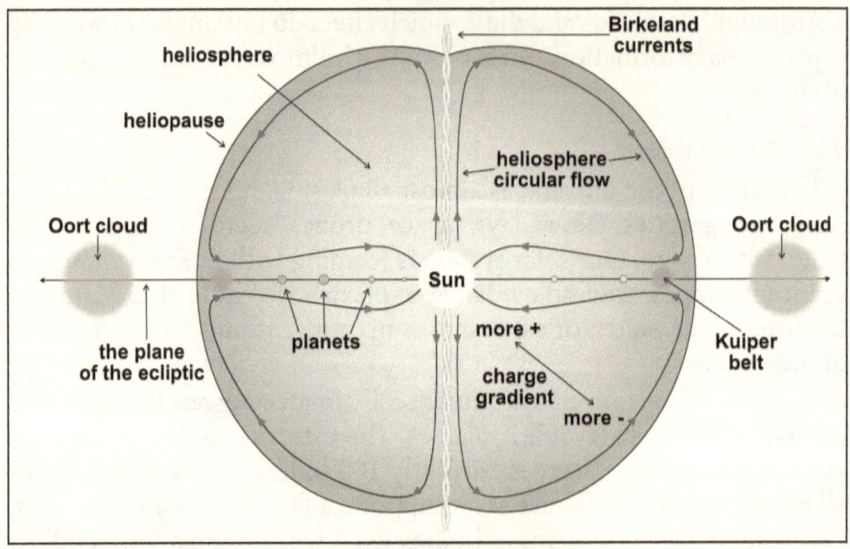

Figure 4. The Solar System

and other positively charged particles ejected from the Sun create the local circuit. They travel through the heliosphere to its edge, the heliopause. Electrons attracted from everywhere within the heliopause back towards the Sun complete the circuit. This circuit occupies a whole sphere but is more concentrated in the plane of the ecliptic.

The Sun is an anode and the heliopause a diffuse cathode. Hence there is a charge gradient between the Sun and its surrounding space that reaches its peak at the heliopause. If it were possible to put one lead of a voltmeter on the Sun and another on the Earth, it would show the Earth as negatively charged in relation to the Sun. The same is true of the other planets.

The negative charge associated with each planet will vary according to its interaction with the local circuit (the solar wind). However, each planet also has a magnetosphere, which insulates it from this circuit. It deflects charged particles to its poles, where the planet receives some of them via the Birkeland currents. The extent to which the electric nature of the planets affect or determine their orbit is not known. However, there is likely an effect.

We calculate the masses of each planet and the Sun on the assumption that gravity is the only force that keeps the planet in orbit. If that assumption is incorrect, then so are those calculations.

CHAPTER 5: OBJECTIVE SCIENCE

The Electric Sun

In *Figure 5*, we depict the inner electric circuit of the Sun created by the interstellar Birkeland currents that arrive at its north and south pole. The Sun's surface is a sea of incandescent plasma powered by these interstellar currents, which ejects positive ions (protons mainly) in all directions.

In the illustration, we envisage a situation where the primary current entering the Sun's poles is increasing. When currents increase, the magnetic fields created by those currents, as illustrated in the diagram, also increase. The change in these magnetic fields will naturally induce a secondary current below the surface of the Sun. This circuit will flow from the pole to the Sun's equator and back to the pole. Scientists using the joint European Space Agency/NASA Solar and Heliospheric Observatory spacecraft detected "rivers" of hot plasma flowing beneath the Sun's surface. They could be such a current.

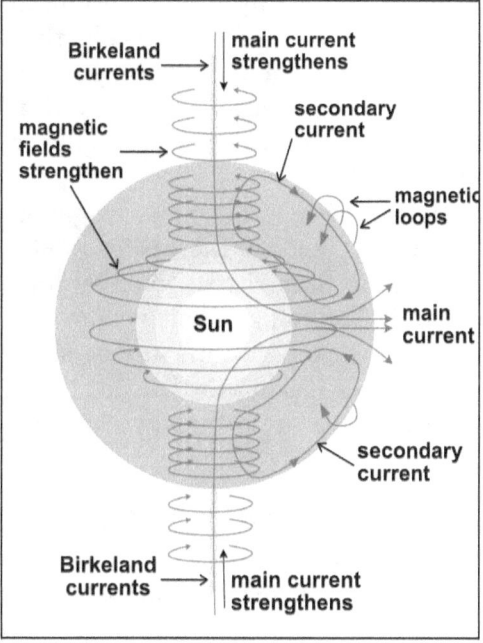

Figure 5. The Electric Sun

A river of hot plasma is, of course, a circuit of some kind. And such a circuit could explain the coronal loops—the huge plasma arches observed on the surface of the Sun that extend out of the photosphere into the corona. The loops, which can be 200,000 km long, are bipolar fields connecting opposite poles.

It works in the following way. If a secondary current "tube" flows southwards from near to the Sun's north pole and it is on or just beneath the Sun's surface, a looping magnetic field will emerge to the east of that current. It will create a north magnetic pole at the point where it emerges. The loop will move out above the Sun's surface and back down into the surface to the west of the "tube."

In the Sun's southern hemisphere, the opposite occurs because the magnetic fields run in the opposite direction. These magnetic loops reverse their orientation with the 11-year sunspot cycle. The explanation is that if the primary current begins to decrease rather than increase, the induced circuit will reverse its direction, and the magnetic loops will also reverse. The Sun appears to breathe in and out every 11 years.

The strength of the Sun's magnetic field has doubled during the Twentieth Century. There is no good theory as to why. Neither do we know how the constant bombardment of the Sun by cosmic rays affects it. Incoming cosmic ray protons are individual plasma currents that impinge on the Sun's surface, supplying it with energy.

For those seeking further details, a more complete description of electric universe cosmology can be found in *Gurdjieff's Hydrogens Volume 1*.*

The SAFIRE Project: An Electric Sun

The scientific establishment invests tens of billions of dollars every year into mainstream astronomy and astrophysics. The study of the electric universe receives almost no funding at all.

In 2012 there were just two scientific hypotheses concerning the nature of the universe.

- One asserted the universe was gravity-driven and the stars were thermonuclear phenomena. This Standard Model of the universe was taught in schools as if it were true. Yet, despite a vast amount of funding, it had never been proven.
- The alternative theory asserted that the universe is electrically driven at every level from galaxies down to planets. In particular, it maintained that stars were electrical phenomena. It had never been proven.

Until that time, nobody had formulated an experiment that could reliably test either hypothesis. That changed in 2012. Montgomery Childs formulated a means of testing a physical model of an electric sun. This gave birth to the SAFIRE Project,† which attracted private funding from the Mainwaring Archive Foundation.

The SAFIRE Project has been in progress since then. It has confirmed the Electric Sun Model, having mimicked an electric sun in

---

* *Gurdjieff's Hydrogens Volume 1: The Ray of Creation* by Robin Bloor
† Visit safireproject.com for more details.

Chapter 5: Objective Science

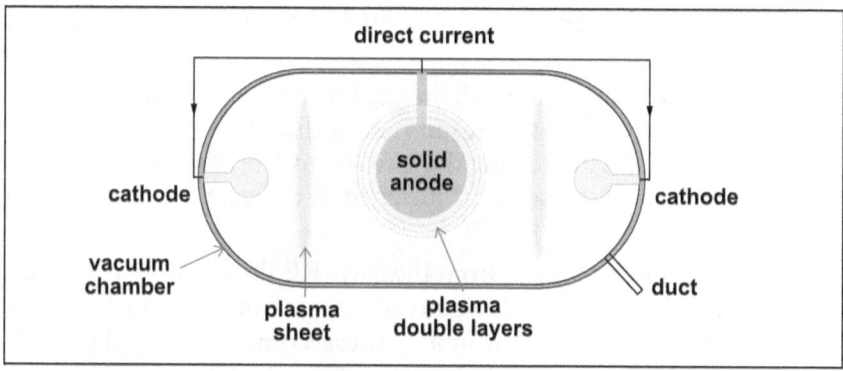

Figure 6. The SAFIRE Reactor Chamber

laboratory conditions. It found no disparities. The project continues because it has made many surprising discoveries.

Figure 6 provides a simple diagram of the experimental reactor chamber used in the SAFIRE project. Towards the center of the chamber is a solid spherical metal anode, and towards the edges of the chamber are two cathodes. The anode and cathodes are supplied with a direct current, as shown. The vacuum chamber can be emptied almost completely using a vacuum pump attached to the duct. If desired, small amounts of gas can be introduced into the chamber. So it is possible to vary the gas mixture, the pressure, and the voltage and current. This facilitates a variety of plasma discharges.

The diagram illustrates a situation where several plasma double layers form around the anode, and plasma sheets form in the chamber between the anode and the two cathodes. We provide a link below* to a 20-minute video that offers much greater detail.

The project has established the Electric Sun and Electric Universe as a credible, perhaps soon to become a dominant, theory. However, it has yielded other important and surprising results.

- The design of a new, clean and efficient power generation capability to build power plants based on plasma interactions. This has very promising commercial application.
- The discovery of a means to neutralize nuclear waste. This is achieved by exposing the radioactive waste to the nuclei of hydrogen isotopes within the vacuum chamber. The process generates energy and could be the basis for a power generating

---

* Visit safireproject.com.

device with nuclear waste as its fuel. It has obvious commercial application.
- A means of transmuting elements. From a commercial perspective, the most important result here is that the SAFIRE team has found a means of creating the rare earths lanthanum and cerium. The cost of doing so is far lower than the cost of mining these elements.

The most important result from the SAFIRE Project is its validation of the Electric Sun model. Mainstream science might want to ignore the science, but they cannot ignore these commercial applications. Neither will they be able to ignore the transmutation of elements. A revolution in mainstream astrophysics will thus occur in time.

Some of the Propositions of Objective Science

We are not attempting here to provide a broad summary of all the propositions of Objective Science. That task is reserved for another volume in this series. However, in this chapter we have identified some of the propositions of Objective Science, so it is worth simply listing those elements so that the reader can peruse them.

- There is an ether.
- Time is subjective, but the flow of time is objective in a given location as experienced by a single observer.
- The whole megalocosmos operates according to two laws: Heptaparaparshinokh (the law of seven) and Triamazikamno (the law of three), assisted by the will of the Absolute manifested as Theomertmalogos. The creation was a consequence of a change to these two laws which was initiated by the Absolute.
- Elements are defined to be substances that have different properties. The atom of an element is the smallest quantity of that element which retains all its properties including its cosmic properties.
- Within our solar system and all other solar systems, the sun, the planets and their moons grow of their own accord.
- The evolution of life on Earth is governed by the influence of the planets. Great Nature, in her entirety, transmits the influence of other planets directly to the Earth itself.

Chapter 6: Language And Style

"Even I, who had then learned perfectly eighteen of their different languages, found myself during my travels under conditions at times where I had not even the possibility of getting fodder for my horse, in spite of the fact that my pockets were full of what is called there 'money, for which in general they will give you with the greatest joy there anything you please.

Gurdjieff ~ Extract from *The Tales*

If *Beelzebub's Tales To His Grandson* had been written by an unknown author, it is unlikely that it would ever have been published commercially. It is too difficult to read for the casual reader for that to be possible. However, Gurdjieff had a personal reputation; he had a sufficient body of pupils to ensure that publishing the book would be a commercial proposition and he was associated with many recognized authors who could vouch for the value of his work, if need be.

If it had been possible for Gurdjieff to write a textbook that comprehensively explained the concepts of The Work and the techniques for self-perfection that he had learned or invented, he would doubtless have done so. The fact that he did not implies that it could not be done, or, if done, would not serve Gurdjieff's aim.

Instead he wrote *All and Everything*, the first series of which is one of the most difficult books to read that any of us has encountered. For a reader, the effort to read and glean some understanding of it is, in some sections of the book, almost as great as if it had been written in a foreign language that needs to be translated word by word and line by line. Yes, we can read it as we might read any other book, and if we do so we will gain some appreciation of what Gurdjieff wrote, but – as we have become mechanized to do with other books – we will skip sentences and paragraphs, and leap over words that we do not understand. At times we will lack attention so completely that after reading several pages we will not have the faintest idea of what we have read.

This forces the reader either to give up or to pay far more attention than he would pay to any other book. Gurdjieff recommends that the first reading of the book be done in our habitual manner. The second reading of the book is to be done "as if reading aloud to another." This demands a dividing of one's attention, since in that style of reading one must keep the experience of the listener in mind. If you read it in that way, you will read it more slowly than in the first mode of reading. The third mode of reading the book takes even longer, since now one has to consider the intended meaning on many levels: the intended meaning of each word, the intended meaning of each phrase, the intended meaning of each sentence and each paragraph.

And that is just the beginning, since in trying to fathom the gist at any point in our "third reading" of the book, we may need to bear many things in mind: the current tale that Beelzebub is telling, how it relates to other tales, how it relates to the overall story, how it relates to various concepts we have begun to appreciate, how it relates to our personal work and so on.

Non Bon Ton

In the first chapter of *The Tales*, Gurdjieff announces his intention to eschew the "bon ton literary language." It might seem then that he will not employ many sophisticated literary techniques. However, this is not the case at all. He deploys almost every literary style device available: tone, euphuism, alliteration, imagery, leitwortstil, irony, metonymy, metaphor, overstatement, understatement, onomatopoeia, asyndeton, paradox, pathos, satire, wordplay and so on. *The Tales* flits from serious to sorrowful, to amusing, to bewildering. It is alive with allegory and peppered with historical references and philosophical ideas. It is a tour de force. It is unique.

It is our conviction that to appreciate *The Tales*, we need to penetrate and appreciate Gurdjieff's writing style – a writing style that has no precedent. We discuss many aspects of it throughout this book. In this chapter, we focus on what we can glean from his use of typography, words, phrases, lists, repetition and variation. We analyze his writing style.

We are not attaching deep significance to this analysis. All we are attempting to do is clarify Gurdjieff's style so that the reader is better

Chapter 6: Language And Style

able to appreciate its nuances. In our experience, knowing the techniques that Gurdjieff–and perhaps also his English editors–used makes *The Tales* easier to grapple with.

It is our considered view that Gurdjieff chose each word and every mode of expression deliberately and meticulously. The final work may not have been absolutely perfect, but it exhibits so few errors that at times one is obliged to wonder whether an anomaly one encounters, which plausibly could be an editorial error, actually is one, or whether Gurdjieff intended it.

His Chosen Style

When one reads *The Tales*, or *The Herald of Coming Good*, or *Life Is Real Only Then, When I Am*, especially if one reads any of these books in a superficial manner, one might conclude that Gurdjieff simply wasn't good at expressing himself.

However, we see that this is not at all so when we read *Meetings with Remarkable Men*, where the style presents few obstacles to the reader. This is even more obvious when we read the scenario of the ballet for *The Struggle of the Magicians*.

The Defects of the Reader

We may believe that we have an excellent grasp of the English language. We may even have certificates to "prove" that our skill is at the highest level. And for normal purposes that may be true. It may even be so in respect of our ability to appreciate the best of English literature. Nevertheless, as we are, we are ill-equipped to appreciate *The Tales*.

Our real skill with our native language, whether English, Russian or any other European language, is described by Gurdjieff in a talk to his St. Petersburg group, reported in *In Search of the Miraculous*:

> This language is full of wrong concepts, wrong classifications, wrong associations. And the chief thing is that, owing to the essential characteristics of ordinary thinking, that is to say, to its vagueness and inaccuracy, every word can have thousands of different meanings according to the material the speaker has at his disposal and the complex of associations at work in him at the moment. People do not clearly realize to what a degree their language is subjective, that is, what different things each of them says while using the same words. They are not aware that each one of them speaks in a language of his own, understanding other

> people's language either vaguely or not at all, and having no idea that each one of them speaks in a language unknown to him. People have a very firm conviction, or belief, that they speak the same language, that they understand one another.
>
> Actually this conviction has no foundation whatever. The language in which they speak is adapted to practical life only. People can communicate to one another information of a practical character, but as soon as they pass to a slightly more complex sphere they are immediately lost, and they cease to understand one another, although they are unconscious of it. People imagine that they often, if not always, understand one another, or that they can, at any rate, understand one another if they try or want to; they imagine that they understand the authors of the books they read and that other people understand them. This also is one of the illusions which people create for themselves and in the midst of which they live. As a matter of fact, no one understands anyone else.

We previously quoted the excerpt from *The Tales*, where Gurdjieff specifically criticizes how we three-brained beings might subjectively understand the word "love" (see Chapter 4, Background Research). Our problem is that our comprehension of words is unpredictably subjective. Gurdjieff attempts to circumvent this subjectivity in a variety of ways.

In particular, we may find it useful to take notice of the words that Gurdjieff chooses to use in *The Tales* where we would probably choose other words. Here are a few examples: manifestation, inherency, vivifyingness, consonances, actualization, cerebrate, elucidation, localities. He deliberately chooses words that other authors rarely use – and hence for which we are unlikely to have formed many subjective associations.

This short list of uncommon words, by the way, was pulled from the first 15 pages of *The Tales*. The reader is less likely to have subjective associations attached to these words, but nevertheless they inevitably make reading the book more difficult, and at times may even force one to consult a dictionary – a habit, by the way, which is worth developing when reading *The Tales*.

Gurdjieff was meticulous in his choice of words. This is clearly demonstrated by the following excerpt from *Life Is Real Only Then, When I Am*:

Chapter 6: Language And Style

> At eleven o'clock, in order to rest a little, I asked the translator to read aloud what he had already translated.
>
> When he came, in the translation, to the expression used by me, "intentional suffering," I interrupted his reading, for he had translated the word "intentional" by the word "voluntary."
>
> As I attempted to explain the great difference between the voluntary and intentional suffering of man, there arose a general philological discussion, as is usual in such cases.

In reading this excerpt we may wish to ask ourselves whether we understand the "great difference" between the words "intentional" and "voluntary."

Do we?

What is the "great difference?"

We might also profit from considering the following excerpt from the same book:

> Here there again arises the question of the poverty of the English language, this time in the sense that the contemporary people belonging to the English race and you Americans also, who have borrowed their language and use it in your ordinary life, totally lack any understanding of the difference between two entirely distinct impulses of an average man, namely, between the impulse of "feeling" and that of "sensing."

It is certainly the case that we often use the verb "feel" in a cavalier manner as in: "I feel cold," "I feel angry" and "I feel stupid." Most English dictionaries give three distinct definitions here: to feel a sensation, to feel an emotion and to experience a belief. We cannot be precise in our meaning by using such a word. In consequence, we have no precise word to describe experiencing an emotion. Gurdjieff provides his definition of this word in a further excerpt from that same book.

> A man "feels" —when what are called the "initiative factors" issue from one of the dispersed localizations of his common presence which in contemporary science are called the "sympathetic nerve nodes," the chief agglomeration of which is known by the name of "solar plexus" and the whole totality of which functioning, in the terminology long ago established by me, is called the "feeling center"; and he "senses" —when the basis of his "initiative factors" is the totality of what are called "the motor nerve nodes" of the

spinal and partly of the head brain, which is called according to this terminology of mine the "moving center."

It would no doubt be convenient if Gurdjieff had provided such a definition for every one of the common words of our language that he employs in his writings. However, in many places in his writings, he writes in such a way as to convey what he means precisely without the possibility of ambiguity. This helps to explain some elements of his style of writing, but only some.

The Language Skills of the Author

Gurdjieff claims to have spoken eighteen languages fluently, and in all probability he knew words from many other languages. He spoke Armenian, Greek and Russian from an early age. From anecdotal evidence we have reason to believe that he spoke Turkish, Kurdish, Greek, English, French, Italian, German and Tibetan.

If we wished to learn that many languages, and were willing to devote the time to doing so, then it might be possible, even though it would take years. But even if we did, we would probably only learn the basic words and the usual verb and noun endings from these languages. It is claimed, believably, that the basic knowledge of a language requires maybe 3,000 words. That's about the same number of words that an average seven-year-old child will know.

Such a level of competence would probably equip you to read a newspaper in the language. But it is unlikely that it would allow you to carry out religious or philosophical discussions in the language. This is not a matter of whether we would have sufficient vocabulary for such a discussion, but whether we would truly appreciate the normal context of the words we would try to use in such discussions. And the irony is – if we accept what Gurdjieff said – that if we did have such an appreciation, we still would not understand the other because of their individual associations with such words.

It is likely that Gurdjieff was far more proficient in the languages he claimed fluency in than that. Why? Aside from Beelzebub's claim, "Even I, who had then learned perfectly eighteen of their different languages" (*The Tales*) or Gurdjieff's direct statement "I, who then spoke eighteen languages perfectly." (*Meetings With Remarkable Men*) there are many anecdotal recollections of Gurdjieff's precision with the languages he spoke. Can we claim to know even one language well?

Consider this excerpt from *In Search of the Miraculous*:

Chapter 6: Language And Style

I remember yet another talk that took place during the same period. Someone asked him about the possibility of a universal language— in what connection I do not remember.

"A universal language is possible," said G., "only people will never invent it.

"Why not?" asked one of us.

"First because it was invented a long time ago," answered G., "and second because to understand this language and to express ideas in it depends not only upon the knowledge of this language, but also on being. I will say even more. There exists not one, but three universal languages. The first of them can be spoken and written while remaining within the limits of one's own language. The only difference is that when people speak in their ordinary language they do not understand one another, but in this other language they do understand. In the second language, written language is the same for all peoples, like, say, figures or mathematical formulae; but people still speak their own language, yet each of them understands the other even though the other speaks in an unknown language. The third language is the same for all, both the written and the spoken. The difference of language disappears altogether on this level"

The first of the three universal languages, then, does not require us to learn any other language. It can be spoken and written in our first language, the one we are familiar with. In the second language we converse in "figures or mathematical formulae." This suggests that in this language we use symbols, which people who speak different languages can understand. And the third language, both written and spoken, is the same for everyone.

We need only be concerned here with the first of these three languages. The second and third may be out of our reach anyway. It is possible that both of these languages are used by Gurdjieff in *The Tales*, but if so, we have not as yet found evidence of it. It is possible – it is a theory, just a theory that *The Tales* was written in this first universal language. If so, then as we refine our own inner use of our language, we may begin to comprehend more and more as we read, study, and reread *The Tales*. We may start to become familiar with this first universal language.

Loan Words and Foreign Words

The Tales is not written entirely in English. Occasionally Gurdjieff deliberately chooses words and expressions that derive from other languages. It seems likely that he made these choices because if he had used a more familiar English equivalent, it would not have served the reader well.

Consider, for example, "Bon Ton." He first uses this term in the following excerpt from *The Tales*:

> ...although I am now about to become a professional writer, yet having had no practice at all either in respect of all the established professional rules and procedures or in respect of what is called the "bon ton literary language," I am constrained to write not at all as ordinary "patented-writers" do, to the form of whose writing you have in all probability become as much accustomed as to your own smell.

"Bon Ton" is a loan phrase from French, which in that language means "good tone," as one might expect. *The Merriam-Webster Dictionary* gives the meaning as:

1. (a) *fashionable manner or style,*
1. (b) *the fashionable or proper thing, or*
2. *high society.*

Clearly he expects us to apply the first of these meanings in the example given. He could have simply chosen the word "fashionable," but he did not. We believe he decided that the expression "bon ton" was more appropriate for the meaning he wanted to convey. We are inclined to believe that because he uses this expression no less than eight times in *The Tales*. On just one occasion he uses the word more in the sense of the second definition given by *The Merriam-Webster Dictionary*. This is from the section where Beelzebub is being taught how to have an audience with the czar.

> "This former mama's darling, when he arrived and began to speak to me, manifested himself at first towards me quite automatically according to the data fixed in his common presence by the rules enforcedly inculcated into him of what are called bon ton...

Now consider the word "Ersatz." This word is used three times, twice in *Chapter 1, The Arousing of Thought* and once in *Chapter 29, The Fruits of Former Civilizations and the Blossoms of the Contemporary* as follows:

Chapter 6: Language And Style

- ...and the mid-wife had in her mouth a lozenge saturated with cocaine of German make, and moreover not "Ersatz" and was sucking this lozenge to these sounds without the proper enjoyment.
- He discharged the last words with such a shower of saliva that it was as if my face were exposed to the action of an "atomizer"–not of "Ersatz" production–invented by the Germans for dyeing material with aniline dyes.
- "But they used and still use those 'antiques' they collected as 'models' for 'cheap goods' which are everywhere known on that ill-fated planet by the name of 'Ersatz.'

"Ersatz" is a recent loan word from German. The *Merriam-Webster Dictionary* gives the meaning as:

> "being a usually artificial and inferior substitute or imitation."

Its etymology is from the German "ersetzen" which means "to replace." Its first use in German was to describe "units of the army reserve," who were regarded as inferior to regular army soldiers.

The alternatives available in English for this word include: artificial, imitation, synthetic, fake, false, mock, phony and sham. Not only did he not use any of these words, but each time he uses the word he places it within quotes and also capitalizes it. It is also the case that he places "bon ton" in quotes, but does not see fit to capitalize it.

The expression "bon ton" and the word "ersatz" are loan words, and hence the reader may have met with them before, and consequently may already have attached associations to them prior to reading *The Tales*. This is not likely to be the case with the next three non-English words from *The Tales* that we consider here: Solianka, Tzimus and Shachermacher.

Solianka

Solianka appears once in the following excerpt, in reference to the Russian and English languages:

> Both these languages are like the dish which is called in Moscow "Solianka," and into which everything goes except you and me, in fact everything you wish, and even the "after-dinner Cheshma" of Scheherazade.

According to Wikipedia, Solyanka is a thick, spicy and sour soup, with the main ingredient being either meat, fish, or mushrooms, but cooked in brine and also containing pickled cucumbers and sometimes cabbage, salted mushrooms, sour cream and dill. The word derives from the Russian word for "salt."

Tzimus

Tzimus is a curious choice of word. It is first encountered in the following passage:

> It will be useful chiefly because I have decided already to make the "salt," or as contemporary pureblooded Jewish businessmen would say, the "Tzimus" of this story, one of the basic principles of that new literary form which I intend to employ for the attainment of the aim I am now pursuing by means of this new profession of mine.

It may be a corruption of tzimmes (from Yiddish), which is a traditional Ashkenazi Jewish sweet stew usually made from carrots and dried fruits and other ingredients including sugar or honey. This is often served as part of the Rosh Hashanah meal, when it is traditional to eat sweet and honey-flavored dishes. Rosh Hashanah is the first day of the year in the Jewish calendar, and by tradition it is the anniversary of the creation of Adam.

Alternatively, "Tzimus" is Russian slang meaning pith or essence, but it is hard to see how that connects with a pureblooded Jewish businessmen. Either way it suggests the essence of something – and for good measure every time he uses the word (four times in *The Tales*) Gurdjieff spells it with a capital T and wraps quotes around it.

Shachermacher

Shachermacher appears three times as below, but in one instance of its use it is part of a compound word that Gurdjieff has invented:

- All this is done "quite honorably, according to all contemporary commercial rules on the basis of "triple-entry bookkeeping" and "Shachermacher-accounting."
- ...and they began half consciously to insert certain details of this fantastic theory into the Legominisms concerning the holy planet, and afterwards these informations, passing from generation to generation, blossomed out with the additions of these fancies, which again our dear Mullah Nassr Eddin expresses by the one word: 'Kmalkanatonashachermacher.'
- ...fearing to lose their personal welfare which, by the way, I had created for them, deserted the common work and with their tails

between their legs took themselves off to their kennels, where, profiting by the crumbs fallen from my, so to say, "idea-table" they opened their, as I would say, "Shachermacher-workshop-booths," and with a secret feeling of hope and perhaps even joy at their speedy and complete release from my vigilant control, began manufacturing out of various unfortunate naive people, "candidates for lunatic asylums."

Shachermacher is a corruption of *szacher-macher*, which is Polish/Yiddish; *szacher* means "of shady dealings, and a *macher* is an ambitious person, a schemer, someone who can make things happen.

Other Examples

There are other occasions where Gurdjieff chooses foreign words where English words would suffice. In the following example, he chooses the German "milch" rather than the English "milk."

> "They waited for these lost sheep with great impatience, because certain of these latter were transformed into what are called 'milch cows' from which they milk, as was already customary there, that something which they defined by the word 'oof' or 'dough.'

In the example below, Gurdjieff chooses the Italian "cinque-contra-uno" – Italian slang for male masturbation – and even puts the English translation in parentheses. Why?

> "Being together, they had 'various talks. But when everything had been talked out and they felt bored, then one of them suggested that as a relief they should take up the pastime which they called for the first time 'cinque-contra-uno (five-against-one), an occupation which has been preserved down to the present time, under the same name, among their descendants who continue to arise and exist there.

Gurdjieff's Typography

Gurdjieff uses an unusual series of techniques to draw attention to particular words or to emphasize meaning. The fact that he decided to employ such a variety of techniques in the meticulous way that he used them might give us pause for thought. Writing a book is not an easy task to take on, but writing a book in the style that he chose requires an extraordinary effort.

Consider the typography and punctuation in *The Tales*. He deliberately used each of the following techniques, often in ways which, although valid, are likely to be unfamiliar to the reader: quotation marks, initial capitalization, full capitalization, italics, hyphens and footnotes.

Quotation Marks

Gurdjieff uses normal English punctuation conventions to denote speech, alternating from double quotes to single quotes when there is speech within speech (i.e., when Beelzebub is speaking but relating what someone else said). Quotes are also often used by Gurdjieff when giving names to things in a list, as in the following excerpt.

> ...*These new movements of painting are known there by the names of 'cubism,' 'futurism,' 'synthesism,' "imagism,' 'impressionism,' 'colorism,' 'formalism,' 'surrealism,' and many other similar movements, whose names also end in 'ism.'*

We suspect that, in this instance, the quotes could have been left out from this sentence without damaging the meaning that Gurdjieff intended. However, in other situations, the quotes are there for a different purpose. It can be regarded as bad style to emphasize a word using quotes – boldface or underlining is more normal – but Gurdjieff, and/or his editors, chose to use quotes frequently for that 'purpose.'

When he uses quotes in that manner, he is indicating that we should pay specific attention and not apply our mechanized associations in assigning meaning to it. There is potential for confusion between these two uses of quotes and that may be intended, because it obliges the reader to pay attention all the time.

In many situations it simply is not obvious why he uses quotes. For example, in *Chapter 42, Beelzebub in America*, we read the following:

> "In general he always drank more than enough of the 'alcoholic liquids' existing there; and when we happened to be together in Paris in the restaurants of Montmartre where it was obligatory to order champagne, which I neither liked nor drank, he would always drink it all alone with great pleasure.

We are obliged to wonder what he means by applying quote-marks to "alcoholic liquids." Indeed we can wonder why he did not write "alcoholic drinks" or "alcoholic beverages. The first time we read this we might simply accept it as part of Gurdjieff's quirky writing style, but in time we don't think of it in that way.

He chose those words and he wrapped them in quotes, so why?

Chapter 6: Language And Style

Here is another example from the beginning of *Chapter 2, Introduction: Why Beelzebub Was in Our Solar System.*

> It was in the year 223 after the creation of the World, by objective time-calculation, or, as it would be said here on the "Earth," in the year 1921 after the birth of Christ.
>
> Through the Universe flew the ship Karnak of the "transspace" communication. It was flying from the spaces "Assooparatsata," that is, from the spaces of the "Milky Way," from the planet Karatas to the solar system "Pandetznokh," the sun of which is also called the "Pole Star."

In these two short paragraphs, Gurdjieff chooses to employ quotation marks six times on: Earth, transspace, Assooparatsata, Milky Way, Pandetznokh and Pole Star. We can accept this as a convention for invented words like "Assooparatsata" and "Pandetznokh," but why are "Earth," "Milky Way" and "Pole Star" punctuated in this way? There is no obvious reason for this.

In some cases when using quotes, he may be indicating that the word in quotes is the best that the English language had to offer, but that it is not precise. But that is not the case here. In some cases his invented word may somehow be better. That might, at a stretch, explain "Milky Way" and "Pole Star," but why is "Earth" in quotes?

Sometimes, Gurdjieff will put quotes around the first usage of a word (or hyphenated set of words) and then not do so in subsequent usages of the words in the paragraphs that follow, assuming that the careful reader will have taken note of the quote marks. Sometimes the use of quotes continues. To further add to the confusion, Gurdjieff also frequently uses quotes to indicate an ironic meaning. Here is an example from *Chapter 42, Beelzebub in America*:

> "Among the conjuries of this unprecedented German Professor Kishmenhof, there are, as I learned, several indeed most amazing ones.
>
> "This famous German professor, a specialist in this branch, started, as is said, 'inventing' these remarkable conjuries of his quite recently, that is to say, in the early years of the last great general European process of reciprocal-destruction there.
>
> "When a food crisis supervened in his fatherland Germany, he, sympathizing with the plight of his compatriots, invented his first

conjury, which consisted in the preparation of a very cheap and economical 'chicken soup.

In this excerpt, the quotes around both "inventions" and "chicken soup" clearly indicate irony.

Incidentally, Gurdjieff's use of quotes is one of the aspects of his writing that the anonymous revisers of the 1992 revised-and-in-our-opinion-mutilated version of *The Tales* saw fit to change. If that was all that the revisers had done, it would still have been a criminal act of vandalism. It is simply absurd for anyone to assume that they knew better than Gurdjieff which words needed emphasis in this way.

Capitalization

Proper nouns, i.e., names for languages, nationalities, days, months, laws, planets, countries, towns, streets and people, should be capitalized in normal written English. Aside from these, and adjectives deriving from them, the only other grammatically sanctioned uses of capitalization are at the beginning of sentences and in the use of common nouns when they are used to denote an entire class of things as in: "What a piece of work is Man."

> "You must first know that for the definition of Time, the three-brained beings of that planet take the 'year' as the basic unit of their time-calculation, just as we do, and also, like us, they define the duration of their 'year' by the time of a certain movement of their planet in relation to another definite cosmic concentration; that is to say, they take that period in the course of which their planet, during its movement — that is, during the processes of 'Falling' and 'Catching-up'— makes what is called its 'Krentonalnian-revolution' in relation to its sun.

Thus the capitalization of "Time" (as a class of things) and "Falling" and "Catching-up" (as laws), in the above excerpt from *The Tales*, is grammatically regular, but the capitalization of "Krentonalnian-revolution" is not. We need therefore to view that capitalization as the author's emphasis, which, like quotation marks, indicate that we need to give consideration to its meaning. Our readings through *The Tales* suggest that he capitalizes words that relate to the spiritual level or higher level. Thus in the following excerpt he capitalizes "Above" and "Sacred Individuals:"

Chapter 6: Language And Style

> "You yourself will very well understand that although the fundamental causes of the whole chaos that now reigns on that ill-fated planet Earth were certain 'unforeseeingnesses, coming from Above on the part of various Sacred Individuals, yet nevertheless the chief causes for the developing of further ills are only those abnormal conditions of ordinary being-existence which they themselves gradually established and which they continue to establish down to the present time.

He also sometimes capitalizes "Being" and "Reason." The words might in some contexts be capitalized in the sense of a class of things, but in other occurrences they are capitalized for emphasis as in the following excerpts:

> "This is quite enough to show me and to convince me with my whole Being what will eventually become of this Jerusalem, now that they have opened there their own famous university, and, moreover, for Jewish youths.

And,

> "But to the common misfortune of all beings, with just a little Reason, of all our Great Universe, they began gradually to mix into all the counsels and indications of this 'normality-loving' Saint Moses, as it was already proper to them to do, such a mass of what are called 'spices, that the saintly author himself could not with all his wish recognize anything of his own in this, as it were, totality collected by them of all he had explained and indicated.

The normal reason of man is usually described as "bobtailed reason," and is not capitalized. The use of the term bobtailed – meaning "with a truncated tail" – clearly indicates that the tail is a symbol of higher reason.

Aside from the occasional capitalization of normal English words, Gurdjieff chose to capitalize almost all his neologisms, irrespective of whether they denoted something positive or negative. Curiously, there are a small number of his hundreds of neologisms that are not capitalized. They are: centrotino, chinkrooaries, choongary, etherogram, foscalia, karoona, kldatzacht, kroahn, kshtatsavacht, obligolnian, paischakir, restorial, tainolair and vibrosho. Additionally, dionosk and egoplastikoori are sometimes capitalized and sometimes not. We can find no obvious pattern to his choice not to capitalize these words.

Full Capitalization

Full capitalization is used only for extreme emphasis. It is used once in a mundane way by Gurdjieff in displaying what was written on the business card of Mr. Chatterlitz:

SCHOOL OF LANGUAGES
BY THE SYSTEM OF MR. CHATTERLITZ

In almost all other usages it refers to the CREATOR. It is notable that Gurdjieff does not accord such importance to the word "God," to which he usually gives the accepted capitalization. But when, on rare occasions, he uses the word to refer to the CREATOR, he uses full capitalization. This excerpt provides an example of both usages:

> " 'Think,' I told him further, 'think a little, not as you have been accustomed to think during the whole of your existence, like a "Khorassanian-donkey," but think a little honestly and sincerely, as it is proper to think for a being as you call yourself, "in-the-likeness-of-God".'
>
> " 'When GOD created you and these beings whose existence you destroy, could our CREATOR then have written on the foreheads of certain of His creatures that they were to be destroyed in His honor and glory?

He uses the word "god" without capitalization when referring to "gods and idols" and sometimes, but not always, when referring to "their 'inner evil god self-calming." At one point, in Chapter 39, The Holy Planet "Purgatory," he writes "their 'inner evil God self-calming." This is possibly a typographical error or it is possible that he means to make that capitalization in accord with the context of usage.

We have noticed four instances where he uses full capitalization and he is not referring to the CREATOR. The first is where he refers to the ALL-COMMON MASTER THE MERCILESS HEROPASS. The second is where he quotes the words of the CREATOR that are placed over the chief entrance of the holy planet Purgatory:

ONLY-HE-MAY-ENTER-HERE-WHO-PUTS-HIMSELF-IN-THE-POSITION-OF-THE-OTHER-RESULTS-OF-MY-LABORS.

The third is in referring to everything, when he uses the expression the GREAT WHOLE.

Chapter 6: Language And Style

The fourth is in reference to "HIGHER-SACRED-INDIVIDUALS." We note here that Angels, Archangels, Cherubim and Seraphim are not accorded the same respect.

Italics

It is a standard convention to use italics for names of ships, which is what Gurdjieff does with the names of the three spaceships mentioned in the book: *Karnak, Occasion* and *Omnipresent.*

There is no other use of italics except once in *Chapter 1, The Arousing of Thought,* when he refers to the "after-dinner *Cheshma*" of Scheherazade. The word "*Cheshma*" is italicized both in the text and in the footnote that appears at the bottom of the page. This is enigmatic. We are currently unsure as to why, aside from the names of spaceships, he chose to use italics for this word alone throughout the whole of the book.

Quite possibly it is because the word "Cheshma" does not mean what he says it means.

Dashes and Hyphens

Typographically, there are two types of dash: the en dash and the em dash, their names deriving from the space they might take on the page. In theory, the en dash is supposed to be equivalent to the letter "n" in length and the em dash roughly equivalent to the letter "m," although in publishing practice this is rarely true. It is thus simpler to think of the em dash as the long dash and the en dash as the shorter one. Gurdjieff uses em dashes and hyphens extensively, but not en dashes.

He uses the em dash mostly to interrupt the momentum of the sentence, introducing something of relevance, as in the following excerpt:

> "Only now have I come very clearly to understand that everything we have at the present time and everything we use–in a word, all the contemporary amenities and everything necessary for our comfort and welfare–have not always existed and did not make their appearance so easily.

We can note in this excerpt, en passant, that when he uses the expression, "in a word," he doesn't literally mean it, and in fact, gives us 12 words. With any other author, if we noticed such a word usage, we would simply accept it as an error that the author made and that the editor failed to pick up. With Gurdjieff, we should assume it to be intentional.

The hyphen has many contexts of usage on which different authorities on punctuation do not always agree. Gurdjieff's use of the hyphen is remarkably extensive. He uses it frequently in linking a collection of words to provide a specific meaning, as in:

> "There was also there, apart, another independent large appliance, which, as it afterwards appeared, was a 'Soloohnorahoona of special construction, or as your favorites would say, a 'pump-of-complex-construction-for-exhausting-atmosphere-to-the-point-of-absolute-vacuum.

Here he is compounding a whole sentence together to provide a meaning for *Soloohnorahoona*, one of his many invented words. He does this frequently. He also uses the same technique pragmatically to provide a group of words to convey a meaning where English does not have an appropriate word. Here is an example:

> "I shall first demonstrate to you,' he continued, 'one of the results which occur when, for some reason or other, one of the active parts of the Omnipresent-Okidanokh is absent during the process of their "striving-to-reblend" into a whole.

In the following example we see several usages of the hyphen:

> "And he added in a half-sarcastic tone: 'Soon we shall be absolutely isolated from everything existing and functioning in the whole of the Universe; but, on the other hand, owing firstly to my new invention, and secondly to the knowledge we have already attained for ourselves, we have not only now the possibility of returning to the said world, to become again a particle of all that exists, but also we shall soon be worthy to become non-participating eyewitnesses of certain of these World-laws, which for ordinary uninitiated three-centered beings are what they call 'great-inscrutable-mysteries-of-Nature' but which in reality are only natural and very simple results automatically-flowing-one-from-the-other.

We can think of its usage in half-sarcastic as normal usage of such punctuation, but its usage in World-laws and in great-inscrutable-mysteries-of-Nature and automatically-flowing-one-from-the-other is surprising. If he had not used hyphens here, especially in the third of these examples, how would we have read the words differently?

Chapter 6: Language And Style

We are reasonably convinced that when he chooses to use hyphens he wishes the reader to try to consider the words that are connected together as if they were a single concept.

Footnotes

Gurdjieff's use of footnotes is one of the many enigmas of *The Tales*. At many points in the text he happily supplies an explanation for the word that he is using. Yet in some cases he chooses instead to use a footnote. Here is the full set of 13 footnotes:

- Cheshma means veil. (p10)
- The word "Kilpreno" in the language of Beelzebub means a certain period of time, equal approximately to the duration of the flow of time which we call an "hour." (p56)
- The word "Zilnotrago" is the name of a special gas similar to what we call "cyanic acid." (p56)
- "Teskooano" means "telescope." (p62)
- (1) Cold, (2) heat, and (3) water. (p75) (Note: This refers to the text: "unaffectable either by (1) 'paischakir' or by (2) 'tainolair' or by (3) 'saliakooriapa'*
- An "Ornakra" is approximately equal to that period of the flow of time which on Earth we would define as a "month." (p524)
- Toolookhterzinek is similar-of course to a certain degree-to that which on Earth is called a "radiogram." (p1124)
- Zarooaries on the holy planet correspond approximately to what on the planet Earth are called towns and villages. (p1125)
- Kelli-E-Ofoo on the planet Mars is the same thing which on the Earth is called a "note." (p1149)
- Fal-Fe-Foof in Martian speech signifies a dwelling. (p1149)
- The expression "Noorfooftafaf" signifies on this planet something like what is called on the Earth "willllessness." (p1151)
- Hirr-Hirr on the planet Saturn is the name given to that sacred ceremony which is similar to what is called on the planet Earth "baptism." (p1154)
- Lifechakan approximately corresponds to what on Earth is called a "dynamo." (p1156)

Ostensibly Gurdjieff is simply helping us out with the meaning of words in a slightly different way. He normally gives us an indication of meaning in the text, but here instead he uses footnotes. Nevertheless there is something a little suspicious in this.

The first footnote he has highlighted by using italics and it is the only place in *The Tales* where he does that. The final footnote is utterly unnecessary and just as strange.

He first mentions the lifechakan in *Chapter 18, The Archpreposterous*, in the following paragraphs:

> "Meanwhile bear in mind that in the enormous Khrh or workshop of Gornahoor Harharkh there were, besides the already mentioned Hrhaharhtzaha, several other large independent appliances, and among them two quite special what are called Lifechakans which Gornahoor himself called 'Krhrrhihirhi.'
>
> "*It is interesting to note that your favorites also have something like this 'Lifechakan' or 'Krhrrhihirhi'; and they name such an apparatus a 'dynamo.*

Thus he explains Lifechakan in almost the same way here as he explains it in the footnote, which is found much farther on in the book.

Of course, we could assign this anomaly to an editing error – and indeed there are a few anomalies that may well be editing errors or typographical errors, which we will point to later. However, for ourselves, we are not inclined to treat this anomaly as an error at all.

Meaning By Indirect Reference

There are many instances in *The Tales* where Gurdjieff qualifies a word in a way that suggests he is not content with the meaning that the reader will automatically assign to it. There are three specific kinds of word constructions that we have noticed.

One of these is "what they call." This suggests that the word we three-brained beings use is somehow wide of the mark, but he uses our words anyway, perhaps hoping we will question our own concept of what he is referring to. Here are two examples:

> "In reality, the surface of their 'Source-of-Heat, like that of all the ordinary suns of our Great Universe, is perhaps more covered with ice than the surface of what they call their 'North Pole.'

And...

Chapter 6: Language And Style

"Here you might as well, I think, be told, by the way, about an interesting fact I noticed, which occurred in the history of their existence concerning the strangeness of the psyche of the ordinary three-brained beings of that planet which has taken your fancy, in respect of what they call their 'scientific-speculations.'

In another construction, he precedes a word with the qualifiers "what is called" or "something like." Here are some examples:

"In this section of the cave were many other apparatuses as yet unknown to me, among which stood one very strange apparatus to which were attached several what are called 'masks,' from which something like pipes, made of the throats of cows, went somewhere up to the ceiling of the cave.

And...

"You must know that by the time of this second descent of the Most High Commission, there had already gradually been engendered in them—as is proper to three-brained beings-what is called 'mechanical instinct.'

And...

"And this all-gracious promise was given me, as soon as 1 returned from exile and had to present myself first of all to His AllQuarters-Maintainer, the Archcherub Peshtvogner, and prostrated myself to produce before him what is called the 'Essence-Sacred-Aliamizoornakalu.'

We have noticed that he very frequently uses "what is called" when he mentions money, as in the following three examples:

"But soon they felt that without a real result' or as they say there 'in-childlessness, there cannot be full pleasure, and from that time on, without sparing what is called 'money,' they took every kind of measure to obtain such a result.

And...

"For the upkeep of all this wealth and grandeur King Appolis certainly needed both a great deal of what is called 'money' and a great deal of labor from the ordinary beings of that community.

And...

"The beings who were addicted to this passion almost ceased to work; the flow of what is called money into the communal treasury entirely ceased and the ultimate ruin of the community seemed to be inevitable.

Note that in the third example here he does not wrap the word "money" in quotations. Also note that there are also many situations where he does not use this construction when referring to money, as in the following two examples:

> *For example, here in Europe, if some, let us say, painter, happens to paint at some time or other a good picture, and he becomes famous, then ever afterwards, no matter what trash he may produce, the public will always pay a great deal of money for that trash, simply because it is said to be the work of that "famous" painter.*

And...

> *"When we finally handed over our original zimbal to our Sheikh and told him what interested us most of all at that moment, he not only gave us his blessing to leave the monastery for a while for our purpose to occupy ourselves with the question which interested us, but even put at our disposal a large sum of money from the resources accumulated in the monastery.*

The final construction we have noticed is where Gurdjieff seems to suggest that there is no appropriate English word and hence uses the word "something" to indicate this. An alternative theory for his choice of "something" is that a precise English word exists that he could have provided, but he prefers that the reader make the effort needed to understand what he is saying from the context.

No matter which of these theories is true, we are, as readers, forced to make additional effort to discover the meaning. Here is an example drawn from *Chapter 1, The Arousing of Thought*:

> *Suppose it is true that the greatest physical force of the pigeon is concentrated in that big toe, then all the more, what we've got to do is to see that just that toe will be caught in the noose. Only then will there be any sense to our aim-that is to say, for catching these unfortunate pigeon creatures-in that brain-particularity proper to all possessors of that soft and slippery something which consists in this, that when, thanks to other actions, from which its insignificant manifestability depends, there arises a periodic requisite law-conformable what is called 'change of presence,' then this small, so to say, 'law-conformable confusion' which should proceed for the animation of other acts in its general functioning, immediately enables the center of gravity of the whole functioning, in which this 'slippery something' plays a very small part, to pass temporarily*

Chapter 6: Language And Style

from its usual place to another place, owing to which there often obtains in the whole of this general functioning, unexpected results ridiculous to the point of absurdity."

It is not obvious to the reader what Gurdjieff means in his use of the word "something."

Meaning From Distinctive Variation

There are some fundamental words/concepts that are used repeatedly throughout *The Tales* which Gurdjieff seems to want us to ponder. We suspect this to be the case because, when such words/concepts arise, he makes a distinct effort in the text to attract our attention to exactly what he is saying. This is a technique which can provoke considered thought, at least in some readers.

One such word is the word "reason." We have noticed that on many occasions he does not capitalize "reason" and that, when he does, he is referring to a high level of reason. When he refers to the "reason for" something he does not capitalize the word. When he refers to the normal reason of three-brained beings he frequently uses the term "bobtailed reason" also without capitalization. When he refers to higher Reason, he often qualifies the meaning using hyphens and/or quotes, varying his description according to context. Here are the variations we have noticed:

- being-Reason
- able-Reason
- three-centered-being-Reason
- germ-of-Reason
- Objective-Reason
- automatic-Reason
- Reason-of-knowing
- Reason-of-understanding

Attempting to put ourselves in Gurdjieff's shoes, we suspect that he was simply choosing the form of words and typography that he thought appropriate for each context. So we will need to consider the precise context of each example to appreciate the meaning.

Throughout our lives we have accumulated associations for the word "reason" but we probably have a very foggy idea as to what the word means. *The Merriam-Webster Dictionary* provides us with the following meanings for "reason":

1a: a statement offered in explanation or justification < gave reasons that were quite satisfactory>
1b: a rational ground or motive <a good reason to act soon>
1c: a sufficient ground of explanation or of logical defense; especially: something (as a principle or law) that supports a conclusion or explains a fact <the reasons behind her client's action>
1d: the thing that makes some fact intelligible : cause < the reason for earthquakes> < the real reason why he wanted me to stay — Graham Greene>
2a(1): the power of comprehending, inferring, or thinking especially in orderly rational ways: intelligence
2a(2): proper exercise of the mind
2a(3): sanity
2b: the sum of the intellectual powers
3: *archaic:* treatment that affords satisfaction
– in reason: rightly, justifiable
– within reason: within reasonable limits
– with reason: with good cause

Gurdjieff is clearly not comfortable with the English use of this word. In *The Tales*, Gurdjieff considers Reason to have gradations as indicated by the following excerpt near the very end of the book:

> *At first, while just the bare horns were being formed, only a concentrated quiet gravely prevailed among those assembled. But from the moment that forks began to appear upon the horns a tense interest and rapt attention began to be manifested among them. This latter state proceeded among them, because everybody was agitated by the wish to learn how many forks would make their appearance on Beelzebub, since by their number the gradation of Reason to which Beelzebub had attained according to the sacred measure of Reason would be defined.*

Thus, even if our concept of "Reason" is not too distorted by our subjective experience of the word, we are extremely unlikely to have the concept that Gurdjieff offers us. If we wish to understand his meaning, genuine effort is required.

Chapter 6: Language And Style

The Sun Absolute, the abode of the CREATOR, is an idea we may have met with before, but probably as some vision or other of clouds and angelic choirs. Gurdjieff's concept of this abode is distinctive in his choice of the very words "Sun Absolute." Gurdjieff also provides us with a wide variety of descriptions, as follows:

- "Sun Absolute"
- 'Most Holy Sun Absolute,'
- Sun Absolute
- Most Holy Sun Absolute
- Most Most Holy Protocosmos
- Most Great and Most Holy Sun Absolute
- most holy Sun Absolute
- Most Most Holy Sun Absolute or Protocosmos
- Protocosmos
- Omni Most Holy Sun Absolute
- Most Most Holy Sun Absolute
- Most Great and Most Most Holy Sun Absolute
- Most Most Holy Prime-Source Sun Absolute

If nothing else, this variety prevents us from quickly attaching an automatic meaning to the concept.

When he mentions the CREATOR, he is very likely to provoke preconceived notions in the mind of almost every reader. He navigates his way through this minefield by deploying a bewildering number of different forms of description. Some he repeats, the most commonly used ones are ENDLESSNESS and CREATOR. Nevertheless, he uses many different descriptions, more than eighty in total, mixing together in one way or another a multitude of concepts. Here is a list of these descriptions, roughly in the order in which they appear:

- COMMON FATHER CREATOR
- MAKER CREATOR
- ENDLESS CREATOR
- COMMON ENDLESS CREATOR
- CREATOR
- UNIBEING ENDLESSNESS
- ENDLESS MAKER AND CREATOR

- UNI-BEING HIMSELF
- ENDLESS UNI-BEING
- ALL-GRACIOUS ENDLESS CREATOR
- HIS UNI-BEING ENDLESSNESS
- UNI-BEING CREATOR
- UNIQUE-BURDEN-BEARING-ENDLESSNESS
- UNI-BEING ALL-EMBRACING ENDLESSNESS
- COMMON CREATOR
- GOD
- COMMON ALL-EMBRACING CREATOR
- MOST JUST CREATOR
- COMMON ALL-GRACIOUS CREATOR
- ONE
- CREATOR and ALL-MAINTAINER
- ALL-CREATOR HIMSELF
- MOST ALL-GRACIOUS COMMON FATHER
- COMMON ENDLESS UNIBEING
- ALL-GRACIOUS-ENDLESSNESS
- COMMON FATHER AND CREATOR
- FATHER
- OUR CREATOR
- COMMON FATHER
- OMNI-LOVING COMMON FATHER ENDLESSNESS
- OUR ENDLESS CREATOR HIMSELF
- OUR ALMIGHTY OMNI-LOVING COMMON FATHER UNIBEING CREATOR ENDLESSNESS
- ALL-MAINTAINING COMMON FATHER
- OMNI-LOVING AND LONG-SUFFERING-ENDLESS-CREATOR
- OUR COMMON CREATOR
- ALMIGHTY AUTOCRAT ENDLESSNESS
- OUR COMMON ENDLESS FATHER
- COMMON FATHER CREATOR HIMSELF

Chapter 6: Language And Style

- OUR COMMON FATHER CREATOR
- UNIQUE COMMON CREATOR
- UNI-BEING COMMON FATHER
- ALL-MAINTAINING ENDLESSNESS
- ALL-MAINTAINING CREATOR
- COMMON UNI-BEING-ENDLESSNESS
- ENDLESSNESS
- ALL-FORESEEING COMMON ENDLESS FATHER
- ALL-JUST CREATOR OMNIPOTENT ENDLESSNESS
- ABUNDANTLY LOVING COMMON FATHER
- HIS ENDLESSNESS
- LORD CREATOR
- COMMON CREATOR GOD
- THAT ONE
- WHO
- ALL-LOVING
- ENDLESSLY-MERCIFUL AND ABSOLUTELY-JUST CREATOR ENDLESSNESS
- COMMON-FATHER-CREATOR-ENDLESSNESS
- CREATOR ALL-MAINTAINER
- OMNIPOTENT CREATOR
- CREATOR OMNIPOTENT
- ALMIGHTY ENDLESSNESS
- COMMON FATHER OMNI-BEING ENDLESSNESS
- COMMON FATHER CREATOR ALMIGHTY
- ALMIGHTY UNI-BEING ENDLESSNESS
- COMMON FATHER ENDLESSNESS
- ALL-EMBRACING ENDLESSNESS
- CREATOR ENDLESSNESS
- INCOMPARABLE CREATOR ENDLESSNESS
- COMMON FATHER CREATOR ENDLESSNESS
- ALL-LOVING CREATOR
- OMNIPOTENT ALL-JUST COMMON FATHER

ENDLESSNESS
- COMMON FATHER ENDLESSNESS HIMSELF
- COMMON-FATHER-ENDLESSNESS
- ALL-COMMON FATHER MAINTAINER
- UNIVERSAL FATHER
- ALL-MOST-GRACIOUS CREATOR
- HIS ALL-MOST-GRACIOUS ENDLESSNESS
- ALL-MOST-GRACIOUS CREATOR ENDLESSNESS
- CREATOR HIMSELF
- HIS ALL-MAINTAINER
- MAKER-CREATOR
- UNIBEING COMMON FATHER
- LOVING CAUSE
- ENDLESS ENDLESSNESS
- ONE COMMON FATHER
- UNI-BEING ENDLESSNESS
- HIS ENDLESSNESS HIMSELF THOU ALL and the ALLNESS of my WHOLENESS.

One effect, perhaps the intended effect, of this aspect of Gurdjieff's writing style is that we are repeatedly presented with the same phenomenon or concept, but it is usually described in a slightly different way each time we encounter it. As a consequence we tend not to form a completely fixed idea of it – we are not hypnotized into assigning a single simple meaning.

Meaning from Distinctive Qualifications

In the previous examples of variations, Gurdjieff has described or qualified particular things (Reason, the Sun Absolute, the CREATOR) in multiple ways so that, we presume, the reader is likely to consider these important concepts from slightly different perspectives. He does the same thing with the concepts of "being" and "essence," but he does it in a different way by using the two words as adjectives, and in each instance he joins the word to the word or words that follow with a hyphen.

Here is the list of his many uses of "being-" as an adjective:

Chapter 6: Language And Style

being-ableness
being-act
being-action
being-active-elements
being-actualization
being-Afalkalna
being-age
being-Aimnophnian
-mentation
being-Ansanbaluiazar
being-apparatuses
being-articulate-sounds
being-aspects
being-association
being-associative-mentation
being-astonishment
being-attainments
being-Autokolizikners
being-awareness
being-bird
being-blessings
being-blood
being-body
being-body-Kesdjan
being-brain
being-capacity
being-center
being-confrontative
-associations
being-confrontative-logical
-mentation
being-conscience
being-consciousness
being-consonance
being-contemplation
being-convictions
being-data

being-Defteroëhary
being-Diardookin
being-Dimtzoneero
being-duty
being-effort
being-Egoaitoorassian-will
being-egoplastikoori
being-energy
being-Exioëhary
being-existence
being-experiences
being-experiencing
being-factor
being-feeling
being-food
being-fulfillments
being-function
being-Hanbledzoin
being-Havatvernonis
being-Heptaparaparshinokh
being-Hikhdjnapar
being-horizon
being-I
being-ideas
being-Impulsakri
being-impulse
being-individuality
being-instinct
being-invention
being-joy
being-judgments
being-Kalkali
being-labors
being-localizations
being-logic
being-logical
being-logical-mentation

being-logical-reflection
being-love-of-knowledge
being-man
being-manifestation
being-mentation
being-Mirozinoo
being-morality
being-necessity
being-need
being-Nerhitrogool
being-notion
being-nourishment
being-objective-conscience
being-obligations
being-obligolnian-strivings
being-organ
being-Oskolnikoo
being-part
being-particularities
being-Partkdolg-duty
being-piandjohary
being-picturings
being-pity
being-pondering
being-productions
being-property
being-Protoëhary
being-psyche
being-qualities

being-Reason
being-reflection
being-relationships
being-representation
being-rumination
being-sane-mentation
being-Sarpitimnian
-experiencing
being-self-appreciation
being-self-consciousness
being-self-perfecting
being-self-shame
being-sensation
being-shame
being-sight
being-Skernalitsionniks
being-snakes
being-state
being-substance
being-Tetartoëhary
being-Triamazikamno
being-Tritoëhary
being-understanding
being-usage
being-vocal-chords
being-welfare
being-wish
being-world-outlook

This happens again and again throughout the book, on page after page with some usages, "being-experience" for example, employed many, many times. Sometimes he is attaching the noun "being" to words that are familiar to us, and sometimes to wholly new words he has invented. And yet how many of us have an understanding of what this noun adjunct "being-" actually means? (Using a noun as an adjective is referred to as a noun adjunct, linguistically.) The use of a noun adjunct

Chapter 6: Language And Style

implies a distinction. So when we read the words "being-morality," it can suggest that there is also morality that does not qualify as relating to being. Similarly "being-logic" could suggest that there is logic that does not relate to being.

This ought to cause us to ponder.

What does "being" mean?

Perhaps we do not know for sure. If we do not, perhaps we should make an effort to do so, because if we don't then there are hundreds of instances in *The Tales* where we cannot properly absorb what is written on the page.

The same applies to Gurdjieff's use of "essence-" as an adjective. It is not as extensive as his use of "being-" but it is still very extensive. Here is a list of its different usages:

essence-questions	essence-opinion
essence-friend	essence-functions
objective-essence-satisfaction	essence-individuality
Essence-Sacred	essence-conviction
-Aliamizoornakalu	essence-center-of-gravity
essence-attitude	essence-initiative
essence-grief	essence-egoism
essence-relations	essence-place
essence-obligations	essence-understanding
essence-values	Essence-oath
essence-doubt	essence-attitude
essence-hope	essence-criticism
Essence-loving	essence-loving-hope
essence-power	essence-anxiety.
Essence-word	

In respect of this extensive usage we could also ask whether we really comprehend the word "essence." You will, we presume, have met this word when reading *In Search of the Miraculous* and hence are likely to think in terms of the duality of essence and personality; essence is what we are born with and personality is what we acquired as we grew. The idea then, is that our essence and personality are distinctly different in their manifestations. Our goal in The Work is to grow essence, a process which involves the gradual subjugation and, perhaps to some degree, the slow consumption of personality by essence. Being is associated with essence, and growth in being implies growth of essence. So the two words "being" and "essence" are closely associated with each other.

Yet if we look at Gurdjieff's use of these two words as adjectives, we see very little overlap between his use of "essence-" and "being-" It occurs only with these five words: obligation, function, individuality, conviction and understanding.

In our view, we should presume that Gurdjieff is attempting to be meticulously accurate in his use of words and thus he chooses "being-" or "essence-" according to whether it is the most appropriate word available to him. This naturally raises the question as to whether a being-obligation and an essence-obligation are exactly the same. It is similar for all the other words (function, individuality, conviction and understanding) where both adjectives are used.

Do they mean the same?

And in the many instances where there is no overlap, would substituting "being-" for "essence-" or vice versa, produce meaningless confusion?

Meaning by Repetition

Perhaps the most bewildering idea in the whole of *The Tales* is that a 'High Commission' chose to implant the organ Kundabuffer into man. The following paragraphs describe this decision, and the reason for it:

"You must know that by the time of this second descent of the Most High Commission, there had already gradually been engendered in them—as is proper to three-brained beings-what is called 'mechanical instinct.'

"The sacred members of this Most High Commission then reasoned that if the said mechanical instinct in these biped three-brained beings of that planet should develop towards the attainment of objective Reason—as usually occurs everywhere among three-brained beings- then it might quite possibly happen that they would prematurely comprehend the real cause of their arising and existence and make a great deal of trouble; it might happen that having understood the reason for their arising, namely, that by their existence they should maintain the detached fragments of their planet, and being convinced of this their slavery to circumstances utterly foreign to them, they

Chapter 6: Language And Style

would be unwilling to continue their existence and would on principle destroy themselves.

> "So, my boy, in view of this the Most High Commission then decided among other things provisionally to implant into the common presences of the three-brained beings there a special organ with a property such that, first, they should perceive reality topsy-turvy and, secondly, that every repeated impression from outside should crystallize in them data which would engender factors for evoking in them sensations of 'pleasure' and 'enjoyment.'
>
> "And then, in fact, with the help of the Chief-CommonUniversal-Arch-Chemist-Physicist Angel Looisos, who was also among the members of this Most High Commission, they caused to grow in the three-brained beings there, in a special way, at the base of their spinal column, at the root of their tail-which they also, at that time, still had, and which part of their common presences furthermore still had its normal exterior expressing the, so to say, 'fullness-of-its-inner-significance-a 'something' which assisted the arising of the said properties in them.
>
> "And this 'something' they then first called the 'organ Kundabuffer.'

The idea of Kundabuffer will be a surprise to the first-time reader of *The Tales*. A question that may immediately occur to the reader is: "Does he really mean that?"

Gurdjieff introduced the idea that man feeds the Moon to his early groups, and in *The Tales* he expands on that idea, suggesting that man was biologically manipulated at some time to ensure that the Moon was fed. It may simply be a myth that Gurdjieff invented to explain many of man's behaviors. Nevertheless, Gurdjieff repeats this idea constantly throughout *The Tales*. It is one of the major themes of the book.

The phrase "the consequences of the properties of the organ Kundabuffer" occurs more than sixty times in the book. We previously drew attention to the fact that when Gurdjieff repeats a concept or an idea, he tends to vary the words that he uses to provide slightly different perspectives. But with Kundabuffer he simply repeats that phrase again and again. It is hypnotic.

There are several other repetitions of this kind. Another one is the phrase "three-brained beings who have taken your fancy." The reader also meets with this phrase, or slight variances of it, over sixty times–

and the variances simply add "of planet Earth" into the phrase or refer to "freaks" rather than "three-brained beings."

A third repetition is the phrase "them themselves," which occurs 40 times, usually as "established by them themselves."

In our view this element of Gurdjieff's style is intended to fix some ideas as firmly and as clearly as possible in the mind of the reader. Taking these three examples together we have:

- "who have taken your fancy" – He is speaking to Hassein throughout, of course, but the style of narrative is as if he were addressing the reader. So the reader is gradually having the suggestion reinforced that these three-brained-beings are of great interest.
- "the consequences of the properties of the organ Kundabuffer" With this idea, no matter whether we take it as a fact or a myth, we are gradually being persuaded that the behavior of man is not entirely man's fault.
- "established by them themselves" – With this phrase we are gradually persuaded that some of the behavior of man really is our fault.

Lists and Their Meanings

Consider the following extract from *The Tales* where Gurdjieff gives a list of seven of our human weaknesses, which in Beelzebub's opinion are crystalized in every one of us:

"Besides this chief particularity of their common psyche, there are completely crystallized in them and there unfailingly become a part of their common presences— regardless of where they may arise and exist-functions which exist under the names 'egoism, 'self-love, "vanity, 'pride, 'self-conceit, 'credulity, 'suggestibility, and many other properties quite abnormal and quite unbecoming to the essence of any three-brained beings whatsoever.

This list may be useful for us to contemplate. If we choose not to focus on that list when we read that page, it may not matter too much, because we will meet other versions of that list eleven times as we read through the book. The other versions of it are as follows:

- called 'self-love, 'pride, vanity, and so on.
- which they call "vanity, "self-love," "pride," "self-conceit," and so forth.

Chapter 6: Language And Style

- "Self-love," "vanity," "pride," "swagger" "imagination," "bragging," "arrogance," and so on.
- namely, 'self-love,' 'pride, and so on, • such for instance as vanity, 'self-love, self-calming, and so on.
- under the names of 'vanity, 'self-love, swagger, and so forth
- they now themselves call 'swagger, 'pride, 'self-love, 'vanity, 'self-conceit, 'self-enamoredness, 'envy, 'hate, 'offensiveness, and so on and so forth.
- namely, 'envy, 'pride, 'self-love, 'vanity, lying, and so on.
- such as 'vanity, 'pride, 'self-conceit, 'self-love, and others,
- under the names of 'egoism, 'partiality, 'vanity, 'self-love, and so on.
- such as their self-love, pride, vanity, and still many others

As with his descriptions of the CREATOR, there is variety in these repeated lists of the weaknesses of personality. This is the only list that Gurdjieff provides that is repeated many times, and thus it conforms to the idea that Gurdjieff intended to give us slightly varying views of one phenomenon.

Many of the other lists that are found in *The Tales* are more enigmatic. There are three lists of animals. The first simply lists wild beings (implying predators) as 'tigers, 'lions' and 'hyenas, which does not seem remarkable on the face of it. The second is this:

> "Even many two-brained and one-brained beings of this same planet, such as for instance the beings called there 'hyenas, 'cats, 'wolves, lions, 'tigers, wild dogs, 'bagooshis, 'frogs, and many others who have not in their what are called 'law-conformable-presences' any data at all which give the possibility of 'comparative logic, at the present time still continue, of course only instinctively, to sense this act as sacred, ...

He is writing here about the act of conception, but provides what can only be regarded as a strange list of two-brained and one-brained beings, consisting of three varieties of canine, three varieties of feline, one amphibian and bagooshis – what exactly are bagooshis?

The third is where he is listing one-brained and two-brained beings that sense fear in other beings as enmity. He writes:

> "Although these being-data are still formed in the presences of certain terrestrial one-brained and two-brained beings of other

exterior forms, as for example those named by them 'tigers,' 'lions,' 'bears,' 'hyenas,' 'snakes,' 'phalangas,' 'scorpions,' and so on, . . .

This list of animals that are inimical to man seems fine, except when we encounter the unfamiliar word 'phalangas.' The word "phalanga" also appears in *Meetings with Remarkable Men*, as follows:

> Suddenly Pogossian jumped up with a shout and I saw darting away from under him a big yellow phalanga. I at once understood the cause of his cry and, springing up, killed the phalanga and rushed to Pogossian. He had been bitten in the leg. I knew that the bite of this insect—a kind of tarantula-is often fatal, and so I instantly tore away the clothes to suck the wound.

Gurdjieff's choice of the word "phalanga" is curious. Indeed this whole list, like the previous one, is curious.

There are other enigmatic lists in *The Tales*.

They include:

- the list of the names of the days of the week on the continent Atlantis
- the list of emanations and radiations issuing from cosmoses of different scales
- the list of 'center-of-gravity active elements'
- the list of the 42 active elements of opium
- the list of fish that Russian Orthodox Christians eat during Lent
- the first and second fundamental aspects of each whole phenomenon
- the names of the octaves of the Lav-Merz-Nokh
- also the notes within those octaves
- the names given to the 'intelligensics'

Some of these lists are constructed from Gurdjieff's newly invented words. Most of them are notable for the reason that they appear not to be necessary, in the sense that if they had been omitted from the book then "what would have been lost?" Yet he included them in the book, so they are probably intended to convey some specific meaning.

Gurdjieff's Long Sentences

In *The Tales*, Gurdjieff frequently uses long and difficult sentences. Why? Certainly such sentences demand effort from the reader. But is that the only reason for him inventing this literary style? Consider the

Chapter 6: Language And Style

following paragraph which concerns Hamolinadir and the question of whether or not man has a soul. It consists of two sentences:

> "So that you may be able to put yourself in the place of that sympathetic Assyrian, I shall also explain to you that in general on your planet, then in the city of Babylon as well as at the present time, all the theories on such a question as they call it of 'the beyond, or any other 'elucidation-of-details' of any definite 'fact,' are invented by those three-brained beings there in whom most of the consequences of the properties of the organ Kundabuffer are completely crystallized, in consequence of which there actively functions in their presence that being-property which they themselves call 'cunning.' Owing to this, they consciously— of course consciously only with the sort of reason which it has already become long ago proper for them alone to possess— and moreover, merely automatically, gradually acquire in their common presence the capacity for 'spotting' the weakness of the psyche of the surrounding beings like themselves; and this capacity gradually forms in them data which enable them at times to sense and even to understand the peculiar logic of the beings around them, and according to these data, they invent and propound one of their 'theories' concerning this or that question; and because, as I have already told you, in most of the three-brained beings there, owing to the abnormal conditions of ordinary being-existence established there by them themselves, the being-function called 'instinctively-to-sense-cosmic-truths' gradually atrophies, then, if any one of them happens to devote himself to the detailed study of any one of these theories, he is bound, whether he wishes or not, to be persuaded by it with the whole of his presence.

Reading through this paragraph of 284 words – it may be necessary to do so several times – we should be able to determine the following:

- All the theories of the existence or not of a soul were invented at that time by dubious individuals who knew nothing.
- Such individuals identify psychological weaknesses in others and invent theories to take advantage of such weaknesses.
- We have a being function that enables us 'instinctively to sense cosmic truths' but it has become atrophied.
- Because of this, like it or not, if we study such invented theories we will become convinced of their verity.

Those are the bones of what is written in that paragraph, but there are other details to notice, as follows:

- You are told this so you can put yourself in the place of Hamolinadir.
- That's how it was at the time of Babylon and it is the same now.
- The theoreticians invent 'facts' (the quotes suggest irony).
- The consequences of the properties of the organ Kundabuffer are crystallized in these theoreticians, and because of that they have developed a kind of cunning.
- This cunning is developed gradually and automatically.
- It forms data about the psychological weaknesses of others and the way their logical faculties are applied. So these theoreticians know how to gull others intellectually.
- We live in an abnormal way and it is, to some extent, our fault.

So here it took eleven sentences to describe what Gurdjieff wrote in two sentences.

We can ask a whole series of questions about the contents of this paragraph:

- Are all modern theories about the existence-or-not of the soul just invented or are some actually based on something real?
- Is the "cunning" that Gurdjieff points to a real phenomenon?
- Do these theoreticians actually know that they are just wiseacring or do they think they know something – in other words are they lying to themselves as well?
- Do we really have a being-function that allows us "instinctively to sense cosmic truths?"
- Are we so gullible that if we read a book that advocates some view or other about the existence of the soul, we are likely to believe what it suggests?

In the selected paragraph we also see the emergence of several of Gurdjieff's repeated themes, specifically:

- The consequences of the properties of the organ Kundabuffer
- Our normal reason is weak and we are suggestible
- There are cosmic truths
- The abnormal conditions of being-existence were established by "them themselves"

Chapter 6: Language And Style

On reflection, those two sentences seem like a musical phrase from a symphony. The style is unique.

Grammar

Grammar is the collection of principles that govern the formation of clauses, phrases, and words in order to convey meaning. It is presumed to be a framework that enables speakers to create and understand collections of words that make sense.

It is distinct from "syntax," which refers to the rules that govern the structure of sentences in a language (or the arrangement of symbols in a formal system such as a programming language). Syntax governs word order, how words group into phrases and the grammatical relationships between words in a sentence (e.g., subject-verb agreement).

So a sentence can be syntactically correct but meaningless. An example of this (invented by Noam Chomsky) is "colorless green ideas sleep furiously."

Modern academic grammars owe their existence to Latin grammar. By the time the Middle Ages arrived the use of Latin had become problematic – because it was no longer spoken. And yet, it was the Lingua Franca (i.e., the bridge between all other languages): it was the essential language of the Church (for liturgy, scripture, and theology), and also the language of scholarship, education, diplomacy, and to some extent, administration throughout Western Europe.

Different dialects of Latin developed, degrading its role as the Lingua Franca, and consequently there was a movement to standardize how it was used. It began with Charlemagne in the 8th century and continued for hundreds of years, and it worked.

By the 16th century academics turned their attentions to English, French, German and other languages, believing that a formal grammar for all languages was necessary. Gurdjieff had a negative view of such grammars. He writes:

> ...yet the real fact, illuminated from every side like an American advertisement, and which fact cannot now be changed by any forces even with the knowledge of the experts in "monkey business," is that although I, who have lately been considered by very many people as a rather good teacher of temple dances, have now become today a professional writer and will of course write a great deal—as it has been proper to me since childhood whenever

> "I do anything to do a great deal of it"—nevertheless, not having, as you see, the automatically acquired and automatically manifested practice necessary for this, I shall be constrained to write all I have thought out in ordinary simple everyday language established by life, without any literary manipulations and without any "grammarian wiseacrings."

Gurdjieff is asserting that meaning is conferred by the living language and not invented rules of meaning. A few pages later we read:

> and in everything, I shall avoid what I have called the "bon ton literary language."
>
> In this respect, the extraordinarily curious fact and one even in the highest degree worthy of your love of knowledge, perhaps even higher than your usual conception, is that from my earliest childhood, that is to say, since the birth in me of the need to destroy birds' nests, and to tease my friends' sisters, there arose in my, as the ancient theosophists called it, "planetary body," and moreover, why I don't know, chiefly in the "right half," an instinctively involuntary sensation, which right up to that period of my life when I became a teacher of dancing, was gradually formed into a definite feeling, and then, when thanks to this profession of mine I came in contact with many people of different "types," there began to arise in me also the conviction with what is called my "mind," that these languages are compiled by people, or rather "grammarians," who are in respect of knowledge of the given language exactly similar to those biped animals whom the esteemed Mullah Nassr Eddin characterizes by the words: "All they can do is to wrangle with pigs about the quality of oranges."
>
> This kind of people among us who have been turned into, so to say, "moths" destroying the good prepared and left for us by our ancestors and by time, have not the slightest notion and have probably never even heard of the screamingly obvious fact that, during the preparatory age, there is acquired in the brain functioning of every creature, and of man also, a particular and definite property, the automatic actualization and manifestation of which the ancient Korkolans called the "law of association," and that the process of the mentation of every creature, especially man, flows exclusively in accordance with this law.

Here Gurdjieff draws our attention to the nature of associations and how they govern the way we receive and digest information, whether

Chapter 6: Language And Style

we do so automatically with little or no attention or actively pondering the words we have heard or read. We have stored within a vast library of associations which we have grown since our birth and a good deal of it relates to language.

Gurdjieff writes:

> In view of the fact that I have happened here accidentally to touch upon a question which has lately become one of my so to speak "hobbies," namely, the process of human mentation, I consider it possible, without waiting for the corresponding place predetermined by me for the elucidation of this question, to state already now in this first chapter at least something concerning that axiom which has accidentally become known to me, that on Earth in the past it has been usual in every century that every man, in whom there arises the boldness to attain the right to be considered by others and to consider himself a "conscious thinker," should be informed while still in the early years of his responsible existence that man has in general two kinds of mentation: one kind, mentation by thought, in which words, always possessing a relative sense, are employed; and the other kind, which is proper to all animals as well as to man, which I would call "mentation by form."
>
> The second kind of mentation, that is, "mentation by form," by which, strictly speaking, the exact sense of all writing must be also perceived, and after conscious confrontation with information already possessed, be assimilated, is formed in people in dependence upon the conditions of geographical locality, climate, time, and, in general, upon the whole environment in which the arising of the given man has proceeded and in which his existence has flowed up to manhood.

Gurdjieff's challenge, then, is to write in such a way that he changes the "mentation by form" of the reader. He uses a new kind of grammar to achieve this: the grammar of associations. The simple fact is that we digest meaning through our associations and Gurdjieff uses this fact to reach out to the reader. Almost all of the techniques of style discussed in this chapter are aimed at this.

The Role of Literary Analysis

In this chapter we have carried out a fairly extensive analysis of the literary style that Gurdjieff employed in writing *The Tales*. This has not been done after the fashion of literary criticism, although at times it may read like literary criticism. The goal of this short analysis is to assist the reader to read *The Tales* more productively.

Gurdjieff has applied a remarkable number of literary techniques in writing *The Tales*. If we know what these are and have some idea of how they are intended to convey meaning, then it is possible that we will be better able to "hear what he is telling us."

There is virtue in becoming familiar with Gurdjieff's use of typography because it is fundamental to being able to weigh the meaning of any given word. There is also virtue in appreciating his precision as an author. Without familiarity with that we will not know how much attention we need to pay to the words.

In our view there is little value in knowing that a particular word or concept occurs, say, exactly 67 times in the book. Nevertheless, there is value in knowing that particular concepts occur very frequently, and that some concepts are described in many distinct ways, whereas others are described in a more standard repetitive way.

Most of all we believe there is virtue in appreciating how Gurdjieff has woven together multiple themes, in a way that is more reminiscent of composing music than writing a long novel.

Chapter 7: Intentional Inexactitudes

In the course of our travels in Central Asia we found, in the desert at the foot of the Hindu Kush, a strange figure which we thought at first was some ancient god or devil. At first it produced upon us simply the impression of being a curiosity. But after a while we began to feel that this figure contained many things, a big, complete, and complex system of cosmology. And slowly, step by step, we began to decipher this system. It was in the body of the figure, in its legs, in its arms, in its head, its eyes, in its ears; everywhere. In the whole statue there was nothing accidental, nothing without meaning.
Gurdjieff to Ouspensky ~ In Search of the Miraculous

In *In Search of the Miraculous*, Gurdjieff explains Objective Art to his Russian pupils. He says:

"In real art there is nothing accidental. It is mathematics. Everything in it can be calculated, everything can be known beforehand. The artist knows and understands what he wants to convey and his work cannot produce one impression on one man and another impression on another, presuming, of course, people on one level. It will always, and with mathematical certainty, produce one and the same impression.

"At the same time the same work of art will produce different impressions on people of different levels. And people of lower levels will never receive from it what people of higher levels receive. This is real, objective art. Imagine some scientific work—a book on astronomy or chemistry. It is impossible that one person should understand it in one way and another in another way. Everyone who is sufficiently prepared and who is able to read this book will understand what the author means, and precisely as the author means it. An objective work of art is just such a book, except that it affects the emotional and not only the intellectual side of man."

Gurdjieff himself claimed that his writings were objective art and we have little reason to doubt him. Consequently, we are obliged to make the appropriate efforts to assimilate them. Gurdjieff gives us specific instructions on how to do this. If we put in the effort to read the books in the three different ways he recommends, then we can discover for ourselves whether there is something objective about them. If we depend on someone else's opinion, then we will never know.

In *Chapter 30, Art*, Beelzebub explains the Legominisms that were created by the Club of the Adherents of Legominism in Babylon to reveal knowledge hidden within their various productions. In particular, they chose to introduce inexactitudes in the expression of the Law of Sevenfoldness within these various productions.

> "In all the productions which we shall intentionally create on the basis of this Law for the purpose of transmitting to remote generations, we shall intentionally introduce certain also lawful inexactitudes, and in these lawful inexactitudes we shall place, by means available to us, the contents of some true knowledge or other which is already in the possession of men of the present time.

Our experience suggests that Gurdjieff introduced such inexactitudes in *The Tales*. Whether he did so or not is for the reader to determine. There are many anomalies and surprising assertions in his writings that quickly become apparent to every reader. In our view these anomalies are indications that something important lies beneath the surface meaning. They are there to attract our attention, so that we will try to find a reason for the anomaly. On many occasions such anomalies simply indicate that what we are reading should be taken allegorically.

At times Gurdjieff almost forces you to abandon the idea of taking some things that he writes literally. And yet, in other parts of the book, he provides assertions that he apparently wishes us to take literally and to take seriously. The reader is thus thrown back on having to make an individual decision on what can be taken literally and what must be considered as allegory. It is the reader's choice.

The reader's difficulty is exacerbated by the fact that the original manuscript of the book was known to have errors. Although the Penguin Arkana edition (1999) of the 1950 version edition corrected known errata, there is no guarantee that this text is perfect.

As we have already mentioned, Gurdjieff made extensive use of punctuation (quotes, hyphens, capitalization) and the reader is

Chapter 7: Intentional Inexactitudes

obliged on the one hand to take note of this element of his style, but on the other to be wary of any errors that may still persist in the text. What the reader may suspect is an intentional inexactitude might simply be a typographical error.

Is this a bad thing?

It is a stick with two ends.

Typographical Errors

The Tales is a complex book to edit perfectly, so it is possible that some apparent typos are not typos at all, but intentional inexactitudes. In the following cases we are reasonably sure that the differences are intentional. Common sense suggests that any differences in respect of surnames would have been pointed out to Gurdjieff and that he insisted that the differences remain:

Brade and Braid

James Braid (1795–1860) was a Scottish physician and surgeon, who became an influential pioneer of hypnotism and hypnotherapy and invented the term "hypnotism," from "neurohypnotism," a term that means nervous sleep. He is sometimes described as the "Father of Modern Hypnotism."

We conclude that it was Gurdjieff's intention that it be spelled "Brade." A possible reason for this, is that "Brade," etymologically, can be taken to mean "prize," from the Latin *bradium*. Braid was, in Beelzebub's terms, a Hasnamuss who saw an opportunity to reach for one of the "glittering prizes of life," and thus wrote his name into history on the back of Mesmer.

Cognar and Cagniard

Baron Charles Cagniard de la Tour (1777–1859) was a French engineer and physicist renowned primarily for his invention of the siren in 1819. His scientific endeavors spanned various fields, including acoustics, the study of yeast and fermentation, and the critical point of fluids.

He named his invention "sirène," after the mythical Greek creatures whose enchanting songs lured sailors and particularly Ulysses and his ship towards disaster.

"Cognar" is possibly a shortening of the French word *cognard*, which is an insult roughly equivalent to the American "asshole." Cognar-de-la-tour would thus possibly mean "asshole of the tower."

Seebeck and Zehbek

Ludwig Friedrich Wilhelm August Seebeck (1805–1849) was a German physicist best known for his significant contributions to the field of acoustics, particularly his work on sound perception and the acoustic siren.

His surname was never spelled Zehbek. However we have been unable to discover any meaning for the word "Zehbek," so we are not even sure it is an insult.

Ten Books in Three Series

This is a glaring anomaly. The first page of *The Tales* and the first page of *Life Is Real Only Then, When 'I Am,'* state that ALL AND EVERYTHING comprises ten books divided into three series. The first series consists of three books, the second of three books and the third of four books. This is a glaring inexactitude. Gurdjieff published the First Series at the end of his life and made arrangements for the later publishing of the first book of the Second Series and the first book of the Third Series.

So there are five official books, while Gurdjieff states categorically that there will be ten, and does so on the first page of every one of his books, as follows:

- FIRST SERIES: Three books under the title of "An Objectively Impartial Criticism of the Life of Man," or, "Beelzebub's tales to his grandson."
- SECOND SERIES: Three books under the common title of "Meetings with Remarkable Men."
- THIRD SERIES: Four books under the common title of "Life is Real Only Then, When 'I Am.' "

Gurdjieff was precise in his use of language and particularly in his choice of words. This becomes very clear the more familiar one becomes with his writing. So the second series, where we only know of one book, and the third series, where we only know of one book, are described as "under the common title," whereas the first series is described simply as "under the title."

So, what are the other books under these common titles?

At three different points in *Meetings with Remarkable Men*, Gurdjieff announces the titles of three chapters, that he claims will be included

Chapter 7: Intentional Inexactitudes

in the third series. But these chapters do not appear in *Life Is Real Only Then, When 'I Am'*.

The chapter titles are:
- The physical body of man, its needs according to law, and possibilities of manifestation;
- The astral body of man, its needs and possibilities of manifestation according to law; and
- The divine body of man, and its needs and possible manifestations according to law.)

There is little indication that there were any other books in the Second Series, aside from *Meetings With Remarkable Men*.

In *The Tales* he refers to another book which he suggest he might write, with a footnote that contains the following words:

> Note: If anyone is very interested in the ideas presented in this chapter, I advise him to read, without fail, my proposed book entitled *The Opiumists*, if, of course, for the writing of this book there will be sufficient French armagnac and Khaizarian bastourma.
>
> THE AUTHOR

As far as we are aware, there is no evidence that this book was ever written. Gurdjieff's main writing activities began after his near-fatal car accident in the summer of 1924 and continued until 1933, when he published *The Herald of Coming Good*. Many people in The Work ignore this book, mainly because Gurdjieff seems to request that you do that in *Life is Real Only Then, When 'I Am'*, where he writes:

> If you as yet have not read this book entitled *The Herald of Coming Good*, then thank the circumstance and do not read it.

However, Gurdjieff contradicts himself later in *Life is Real Only Then, When 'I Am'*. His initial suggestion not to read *The Herald of Coming Good* can thus be taken as an intentional inexactitude that is actually drawing attention to that book.

As such, we might be inclined to theorize that *The Herald of Coming Good* is one of the "missing" books of the second or third series. However, we do not think this to be the case, partly because Gurdjieff insists on describing *The Herald of Coming Good* as a "booklet" rather than a book throughout its text, and partly because it does not have the character of the second series of his writings, which are primarily allegorical and written in an easily accessible style. He also writes several other things in this booklet that might cause us to pause for thought. Here is one such excerpt:

> In this booklet I shall not say anything more about this Institute, which I first founded in Russia, where the unexpected and catastrophic events of the World War destroyed it at the very height of its earlier activities and with it all the results hitherto obtained. I shall not describe also the further "peripeteias" or the attempts to organize such an Institute again in various other towns in Russia, as well as in other countries, attempts which all came to nothing because of all the various consequences of the War and each time with a "crash" involving enormous material and other loss; and its fundamental and successful establishment seven years later in noble France, where it existed without hindrance until its general liquidation following my serious motor-accident.
>
> I shall not speak about these events and all the consequences flowing from them, because I have already described them in sufficient detail, partly in the third book of the second series of my writings, and partly in the first book of the third series.

Here he states that, when *The Herald of Coming Good* was published, he had already written "the third book of the second series," which has either never been published or, possibly, doesn't exist. His second assertion, that he partly described these events in the first book of the third series, *Life Is Real Only Then, When 'I Am'*, is accurate.

In *The Herald of Coming Good*, he also states:

> To give the reader immediately, in this booklet, an idea of this finally selected form of all my writings, and at the same time not to strain again my poor brain, which is already tired out, I shall simply give here the first six title-pages of the writings of my first book, which is completely finished and given to the printer.

This is not, as far as we can tell, literally accurate. A draft of the English version of the book had certainly been finished and edited, primarily by Orage and Toomer, but it was not given to the printer – unless one chooses to categorize Orage as the printer, since copies of the initial draft were circulated to select members of Orage's American groups.

The chapter titles for *The Tales* that are listed in *The Herald of Coming Good* neither accord with the drafts of *The Tales* that Orage circulated, nor with the chapter titles in the final release of the book. From 1933 until his death in 1949, Gurdjieff and his assistants gradually edited

Chapter 7: Intentional Inexactitudes

The Tales, making significant changes. The writings of Gurdjieff that have been published publicly consist of:
- An introductory booklet: *The Herald of Coming Good*
- The three books of the first series: *An Objectively Impartial Criticism of the Life of Man or Beelzebub's Tales to his Grandson*
- The first book of the "three books of the second series." *Meetings with Remarkable Men*
- The first book of "the four books of the third series": *Life Is Real Only Then, When 'I Am'*

Aside from that, the only other published work we are aware of is the scenario of the ballet, *The Struggle of the Magicians*.

The difference between what Gurdjieff proclaims will be published and what actually has been published stands out like a sore thumb. We know that he personally ensured that the final manuscript of *The Tales* went to the publisher before his death in 1949, and in that book, as well as what has been published of the second and third series, we are met on the first page with this wild anomaly.

What was he trying to convey by this?

We can certainly invent theories. Perhaps these books exist under the control of some group which will eventually publish them, even this late in the day. Perhaps they were never written. Perhaps they were written but later destroyed. Perhaps they were published, but in some secretive private manner to advanced adepts of The Work. Perhaps we have to write these books within ourselves. Perhaps we should not take this literally, but allegorically.

The Sun Neither Lights Nor Heats

The Tales contains some anomalies that can only be described as "absurdities." First, and perhaps foremost, is the proclamation that "the sun neither lights nor heats." The most definitive statement of this is in the following extract:

> And yet, if you should chance to be there among them, you would be unable to prevent the process in yourself of the 'being-Nerhitrogool, that is, the process which, again there on the Earth, is called 'irrepressible inner laughter'; that is to say, you would not be able to restrain yourself from such laughter, if in some way or another, they were suddenly clearly to sense and understand, without any doubt whatever, that not only does nothing like 'light, 'darkness, 'heat, and so on, come to their planet from their Sun

itself, but that their supposed 'source of heat and light' is itself almost always freezing cold like the 'hairless-dog' of our highly esteemed Mullah Nassr Eddin.

"In reality, the surface of their 'Source-of-Heat,' like that of all the ordinary suns of our Great Universe, is perhaps more covered with ice than the surface of what they call their 'North Pole.'

This is an assertion that has a stunning impact on most if not all readers. The statement, taken literally, has set some readers off on a wild scientific goose chase trying to find some way to explain that the heat we apparently receive from the Sun is not caused by an internal process of the Sun, but somehow prompted by radiations coming from elsewhere. Such a goose chase will not, in our view, result in the catching of a goose.

Others have wiseacred about the details of Beelzebub's statement, trying to explain somehow that the Sun doesn't light and heat directly but causes light and heat to occur on Earth through the process of Djartklom in local Okidanokh. Wiseacring is wiseacring.

Our view is simply that the purpose for this absurdity is to draw attention to one of the important allegorical themes of *The Tales*. We will discuss the possible allegorical meaning of this in the next chapter. Here we will simply nail down the absurdity.

Gurdjieff writes:

"In reality, the surface of their 'Source-of-Heat, like that of all the ordinary suns of our Great Universe, is perhaps more covered with ice than the surface of what they call their 'North Pole.'

The surface of the Sun of our solar system varies in temperature between about 4,000° C and 10,000° C, except when solar flares occur, when the temperature rises way beyond those figures. This is not new information. It was well known in Gurdjieff's time and the accuracy of this data has been confirmed many times by satellite data. There is never any ice on the surface of the Sun and no credible scientific speculation has ever suggested that there could be.

As regards the heating and lighting of the Earth, the Sun emits massive volumes of electromagnetic waves across the whole spectrum. Some arrive at the surface as infrared waves and heat the surface directly. Some arrive as light and light up the surface and the atmosphere. But we note that Beelzebub does not say that the Sun does not light and heat the planet Earth. Nowhere does he say that.

Chapter 7: Intentional Inexactitudes

The "Ape Question"

Beelzebub introduces the "Ape Question" in the following passage from *The Tales*:

> ...the three-centered beings of the planet Earth have again begun to revive what is called the 'Ape question.'
>
> "I must tell you first of all, that on account of a cause also ensuing from the abnormal being-existence there, there was long ago crystallized, and there is periodically intensified in its functioning in the presences of those strange three-brained beings arising and existing on the planet Earth, a strange factor which from time to time produces in their presences a 'crescendo impulse,' owing to which, during the periods of its action, they wish at all costs to find out whether they have descended from these apes or whether these apes have descended from them.

The idea that apes may have descended from humans is a surprise for the reader, who will probably only have known the alternative that men descended from apes. This statement of descent, by the way, is slightly inaccurate as a statement of Darwinian theory, which suggests that both men and apes descended from a common ancestor. However, that is a minor point.

Beelzebub examines the two theories for Hassein and eventually "reveals" that, in fact, neither did apes descend from men, nor men descend from apes, but that apes descended from women, through their mating with other two-brained beings. If this suggestion does not shock the first-time reader of *The Tales*, then probably nothing will. Beelzebub explains the circumstances as follows:

> "I must tell you first of all that the species of terrestrial apebeings now arising there under several different exterior forms, never existed at all before the second 'Transpalnian perturbation'; only afterwards did the genealogy of their species begin.

If we take the idea of Atlantis sinking beneath the waves literally, then Beelzebub is suggesting that apes never existed at all prior to roughly 12,500 years ago – assuming we accept that date as the probable time that Atlantis sank. This is itself an absurd suggestion if we check the fossil record for ape bones. There were species of apes and humans well before that time. Later in the text, Beelzebub says:

> "During that same period many of your three-brained favorites who chanced to survive, together with various one-brained and

two-brained beings of other forms, unexpectedly struck upon other newly-formed terra firmas in entirely new places unfamiliar to them.

"It was just at this period that many of these strange Keschapmartnian three-brained beings of active and passive sex, or, as they say, 'men' and 'women, were compelled to exist for some years there apart, that is to say, without the opposite sex.

If we take this literally, it is a clear absurdity. There is no possibility that men and women would be separated by any catastrophe in this way, unless they lived entirely separately, which is itself unlikely. Beelzebub then relates that because of this separation for "some years" of men from women their sexual behavior changed, and they:

...began to turn to various antinatural means for the removal from themselves of the sacred substance Exioëhary formed in them.

"The beings of the male sex then turned to the antinatural means called 'Moordoorten' and 'Anderoperasty, or, as the contemporary beings would say, 'onanism' and 'pederasty, and these antinatural means fully satisfied them.

"But for the three-brained beings of the passive sex, or, as they are called, 'women, the said antinatural methods proved to be not sufficiently satisfying, and so the poor 'women orphans' of that time, being already then more cunning and inventive than the men there, began to seek out and accustom beings of other forms of the given place to be their 'partners.'

"Well then, it was after these 'partnerships' that those kinds of beings also began to appear in our Great Universe who in themselves are, as our dear Mullah Nassr Eddin would say, 'neither one thing nor the other.'

Biologically this is also an absurdity. We are not aware of any experiments that have been specifically done to prove the point, but it is usually difficult for any species to fertilize any other species successfully. The few examples where it does happen, such as the cross between a horse and a donkey, leads to the birth of a mule (male donkey with female horse), or a hinny (male horse with female donkey), both of which offspring are infertile. Beelzebub's suggestion is thus absurd, even if women were physically able and willing to create such offspring.

Chapter 7: Intentional Inexactitudes

In short, everything here is an anomaly. And, Beelzebub indicates this quite clearly–which he rarely does in *The Tales*–by saying:

> At this point of his tales, Beelzebub made a long pause and looking at his favorite Hassein with a smile which very clearly expressed a double meaning...

It is our view that Gurdjieff is clearly indicating here that he is providing the reader with an allegory to consider. But what is the meaning of this allegory?

The New York Restaurant

The Tales includes many anomalies that are of a less surprising nature than the two we have discussed so far. Here is one from Chapter 42, America, about Beelzebub's visit to a New York restaurant, which is clearly meant to be read as an allegory:

> "Menu, there on your planet, is the name given to a sheet of paper on which are written the names of all the varieties of food and drink available in the said restaurant.
>
> "Reading the contents of this paper, I found among other things that no fewer than seventy-eight different dishes could be ordered there that day.
>
> "This staggered me, and I wondered what on earth kind of a stove these Americans must have in their kitchens to be able to prepare seventy-eight dishes on it for just one day.
>
> "I ought to add that I had been on every one of the continents there and had been the guest of a great many beings of different castes.
>
> "And I had seen food prepared innumerable times, and also in my own house. So I already more or less knew that to prepare a single dish, at least two or three saucepans were required; and I reckoned that as these Americans prepared seventy-eight dishes in one kitchen they would certainly need about three hundred pots and pans.
>
> "I had the fancy to see for myself how it was possible to accommodate on one stove three hundred saucepans, so I decided to offer what is called there a 'good tip' to the waiter who served me with the orangeade, to let me see the kitchen of the restaurant with my own eyes.
>
> "The waiter somehow arranged it, and I went into the kitchen.

"When I got there, what do you think? . . . What kind of picture did I see? . . . A stove with a hundred pots and pans?

"Not on your life!! . . .

"I saw there only a small what is called there 'midget gas stove,' such as what are called 'old bachelors' and 'man-haters, that is to say, 'worthless spinsters, usually have in their rooms.

"By the side of this 'pimple of a stove sat an extremely fat-necked cook of 'Scotch origin' reading the newspaper inseparable from every American; he was reading, it seems, the newspaper *The Times*.

"I looked around in amazement and also at the neck of this cook.

On some American restaurant menus one sees a long list of dishes, even as many as seventy-eight. Beelzebub's arithmetic about the number of pans required to cook so many different meals is inaccurate, since 78 multiplied by three is only 234, not 300. That could simply be artistic license, which is fine. We may also question why Beelzebub casts himself in such a naive light in this particular part of *The Tales* – since he has already related many times the various deceptive behaviors of human beings.

Even so, this passage is curious. It is absurd to suggest that cooking in any restaurant would be carried out on a 'midget gas stove. The restaurant kitchen might not have been particularly grand but even in 1920 (the time of Beelzebub's visit) it would most likely have had a couple of stoves and possibly other cooking devices.

We are presented with the image of a "fat-necked cook."

Why fat-necked?

And also, why 'Scotch origin'? Technically, the word "Scotch" is used incorrectly, although that usage was accepted in the early twentieth century and Gurdjieff used it frequently in conversation. It should be "Scottish," as appears in *Chapter 34, Russia*, where we read:

> "...whose job it is to grease with what is called 'Scottish cream' the navels of several particularly loud-voiced clamorers,..

Another obvious question is: "Why is this cook reading a newspaper?" This would not happen. Clearly this is an allegory.

What does it mean?

Chapter 7: Intentional Inexactitudes

The Cock Cry

Sometimes when we encounter an anomaly in *The Tales* we may not immediately realize that it is an absurdity. We are so accustomed to people exaggerating, when they write or even speak about their experiences, that we may be inclined to let it pass without even thinking. Sometimes we may simply classify something as satire.

We can view Beelzebub's visit to the New York restaurant in that way. We can say to ourselves: "OK, the kitchen could not have been that pathetic, but he has a point here. There are restaurants which offer many menu choices that probably equate to food in tins and boilable bags that are quickly cooked and served. So he is satirizing such places." And he is, if you read it literally. But not if you read it allegorically.

However, there are some examples in *The Tales* where Gurdjieff doesn't just produce an absurdity, he writes something that is obviously flat-out wrong. In such circumstances we should have no doubt that we are looking at something allegorical. Here is an example:

> "The beings of all other forms of that planet also manifest themselves by voice, but at a definite time. For instance, the cock cries at midnight, an ape in the morning when it is hungry, and so on, but donkeys there bray whenever it enters their heads to do so, and in consequence you may hear the voice of that silly being there at any time of the day or night.

The cock does not cry at midnight. No cocks anywhere of any kind cry at midnight. This is flat-out wrong. It is not just wrong by time of day, it is wrong by use of the verb "cry." Cocks do not cry; they crow. And why does an ape attract ones attention in the morning. And as regards the donkey, what does this mean? Donkeys do not normally make noise at night.

This is allegorical symbolism. What does it mean?

The Elevation of Tibet

Here is another passage from *The Tales* that is flat-out incorrect if taken literally:

> "At that period when I was passing through Tibet for the first time, its heights were indeed also unusually far above the surface of the Earth, but they did not differ particularly from similar elevations on other continents and on the same continent Ashhark or Asia, of which Tibet was a part.

> "But when during my sixth and last personal stay on the planet Earth there, my way again took me through those, for me, extremely memorable places, I just then constated that in the interval of the few score of their centuries, the whole of that locality had projected so far from the planet that no heights on any of the other continents could even be compared with them.
>
> "For instance, the chief range of that elevated region through which we had then passed, namely, the range of elevations which the beings there call a 'mountain-range, had in the interval projected so far from the planet that some of its peaks are now the loftiest among all the abnormal projections of that vainly-long-suffering-planet. And if you climbed them, you could possibly with the aid of a Teskooano 'see clearly' the center of the opposite side of that peculiar planet.

This first paragraph is incorrect. There is no easy way to date Beelzebub's first visit to Tibet. It happens during the third descent, and it is supposed to have occurred after the time of Buddha, whose birth date is usually accepted to be 563 BCE. However, this is anachronistic. Beelzebub's fifth flight to the planet was in the time of Babylon, which is quite difficult to date if we take the text literally, but was almost certainly prior to the time of Buddha. That on its own is an inexactitude.

So is the idea that, at any time after the supposed sinking of Atlantis, the height of Tibet above sea level was not much more than, say, the height of the Andes or the Alps, or any other high range of mountains. The suggestion that in a few score centuries (2000 years) the Himalayas suddenly became much higher is wrong by any interpretation of geological evidence. And the idea that, with any kind of telescope, one could clearly see one side of a planet from the other side, whether from the top of a mountain or not, is also obviously incorrect.

So what does he mean?

The Size of Atlantis

In discussing the continent Asia, Beelzebub says:

> "For my further tales concerning these three-brained beings who have taken your fancy, it will be very useful for you, I think, if I emphasize here that on account of various disturbances during the second terrestrial catastrophe, several parts of the continent Iranan

Chapter 7: Intentional Inexactitudes

entered within the planet, and other terra firmas emerged in their place and attached themselves to this continent, which in consequence became considerably changed and became in size almost what the continent Atlantis had been for the planet Earth before the catastrophe.

Aside from the fact that there is no good geological evidence for any of this, or even for the sinking of Atlantis, Beelzebub equates the size of Asia with the size of Atlantis, implying that Atlantis was even larger than Asia. This obviously cannot be correct in any literal way, even if we accept the existence of an Atlantis somewhere in the past.

So what does he mean by this?

The Beings on Other Planets of Our Solar System

Some parts of *The Tales* are distinctly odd. Gurdjieff will have known that anyone reading Chapter 3, The Cause of the Delay in the Falling of the Ship Karnak, and who knew little about The Work, would wonder whether the author of *The Tales* was utterly mad. Here, as Beelzebub chats to his grandson about his time in the solar system Ors, and says, among other things:

"...on almost all the planets of that solar system also, three-brained beings dwell, and in almost all of them higher being-bodies can be coated.

He then goes on to describe the inhabitants of Mars in the following way:

...the three-brained beings are coated with planetary bodies having the form-how shall I tell you—a form like a 'karoona, that is to say, they have a long broad trunk, amply provided with fat, and heads with enormous protruding and shining eyes. On the back of this enormous 'planetary body' of theirs are two large wings, and on the under side two comparatively small feet with very strong claws.

"Almost the whole strength of this enormous 'planetary body' is adapted by nature to generate energy for their eyes and for their wings.

He proceeds to describe beings of another planet of the system Ors, without naming the planet:

"The three-brained beings breeding on another planet, a little below the planet Mars, owing to the intense cold there are covered with thick soft wool.

"The external form of these three-centered beings is like that of a 'Toosook, that is, it resembles a kind of 'double sphere, the upper sphere serving to contain the principal organs of the whole planetary body, and the other, the lower sphere, the organs for the transformation of the first and second being-foods.

"There are three apertures in the upper sphere, opening outwards; two serve for sight and the third for hearing.

"The other, the lower sphere, has only two apertures: one in front for taking in the first and second being-foods, and the other at the back for the elimination from the organism of residues.

"To the lower sphere are also attached two very strong sinewy feet, and on each of these is a growth that serves the purpose of fingers with us.

He describes the inhabitants of the planet Moon in the following way:

"Though the beings of this planet have very frail 'planetary bodies, they have on the other hand a very 'strong spirit, owing to which they all possess an extraordinary perseverance and capacity for work.

"In exterior form they resemble what are called large ants; and, like these, they are always bustling about, working both on and within their planet.

"The results of their ceaseless activity are now already plainly visible.

"I once happened to notice that during two of our years they 'tunneled, so to say, the whole of their planet.

"They were compelled to undertake this task on account of the abnormal local climatic conditions, which are due to the fact that this planet arose unexpectedly, and the regulation of its climatic harmony was therefore not prearranged by the Higher Powers.

What meaning are we expected to extract from these descriptions? Clearly they are not to be taken literally.

The Titles of Algamatant and Looisos

One cannot help but be surprised by the titles, or forms of address, of two of the angelic characters that appear in the wake of the collision of the comet Kondoor with the planet Earth. One of these, Algamatant, is referred to as the "Great Arch-Engineer of the Universe"

Chapter 7: Intentional Inexactitudes

and "Arch-Engineer" and "His Pantemeasurability." Algamatant is the archangel who provides a theory as to what has happened in the wake of the collision of the comet Kondoor with Earth.

"And the Arch-Engineer Archangel Algamatant was good enough to explain to us personally that in all probability what had happened was as follows:

" 'The broken-off fragments of the planet Earth had lost the momentum they received from the shock before they had reached the limit of that part of space which is the sphere of this planet, and hence, according to the "Law of Falling," these fragments had begun to fall back towards their fundamental piece.

" 'But they could no longer fall upon their fundamental piece, because in the meantime they had come under the cosmic law called "Law-of-Catching-Up" and were entirely subject to its influence, and they would therefore now make regular elliptic orbits around their fundamental piece, just as the fundamental piece, namely, the planet Earth, made and makes its orbit around its sun "Ors."

" 'And so it will always continue, unless some new unforeseen catastrophe on a large scale changes it in one way or another.

" 'Glory to Chance...' concluded His Pantemeasurability, 'the harmonious general-system movement was not destroyed by all this, and the peaceful existence of that system "Ors" was soon re-established.'

However, the Most High Commission concludes that, to ensure continued harmony, the planet Earth will need to send the sacred vibrations "Askokin" to its broken-off fragments.

The second appearance of this Most Sacred High Commission occurs because they are not completely assured that no undesirable surprise will occur in the future from the planet Earth. This is when they decide to implant the organ Kundabuffer in man.

This organ is "devised and actualized" by the Angel Looisos who is referred to as the "Chief-Common-Universal-Arch-Chemist-Physicist" and also "His conformity." Later on in *The Tales* Looisos becomes an archangel. It is not immediately apparent to the reader that these forms of address are actually insults, but it becomes clear late in *The Tales* that Beelzebub is not at all happy with what this Most High Commission did. Indeed he is almost bitter about it. We read:

"Then, namely, for the second time in the whole of my existence, there proceeded in my Being the process of this same being-Sarpitimnian-experiencing, which had engendered in my common presence a revolt on account of various unforeseeingnesses on the part of our Most High, Most Saintly Cosmic Individuals, and of all the objective misfortunes flowing from them, which have already obtained and, maybe, will still continue to obtain on this planet Earth as well as in all our Great Universe.

"How was it possible not to foresee in their calculations of the harmonious movement of cosmic concentrations that the comet Kondoor would collide with this ill-fated planet Earth?

"If those who should have done so had foreseen this, then all subsequent unfortunate consequences issuing one from the other would not have happened and there would not have been the need to implant in the first three-brained beings of that ill-fated planet that, for them, maleficent organ Kundabuffer which was the cause of all subsequent distressing and terrifying results.

"It is true that later when it was no longer necessary and this for them maleficent organ was destroyed, they yet again did not foresee that by the destruction of the organ itself the possibility was not destroyed that in the future the given consequences of its properties would, owing to a certain manner of existence of the beings, become crystallized in the presences of their descendants.

"In other words, they did not foresee for the second time also that even if it were possible to destroy that organ, yet the fundamental Cosmic Law Heptaparaparshinokh with its 'Mdnel-Ins' nevertheless remains, in the sense of the evolutionary process for the three-brained beings of the planet Earth just as for everything existing in the whole Universe.

"It was thanks particularly to the second almost criminal 'unforeseeingness' that this situation, terrifying for the three-brained beings, obtains there, namely, that on the one hand there are in their common presences as in the presences of all the three-brained beings of our Great Universe, all the possibilities for coating the 'higher-being-bodies, and at the same time, thanks to the crystallization which has become inherent in them of the various consequences of the organ Kundabuffer, it is almost impossible for them to carry the higher sacred parts coated in them up to the required degree of perfecting. And since, according to the fundamental common cosmic laws, such a formation as their

Chapter 7: Intentional Inexactitudes

'higher-being-part, coated in the common presences of three-brained beings, is not subject to decomposition on planets, and since the planetary body of the beings cannot endlessly exist on planets and the process of the sacred Rascooarno must inevitably proceed with them at the proper time, therefore, their unfortunate higher bodies arising in the terrestrial three-brained beings must inevitably languish also forever in all kinds of exterior planetary forms.

What are we to understand from this?

When Men Had Tails

In connection with the implanting of the organ Kundabuffer, we read: "...they caused to grow in the three-brained beings there, in a special way, at the base of their spinal column, at the root of their tail-which they also, at that time, still had, and which part of their common presences furthermore still had its normal exterior expressing the, so to say, fullness-of-its-inner-significance–a 'something' which assisted the arising of the said properties in them.

"And this 'something' they then first called the 'organ Kundabuffer.'

When did men ever have tails?

Objective Time Calculation

There are also parts of *The Tales* that we think curious, where the question "why did he include this?" naturally occurs. Chapter 2 of *The Tales* begins with the words:

> It was in the year 223 after the creation of the World, by objective time-calculation, or, as it would be said here on the "Earth" in the year 1921 after the birth of Christ.

Objective time is mentioned only a few other times in the book, with Beelzebub stating its relative value to our time reckoning in *Chapter 16, The Relative Understanding of Time*:

> "From which it follows that our "year, according to the conventionally objective time-calculation, is three hundred and eighty-nine times longer than that period of Time which your favorites consider and call their year.

This 389 is a rather bewildering number. If we use this to calculate when "the creation of the World" occurred, then the answer is 86,747 years before 1921.

What does that mean?

Are we to take this as the time that mankind has been on Earth? If not that, then what?

Another question is: "What does the number 389 signify?"

This is not at all obvious. It is curious, though, that if you divide the approximate radius of orbit of the Earth around the Sun by the radius of orbit of the Moon around the Earth, the answer is roughly 389.

If that is its significance, then what are we supposed to understand from that?

The Mooring of the Occasion

When Beelzebub visits Earth, he moors his transspace ship, *Occasion*, in different places. Why does Gurdjieff take the trouble to tell us in detail where the ship is moored?

On his first visit he moors the ship on the shores of Atlantis. On subsequent visits he moors it at sea. On his final visit he moors it at the North Pole. The text is as follows:

"Having descended onto the locality near this Afghanistan, we decided to send our ship Occasion for mooring somewhere further from those places where your favorites had recently been breeding.

"You must know that to find a suitable mooring place for our ship Occasion on the surface of your planet has already in recent times become anything but easy, since your favorites have furnished themselves with very many kinds of contrivances for what is called 'marine locomotion,' which contrivances they also call ships, and these ships of theirs are constantly flitting about in all directions, mostly around the continents.

"We had, it is true, the possibility of making our ship Occasion invisible to their organs of perception of visibility, but we could not annihilate its presence, and without this it could not remain stationary on the water because of the constant danger that their ships might bump into it.

"Well, for this reason we this time decided to send our ship for mooring to what is called the 'North Pole,' where their ships have as yet no possibility of going.

Clearly, in the early part of the twentieth century ships could not go to the North Pole. This is literally true. But mooring a ship on the huge mass of ice that constitutes the North Pole is a strange idea. And if hiding the ship is all that concerned Beelzebub, then obviously there

Chapter 7: Intentional Inexactitudes

were many places that an "invisible ship" could be located where men would not discover its existence by accident.

There is a progression in this. On the first visit the ship is moored by the shores of Atlantis. On later visits it is moored at sea, and on the final visit it is moored at the North Pole.

Why?

This may connect with Beelzebub's insistence on referring to seas as Saliakooriapnian spaces. And the meaning of that might be clearer if we had an understanding of the meaning of Saliakooriap. The North Pole could be thought of as crystallized Saliakooriap.

The First Transapalnian Perturbation

Beelzebub repeatedly mentions the second Transapalnian perturbation involving the loss of Atlantis. However, he never mentions the first Transapalnian perturbation.

When he refers to the collision of the comet Kondoor with Earth, he does not call this a Transapalnian perturbation. Given that the prefix of this word Transapalnian is "trans" which means "across, implying "across the surface of the planet," we think it unlikely that this collision qualifies as a Transapalnian perturbation. At that time there were no three-brained beings on the planet as indicated in the text:

> "So, my boy, owing to all the aforesaid, there first arose on this planet Earth also, as there should, what are called 'Similitudes-of-the-Whole,' or as they are also called 'Microcosmoses,' and further, there were formed from these 'Microcosmoses,' what are called 'Oduristelnian' and 'Polormedekhtic' vegetations.
>
> "Still further, as also usually occurs, from the same 'Microcosmoses' there also began to be grouped various forms of what are called 'Tetartocosmoses' of all three brain-systems.
>
> "And among these latter there then first arose just those biped "Tetartocosmoses' whom you a while ago called 'slugs.'

The second Transapalnian perturbation is mentioned many times, but why is the first Transapalnian perturbation never mentioned?

And incidentally, what was it?

Word Choices

There are some parts of *The Tales* where Gurdjieff uses a single word that seems distinctly odd. Consider, for example, the following sentence which refers to the establishment of Rome:

> "And thus when, thanks to all this, their numbers had considerably increased and external conditions demanded frequent relations between separate families, they formed their first common place, and this common place they called 'Rimk.'"

It is very unlikely that Rome was ever called "Rimk" for the simple reason that there is no "k" in Latin.

So why did Gurdjieff choose this word, and what does it mean?

His description of the origin of the Romans is also a little bewildering, as he refers to them as Asiatic shepherds. This is anomalous. On the one hand they were not Asiatics. They were European. On the other, there is no evidence we can find that they were primarily "shepherds." Had their farming activity involved sheep in any significant way then they would most likely have been traders in wool, but we can find no evidence of that. The legend of the founding of Rome is the story of the twins Romulus and Remus, who were supposedly suckled by a she-wolf. Together they decided to build the city of Rome. They argued and, as a consequence, Romulus killed Remus. Roman historians give the date for this as 21 April 753 BCE. Rome was thus named after Romulus.

An alternative legend, from Virgil's *Aeneid*, attributes the founding of Rome to Trojan refugees led by Aeneas, who escaped the destruction of Troy. This, at least, would mean that the early Romans were Asiatic. Subsequently in *The Tales* we read, in respect of the Ancient Greeks:

> "The beings of those newly formed groups of three-brained terrestrial beings were then called 'Hellenaki,' a word that meant 'fishermen.'"

This is also distinctly odd. Most Ancient Greeks were actually farmers. Historically, there is more reason to believe that Greeks, rather than the Romans, were shepherds, as the soil in Greece was relatively poor for growing crops. It has been estimated by historians that about 80 percent of the Greek population were occupied with farming.

Additionally, the word "Hellenaki" does not appear to derive from the Greek word for fishermen (alieon) or fisherman (psaras) at all. Its origin is, most likely, from Hellen, the son of Deucalion. If so, the term dates back to the time of The Flood. Hellen and his descendants ruled Phthiotis. In *The Iliad*, Homer uses the word "Hellenes" to describe Achilles and his followers, who came from Phthiotis.

Chapter 7: Intentional Inexactitudes

We note here, in passing, that in The New Testament, the words "shepherd" and "fisherman" have very distinct symbolic meaning. As for the words "Latinaki" and "Hellenaki, the ending "aki" can be diminutive. So we can read "Latinaki" as "the little Latins," and "Hellenaki" as "the little Hellenes."

We could provide many examples of the anomalous use of specific words by Gurdjieff, or even specific punctuation that highlights a given word for special consideration. We give, as a final example here, yet another very strange choice of word.

In *Chapter 42, Beelzebub in America,* we come across a long list of fish eaten during Lent that a Russian Orthodox Christian praises in lyrical terms:

> "*During fasts and especially during Lent, our homes are made happy by the frequent visits of the:*
>
> *Most Honorable 'Sturgeon' and the Estimable 'Sterlet' and the Respected 'Dried Sturgeon' and the Ever-memorable "Turbot' and Her Illustrious Highness The 'Salmon' and the Musical 'White Sturgeon' and the Serenely Plastic 'Mackerel' and the Eternally Angry 'Pike' and the Ever-demure 'Gwyniad' and the Leaping-alive 'Trout' and the Beauty 'Trioshka' and the Proud 'Shamai' and that Worthy Personality 'Bream,' and all our other like benefactors and protectors.*

It is extremely unlikely that any Russian has ever eaten a Gwyniad. Unless he were an ichthyologist, he would not know of the existence of such a fish. The Gwyniad is a freshwater whitefish that is native to Lake Bala in Wales. It is also a protected fish. It is believed to be related to the Eurasian common whitefish that are much more populous.

Why would Gurdjieff include such a fish in this list of "tasty fish"? What does he mean?

To Fathom The Gist: Vol I

Chapter 8: Etymology and Neologisms

—⁂—

"My dear Grandfather, during your tales you have already many times used the expression Hasnamuss. I have until now understood only from the intonation of your voice and from the consonance of the word itself, that by this expression you defined those three-brained beings whom you always set apart from others as if they deserved 'Objective-Contempt?
"Be so kind as always and explain to me the real meaning and exact sense of this word."

Gurdjieff ~ *The Tales*

Gurdjieff had a deep knowledge of language, not just in the sense that he spoke and understood many languages, but it is also our impression that he understood the "spirit of a language,"–not so much in respect of grammar , clearly he had little respect for "grammarians" – but in respect of how meaning is achieved in different languages.

Gurdjieff the Philologist

His depth of knowledge of language is evident from some reported conversations between Gurdjieff and his pupils, but it is also evident in various places in *The Tales*. For example, in *Chapter 1, The Arousing of Thought*, he points out that in English, the nouns "sole" and "soul" are pronounced identically and even written in a similar way. In *Chapter 30, Art*, he discusses the confusion in English and Russian that exists between the Greek letters 'delta' and 'theta.' In *Chapter 36, Just a Wee Bit More About the Germans*, he berates the Germans for placing the particle of negation after an affirmation as in "I want this not." And so on.

Gurdjieff was deeply interested in etymology: the origins and history of individual words. He was an expert philologist and he chose his words meticulously. We have little doubt that he constructed the neologisms (new words) that he invented in a considered way and for a very definite purpose. We will discuss this now, but in order to do so, first we need to provide some information on language construction and the significant differences that exist between languages.

The Diversity of English

If English is the only language you know, you are ill equipped to understand the general nature of languages. English may be the dominant modern language, but it is also a highly irregular language for many reasons. It is worth mentioning a few of its irregularities.

In terms of the words used, English is composed mainly of early German words, as spoken by the German tribes (Angles, Saxons and Jutes) who invaded and settled in Britain in the 5th century. That language was heavily modified by the Normans, who invaded in the 11th century, leading to the addition of many French words. However, their leader, William the Conqueror, was descended from Viking raiders. The Vikings, who periodically invaded the East Coast of Britain for centuries, also gave a Scandinavian influence to the language. All of these influences overlaid the Celtic tongues spoken by the more ancient Britons, which had first been overlaid by Latin after the Romans conquered England–but not Scotland, Ireland or Wales. English thus had many contributing sources for words and varieties of expression. To this mixture we need also to take into account that English speakers have a habit of borrowing words from other languages, often with little or no modification.

The tendency to purloin words from other languages is facilitated by the fact that English has very few imposed word endings–and it has no conventions whatever for forming new words, except in the scientific field, where it happily borrows word roots (morphemes) or whole words from Greek or Latin, and in the field of law, where Latin-Roman legal terms predominate.

It is interesting to note that mankind has a tendency to record knowledge in "the language of the last empire." This can be observed by reviewing written historical documents. The Aramaic languages were dominant at the time of the Babylonian Empire. Nearly all the languages of the Middle East, from Ancient Hebrew to Persian, can be thought of as diverse dialects or descendants of Aramaic. When the Greek Empire was established and dominant, the Holy Books were

Chapter 8: Etymology And Neologisms

written in Aramaic. Even *The New Testament* was written first in Aramaic.

The Greek Empire eventually fell to the Romans, and the Romans adopted the habit of preserving Greek writings and recording what they regarded as important knowledge in Greek. The New Testament was soon translated into Greek. With the rise of the Catholic Church, *The Bible* was translated from Greek to Latin. It remained in that language until the rise of the Protestant movement. So Greek was succeeded by Latin as the language of the last empire.

Gurdjieff describes the persistent influence of the Greek and Roman cultures in *The Tales*. Much of our scientific and philosophical tradition–the tradition of the intellectual center–leans heavily on Greek words and concepts, just as our legal system leans heavily on Latin words and concepts.

A common feature of languages is the "gender classification" of nouns. This is present in about a quarter of all the world's languages, including most European languages. The gender is expressed in noun endings, adjectives and articles. Some languages, like German, also include a neuter form. In English this feature applies to people and animals only, with one or two exceptions. Ships, for example, are regarded as female. In general, the English language does not impose many word endings to provide contextual meaning. A regular English verb conjugates very simply:

I walk
You walk
He/she/it walks
We walk
You (plural) walk
They walk.

Just add an 's' to the third-person singular and you have it. Verb tenses are also fairly simple. For nouns the plural usually requires just the addition of an 's.' There is no other declension of nouns. This is why English adopts words from other languages very easily.

This feature of the language would make learning English relatively simple, were it not for the fact that the language has many irregular verbs and obeys very few general rules. It is highly irregular in its spelling and in the link between spelling and pronunciation.

To mention just one bewildering example, the words:
"though"
"through"
"thought"
"thorough"
"bough"
"cough"
all have the "ough" letter combination and are all pronounced slightly differently.

To add to that, English has a far greater number of words than any other language, often offering two words that have very similar meanings.

Constructed Meaning in Different Languages

If we are to understand the processes that Gurdjieff may have used to construct many of the new words he introduces in *The Tales*, we need to consider languages other than English.

Gurdjieff spoke many of the languages of the Middle East, including Armenian, Persian and Turkish. All these three languages can be described as agglutinative, which means quite simply that new words can be built up by a process of "gluing" morphemes together; a morpheme is a unit of meaning, often a single syllable.

Most of the ancient languages of the Caucasus and Middle East were agglutinative, including Sumerian, Elamite and Urartian, from which Armenian is thought to have descended.

There are some occurrences of agglutination in English. For instance, we have the word "hopelessness" which is constructed from the three morphemes: 'hope,' 'less,' and 'ness.' Antidisestablishmentarianism, one of the longest words in the English language, is another example. It has six morphemes: 'anti,' 'dis,' 'establish,' 'ment, 'arian,' and 'ism.' Nevertheless, agglutination is not a common fundamental mechanism in English for building new words. English often uses prefixes and suffixes, but otherwise it rarely employs this linguistic mechanism.

Agglutinative languages tend to be very regular languages. Turkish, for example, has only one irregular verb and Japanese–also an agglutinative language–has only two.

Linguistically, English is classified as an isolating language, because most words in the language are a single morpheme. However, it has

Chapter 8: Etymology And Neologisms

developed from so many distinct languages that there are traces of many language features that were once more prevalent.

Another feature of languages is "compounding." This is where two words are simply put together to make a third word. English examples of this include: earthquake, waterfall and sunrise; these are compounds that became English words in their own right.

English speakers do not tend to construct words like this as a matter of course, and subsequently write them as a single word. German speakers do. An often quoted and amusing example of this is 'der Donaudampfschifffahrtsgesellschaftskapitän,' which means 'the Danube Steamship Navigation Company Captain,' all written as a single word.

It is our view that when Gurdjieff uses hyphens to concatenate many English words together, as in 'pump-of-complex-construction-for-exhausting-atmosphere-to-the-point-of-absolute-vacuum,' he is trying to impose the sense of meaning that could be achieved in German by extensive compounding. He is creating complex units of meaning for the reader.

In respect of this particular example, we can conclude on reflection that no such pump exists. There are indeed some very effective pumps, but removing every atom from a particular enclosed space is not, as far as we know, achievable. Nevertheless, Gurdjieff wants the reader to imagine such a pump and uses 'concatenation via hyphens' to build a single concept.

A third linguistic mechanism that is worth noting is 'blending,' where two words are joined together but merged, so that elements of one word or the other are lost. One English example of this is "smog," where 'smoke' and 'fog' have been blended together by the removal of four letters. Another example, a very recent word, is co-opetition (also coopetition, coopertition or co-opertition) which fuses the words co-operation and competition.

Lewis Carroll used blending for the sake of amusement, inventing words such as frumious (fuming and furious), slithy (slimy and lithe) and Snark (snake and shark).

Blending may be entertaining, but it can present difficulties for the etymologist, because the loss of letters can obscure the original derivation and hence the original meaning. This happens when blending occurs in words formed by compounding or agglutination. A good illustration of this is provided by the words 'amoral' and 'immoral.' The Greek prefix *an* means "not." We might thus think that

179

'amoral' means "not moral" deriving from an-moral via blending. However the word derives from the Latin prefix *a* or *ab*, which means "from" or "away from." The English word for "not moral" is "immoral," using the Latin prefix *in*, which means "not" (but also means "in" or "into").

We do not intend to say much more about philology and linguistics. Our goal here is not to investigate linguistics in depth; it is simply to provide enough of a basis to help the reader to try to derive the meaning of Gurdjieff's invented words.

Gurdjieff spoke several agglutinative languages and no doubt deeply understood agglutination, compounding and blending. He also understood the meaning of many prefixes, suffixes and various word endings that are used in different languages. It will be clear, when we take a look at some of his constructed words, that he employed this knowledge in writing *The Tales*.

Why?

Why did Gurdjieff choose to introduce so many new and strange words when writing this book?

Common sense suggests that if he could have written the book without introducing hundreds of new words, he would have done so. Creating so many new words must have involved a great deal of effort.

We can suggest theories for this. One theory is that he wanted those who study the book to put in the considerable effort required to unravel the meaning of these words.

This must be true to some degree, for in many situations he simply tells us what the word means. For example, he states that the meaning of the word "Choon" is "Prince." "Prince" is not a complicated word when taken literally. Neither is it particularly hard to fathom, if we take the meaning allegorically. It would have been easy for him not to introduce the word "Choon" and simply use "Prince" but he didn't.

When he gives a word that has a more complex meaning he sometimes provides a whole phrase to explain it. Here is an example:

> "And so, my boy, the chief peculiarity of the Omnipresent Okidanokh, in the given case, is that the process of 'Djartklom' proceeds in it within the presence of every being also but not from being in contact with the emanations of any large cosmic concentration; but the factors for this process in the presences of beings are either the results of the conscious processes of

Chapter 8: Etymology and Neologisms

'Partkdolg-duty' on the part of the beings themselves-about which processes I shall also explain to you in detail later-or of that process of Great Nature Herself which exists in the Universe under the name 'Kerkoolnonarnian-actualization, which process means "The-obtaining-of-the-required-totality-of-vibrations-by-adaptation"

We can assume here that there is no English word that expresses the idea of "Kerkoolnonarnian-actualization," so he explains it with a whole English phrase: "The-obtaining-of-the-required-totality-of-vibrations-by-adaptation." Perhaps we should absorb this word into our vocabulary and use it whenever we wish to express this concept. It may even be that the sound of this word, when pronounced correctly, is precise and resonates with the concept it expresses.

In other situations, Gurdjieff simply provides us with an English phrase, but does not invent a new word for it. Here is an example:

"And further, thanks on the one hand to this clamor and, on the other hand, thanks to the action of always the same cosmic law Solioonensius, which action is always combined abnormally in the presences of all of them, others also begin to clamor. When these clamorers among the ordinary beings begin already, excessively cacophonically, to act upon what are called 'the-effeminate-nerves-of-the-left-half' of several of the power-possessing beings of the given community, and these latter order those whose job it is to grease with what is called 'Scottish cream' the navels of several particularly loud-voiced clamorers, then there begin these excesses of theirs which, progressively increasing, reach their zenith, yet to their misfortune ultimately always lead to nothing."

There is no English word for "the-effeminate-nerves-of-the-left-half," but he does not see fit to invent a new word for this group of nerves. Another very plausible theory is that he has created words that will reveal a specific meaning if we can unravel their etymological roots. This may be the case even when he provides an English explanation of the new word that he created. But in some instances he provides no direct clue to the meaning of a word. Here is an example:

"One of these mentioned copies, as my what is called 'Spipsychoonalian investigations' cleared up for me, was then assigned to that branch of the Church which was situated on the small continent then existing named 'Sinndraga, which lay not far from the still existing continent Africa.

What does 'Spipsychoonalian' mean?

He uses is this word three times and never explains its meaning. In such a situation we have no choice but to investigate the etymological derivation of the word or guess its meaning from the context.

Sakaki and Friends

In *Mister Gurdjieff's Hapax Legomena*, by Nicolas Tereshchenko, Tereshchenko discusses the names of the angels and archangels who were part of the High Commission that ultimately implanted the organ Kundabuffer in Man. He writes as follows:

> *Thus for example, the name of the Commission's Director, the "Most Great Archangel" САККАКИЙ = SAKKAKI, in the Russian original is spelled with TWO KK, not just one as wrongly transliterated in the English and French versions, and so can be divided into two: SAK and KAKI. "Kaki" in Russian is the genitive of the word KAKA originally meaning "ugly and repulsive," but nowadays used for "faeces", and SAK sounds like the French word sac = bag; thus the name could well be interpreted as "Bag of shit."*

Our view is that Tereshchenko has interpreted the meaning of the name Sakaki correctly. Pushing the two Ks together into one is simple blending, and Gurdjieff probably chose to do that in the English version of *The Tales* to obscure the meaning.

Once you break up the blending, the meaning of the two morphemes, "Sak" and "kaki" are fairly obvious. The Russian "CAK" translates to the English "sack," the German "sack" and the French "sac." It's a sack. The Russian "Kaki" translates to "shit." This word is common across many languages since the Greek has "kakos" meaning "bad," from which we get the English "cacophony." The Latin verb "caco, cacare" means to defecate. It is difficult not to conclude that Sakaki means "bag of shit."

We can also consider the meaning of the name Looisos (an angel who later becomes an archangel). "Looisos" breaks up into the two morphemes "Loo," and "isos." The second of these morphemes, *isos* is almost certainly from Greek, meaning "equal to." We find this morpheme in the English word "isosceles," which means "having two sides of equal length." The "Loo" is probably simply the English slang word for a toilet. That English slang word probably derives from the French expression "lieu d'aisance" (place of ease) picked up by British soldiers during the First World War. Thus Looisos' name means "equal to a toilet."

Finally we can consider the name "Algamatant." This breaks into "alga," "mat" and "ant." The *ant* is probably the "ant" in "debutant" indicating "the one doing something." The *mat* is probably Greek, meaning "fits with" or "similar to." This word has come through to several European languages as "mating," as in sexual reproduction. The "alga" is more familiar in its plural, "algae" which derives from the Latin *alga* for "seaweed." This in turn possibly derives from a Proto-Indo-European root word that has the meaning of "rotting or putrefying." In short, Algamatant is "similar to algae." Algamatant is a friend to bacteria.

Incidentally, it is not currently our view that all the names of the "heavenly" characters in *The Tales* are insulting. We note that those three characters, Sakaki, Looisos and Algamatant are the ones most responsible for implanting the organ Kundabuffer in the three-brained beings of planet Earth.

Classifications

In *Mister Gurdjieff's Hapax Legomena*, Tereschenko also classifies some of Gurdjieff's neologisms into categories under separate headings. Realizing that this might be a useful exercise, we did the same. We concluded that it was indeed a useful activity. Some readers of this book may also wish to do this. If so, then we believe the following list of headings will prove to be useful:

- The cast of characters
- Tribes, Peoples, Festivals
- Animals
- Plants
- Substances
- Physical objects
- Devices
- Comets, Planets, Suns, Systems
- Cities, Countries, Continents
- Concepts, Processes
- Laws
- Octaves, Opium derivatives

- Saturnian words
- Martian words
- Foreign words/Loan words
- Miscellaneous

Our intention is that this list should serve as a starting point, rather than be treated as a definitive categorization.

Neologisms and Morphemes

As we have already mentioned, many of the languages that Gurdjieff spoke are agglutinative, with words constructed from morphemes, each of which has a distinct meaning. In our view, many, if not all, of his neologisms are constructed in an agglutinative manner, but constructed from root words that derive from the different languages he spoke or was familiar with.

Gurdjieff uses some morphemes several times. So if we manage to discover or roughly deduce the meaning of a particular morpheme, it may help us to determine the intended meaning of other neologisms that Gurdjieff uses. For example, the morpheme "Noora" can be found in the following words from *The Tales*:

Blagonoorarirnian
Erti-Noora-Chaka
Issi-Noora
Khooti-Noora-Chaka
Nar-Khra-Noora
Ori-Noora-Chaka
Sami-Noora-Chakoo
Shvidi-Noora-Chakoo
Taranooranura
Teleoghinooras

Another example that is found many times is the morpheme 'nokh':

Heptaparaparshinokh
Okidanokh
Olooestesnokhnian
Olooessultratesnokhnian
Koritesnokhnian
Djamtesternokhi

Chapter 8: Etymology And Neologisms

Pandetznokh
Alnokhoorian
Prokhpaioch
Lav-Merz-Nokh
Eknokh
Nokhan

In fact there are many morphemes that are used more than once. For that reason we have provided a list in Appendix E of all the repeated morphemes that we have discovered We note also that some of the neologisms seem to involve a blending of two morphemes, with a letter being dropped. Since, as far as we are aware, the neologisms were originally translated into English from Russian, there is some justification for examining the original Russian text. This effort requires a familiarity with Russian script and the sound the individual Russian letters stand for. Those who wish to take a shortcut here are advised to obtain a copy of *Guide and Index to G. I. Gurdjieff's Beelzebub's Tales to His Grandson*, published by Traditional Studies Press in Toronto, which provides advice on the phonetics of the Russian versions of these words. One or two of the neologisms are not difficult to fathom.

Orage, in his notes on *The Tales*, reveals that Partkdolg-duty is Dutyduty-duty, with *Partk* being Armenian for duty and *dolg* being Russian for duty.

Similarly the word "Havatvernoni" breaks down into *havat* (Armenian for faith) and *vera* (Russian for faith). The morpheme *noni* may mean godfather or godmother (Greek).

Our experience of investigating the meaning of Gurdjieff's neologisms suggests that he uses morphemes from German, French, Dutch (possibly), Persian, Arabic, English, Italian, Russian, Greek, Yiddish, Turkish and maybe many other languages.

Word Pronunciation

One of the neologisms that stands out for many readers is "Aieioiuoa," because the word consists entirely of vowels. It is perhaps worth noting that the Ancient Greeks used the seven vowels of the Greek language, A (*alpha*), E (*epsilon*), H (*eta*), I (*iota*), O (*omicron*), Y (*upsilon*) and Ω (*omega*) to denote the seven notes of their musical scale and that these vowels were chanted as part of some religious rituals.

"Aieioiuoa" contains every English vowel and means "remorse." It is a large and important word in *The Tales*. It may be that its meaning is somehow reflected in its sound. We were told, anecdotally, that Gurdjieff insisted that this word be pronounced as a "sigh."

This naturally raises the question of pronunciation of Gurdjieff's new words. We need to be able to pronounce them in order to read from the book. So what can act as our guide?

Guide and Index to G. I. Gurdjieff's Beelzebub's Tales to His Grandson, published by the Traditional Studies Press, includes a pronunciation guide as its first appendix. For each of Gurdjieff's neologisms, it gives the English spelling of the word, followed by the Russian spelling, followed by a phonetic guide to the pronunciation. There is also a compact disc (CD ROM) that has recordings of the pronunciations that was designed to accompany the book.

It seems that Gurdjieff wanted these words to be pronounced in a designated way. Consequently, the following question may arise in the reader: "Are the sounds of these words themselves objective?"

We have no idea. However, we see no problem in assuming that it is indeed so, since we lose little by that if it is not.

The Use Of Information Technology

Today, there is a wealth of information technology that can be put to effective use by the reader of *The Tales*. In our view there is nothing wrong with taking as much advantage of this as is possible. As such we describe below the main capabilities we use and have found useful.

A Searchable Version of The Tales

We took the time to create a searchable version of *The Tales* on our computer. Having such a version reduces the effort involved in many activities, particularly, for example, finding every place where a specific word is used.

In creating this electronic version, we removed from the book every "publisher's hyphenation," by which we mean every hyphen added to help text flow neatly from line to line. Such hyphens can cause omissions when one searches for a particular word.

Chapter 8: Etymology And Neologisms

Because this has proved so useful for us, we decided to also publish it as an e-book, under the title Beelzebub's Tales to his Grandson, The 1951 Version in Searchable Form.

Wikipedia

The web link for Wikipedia will doubtless be familiar to most readers of *The Tales*. (http://en.wikipedia.org/wiki/Main_Page). It probably needs no recommendation either. It is worth mentioning though that it has, on one or two occasions, proved useful to simply enter a single word or a name or a single morpheme into Wikipedia to see what results are returned.

Dictionary (Words And Morphemes)

If we just need to know the meaning of an English word we are not sure of, we use a dictionary provided on our PC. If we need precision, www. oxforddictionaries.com or www.merriam-webster.com are better. We also frequently use the web site www.onelook.com. This is a dictionary of dictionaries with the useful feature that it offers a wild card search. You can, for example, enter *hepta* and it will provide you with a list of words containing "hepta." For each word, it will provide links to every Internet dictionary it has found which contains that word. This has proved useful to us in discovering the meaning of some morphemes.

Etymology

We use www.etymonline.com to investigate the etymology of words. We usually use www.dictionary.com if we need a second opinion on etymology. We have found the tracing of etymology to be useful, both in trying to discover the meaning of Gurdjieff's neologisms, and in understanding some of the English words that Gurdjieff (or Orage) chose.

Translation

We use Google Translate (translate.google.com) to try to find words from other languages. For some languages that have different alphabets, such as Armenian and Russian, it gives phonetic English versions of the foreign language word. Google translate currently covers 65 languages, including Arabic, Azerbaijani, Czech, Dutch, English, French, Georgian, German, Greek, Hebrew, Hungarian, Italian, Latin, Persian, Polish, Romanian, Russian, Serbian, Slovak, Slovenian, Turkish, Urdu and Yiddish.

It is a fairly rough capability, but it is easy to use. It helps also to use word-for-word translation dictionaries especially for Russian, Turkish, Persian, Armenian and Greek, although we have found few capabilities that make it easy to identify morphemes from these languages. There are many resources that help with identifying the meaning of specific endings in languages like Russian, Turkish, Latin and Greek, where noun endings confer meaning.

Internet Search

When researching a topic we tend to look for more than one source of information, so we naturally use Google Search. And, with Google, it can be worthwhile to enter a single word or morpheme.

AI

The recent advent of AI engines, like ChatGPT and Google's Gemini, can be thought of as enhancements to the earlier search capabilities of the Internet. We recommend their use.

An Exercise: The Word "Pirmaral"

The word "Pirmaral" is first mentioned in the following passage:

> "A long, long time before that period to which my present tale relates, namely, long before that second great catastrophe to that ill-fated planet, while the continent Atlantis was still existing and at the height of its splendor, one of the ordinary three-centered beings of that continent 'invented'—as my latest detailed investigations and researches cleared up—that the powdered horn of a being of that particular exterior form then called a 'Pirmaral' was very effective against what they call 'diseases' of every kind. His 'invention' was afterwards widely spread by various 'freaks' on your planet, and also there was gradually crystallized in the Reason of the ordinary beings there an illusory directing factor, from which, by the way, there is formed in the whole of the presence of each of your favorites, especially of the contemporary ones, the Reason of what is called their 'waking-existence,' which factor is the chief cause of the frequent change in convictions accumulated in them.

It is not too difficult to discover the etymological meaning of this word using some of the information resources listed above. We recommend that you do this now.

Chapter 9: Allegory

"They do not consider that at that period 'being-mentation' among the beings of this planet was still nearer to that normal mentation, which in general is proper to be present among three-brained beings, and that at that time the transmission of ideas and thoughts was in consequence still what is called 'Podobnisirnian,' or, as it is still otherwise said 'allegorical' "

Gurdjieff ~ *The Tales*

An allegory is a work of art or craft that can be experienced in a literal fashion – "it is what it is" – or in another manner that reveals a hidden meaning. The use of allegory in art is extensive and stretches back to prehistoric times. For example, the myths of various cultures (Sumerian, Hindu, Greek, Roman, Nordic, and so on) can be understood as allegories.

Considering just one example, the Greek myth of Narcissus is an obvious allegory. Narcissus is remarkably handsome, but so proud that he disdains even those who admire him and fall in love with him. Echo, a mountain nymph, falls in love with Narcissus, but he repulses her and then ignores her. Nemesis, the goddess of revenge, witnesses this and, invisibly, leads Narcissus to a clear pool where he is able to see his own image on the surface of the water. He is smitten with love for this image, but eventually dies of sorrow because he realizes that he cannot have the object of his desire. The gods transform Narcissus into a flower. Echo fades away until she becomes nothing more than an echo.

The name Narcissus possibly derives from the Greek *narke*, which means "sleep." In this allegory, we see a characterization of the vain personality and the abandoned essence.

The importance of allegory becomes clear when we consider that the mentation of the intellect (mentation by words) contrasts directly with the mentation of the emotional center (mentation by picturings). Allegories are intended to communicate to that other half of us. The

Work and *The Tales* seem to communicate with both parts of us, on the one hand providing the intellect with more accurate psychological words and concepts to employ, and on the other providing psychic picturings for our essence to digest.

We have already remarked upon Gurdjieff's description of the principle of Itoklanoz, by which three-brained beings of the planet Earth evolve. If we read through the seven actualizations described in *The Tales*, we clearly see that, for most of us in The Work, the first six of these are in the past and only the seventh is directly amenable to change. Here are those actualizations again:

"According to this principle, the duration of being-existence and also the whole of the contents of their common presences are in general acquired from the results arising from the following seven actualizations surrounding them, namely, from:

(1) Heredity in general

(2) Conditions and environment at the moment of conception

(3) The combination of the radiations of all the planets of their solar system during their formation in the womb of their productress

(4) The degree of being-manifestation of their producers during the period they are attaining the age of responsible being

(5) The quality of being-existence of beings similar to themselves around them

(6) The quality of what are called the Teleokrimalnichnian' thought-waves formed in the atmosphere surrounding them also during their period of attaining the age of majority-that is, the sincerely manifested good wishes and actions on the part of what are called the 'beings-of-the-same-blood, and finally,

(7) The quality of what are called the being-egoplastikoori of the given being himself, that is his being-efforts for the transubstantiation in himself of all the data for obtaining objective Reason.

Egoplastikoori are "psychic picturings" and if we are to effect a change in those that we have acquired over the years, then we will need to experience *The Tales* as allegory.

Chapter 9: Allegory

Familiar Allegories: B Influence

We have inevitably experienced many allegories. In *In Search of the Miraculous*, Gurdjieff speaks of influences A, B, and C, where A is the influence of normal life, C is the direct influence of conscious individuals and B is the degraded C influence as it gradually involves and passes into life. Many allegories can be regarded as B influence. Gurdjieff tells Ouspensky:

> *"Realizing the imperfection and weakness of ordinary language the people who have possessed objective knowledge have tried to express the idea of unity in 'myths,' in 'symbols,' and in particular 'verbal formulas' which, having been transmitted without alteration, have carried on the idea from one school to another, often from one epoch to another.*
>
> *"It has already been said that the higher psychic centers work in man's higher states of consciousness: the 'higher emotional' and the 'higher mental' The aim of 'myths' and 'symbols' was to reach man's higher centers, to transmit to him ideas inaccessible to the intellect and to transmit them in such forms as would exclude the possibility of false interpretations. 'Myths' were destined for the higher emotional center; 'symbols' for the higher thinking center.*

An effective way for a writer to be successful is to borrow a theme from elsewhere, disguise it slightly, and then present it as original work. Plagiarism of C influence begets B influence. While we might condemn this time-worn practice from the perspective of honesty, it is both inevitable, and, to some degree, a useful influence. Unless the changes to the original story are too extreme, the impact of the allegory can still have effect.

Allegories consist mainly of stories that defy logic. If analyzed by the "rational" mind on the basis of "could this actually happen?" the usual conclusion is "no." But that is also true of most of the entertaining stories that make up modern culture. In life, there is no James Bond or Indiana Jones.

Fairy Tales are almost all allegories. They begin in time "once upon a time," and they end with eternity "and they lived happily ever after." They sometimes involve a princess (the essence) who is ignored or even betrayed, but who is eventually rescued in some way. There are malevolent characters and heroic characters. Most importantly, they are stories for children.

There are even games that are allegories. The English board game, *Snakes and Ladders*, is allegorical and probably derives from *The Old Testament*. We climb Jacob's ladder to ascend and we descend via the Garden of Eden snake. It is interesting to note, in the passing of this game from Britain to America, some well-intentioned American decided, it seems, that snakes were too disturbing for children and changed the name of the game to *Chutes and Ladders* and replaced the snakes with chutes. The allegorical content of the game was thus destroyed in one fell swoop. Children enjoy sliding down chutes.

The pack of cards, deriving from the Tarot, is also a degraded allegorical game.

In these examples, the allegory is not deep or complex and, in fact, has been reduced to a few simple symbols, whereas many allegories are far more involved and complex.

Aside from children's stories, a great deal of literature is allegorical to some degree, although not all such allegories are strongly related to The Work. Spenser's epic poem, *The Faerie Queene*, is primarily an allegorical commentary on 16th-century morals and manners. Swift's *Gulliver's Travels* is mainly an early 18th-century satire that uses allegory. By contrast, John Bunyan's *Pilgrim's Progress* and Cervantes' *Don Quixote* are more direct allegories relating to The Work and the evolution of man.

Shakespeare's Psychic Dramas

Many of Shakespeare's plays can be read as allegories and experienced as allegories. This is, perhaps, why they continue to be popular despite the fact that the Elizabethan English, in which the plays were written, is difficult for most people to comprehend.

Shakespeare is an enigma. His plays and poetry exhibit an extraordinary quality, and yet little is known about him as an individual. At times his writing suggests that he had deep esoteric knowledge. Beryl Pogson, a pupil of Maurice Nicoll, wrote a book titled *In The East My Pleasure Lies*, which discusses the esoteric aspects of many Shakespeare plays, including: *A Midsummer Night's Dream, The Tragedy of Othello, Macbeth, Hamlet* and others. We are inclined to accept her considered opinion, which includes the idea that many of these plays are "psychic dramas."

We use the term "psychic drama" to mean a play where the characters in the play do not represent just individuals within the drama, but also

Chapter 9: Allegory

represent elements of the psyche of man. In one particular play, *The Tragedy of King Lear*, this seems to be particularly evident. Readers who wish to study this in depth are advised to obtain Beryl Pogson's book. Our interest here is to point out only that King Lear himself, and his three daughters, represent the lower parts of the psyche – Lear representing our normal personality, perhaps.

As far as we are aware, nobody who has researched this play has been able to establish an historical figure upon whom King Lear is based. It is possible that the King's name derives from the mythological Welsh Llÿr, but it seems unlikely as the plot of the play bears no resemblance to the myth of Llÿr. So there is no historical King Lear and the action of the play does not mimic any set of events that could be assigned to the rule of any British king. And yet the play is set in England and includes the characters, Gloucester, the Earl of Kent, and the Duke of Cornwall, who appear to be English nobility. There is also the strange character of the Duke of Albany, strange because there never was such a Duke at any time in English history.

Briefly, the plot of the play revolves around King Lear's decision to abdicate his throne. He is old and weary of his position, and wishes to live out the remainder of his life near to his three daughters. His first daughter, Goneril, is married to the Duke of Albany and the second, Regan, to the Duke of Cornwall. His third daughter, Cordelia, unmarried at the start of the play, eventually marries the King of France. Lear summons his three daughters and tells them that he proposes to divide his kingdom between them, but first he wishes to know how much each one of them loves him.

Goneril and Regan profess great love for the king, but Cordelia, disgusted by the insincerity of her elder sisters, says only that she loves her father "according to my duty – no more, no less." Lear, offended by this, decides that he no longer wishes to have anything to do with Cordelia and gives her in marriage to the King of France: "Take her, take her, for I will never see that face of hers again."

So Cordelia becomes Queen of France, and the Earl of Kent, who took her side, is banished from the kingdom.

The King then goes to stay with Goneril, who now treats him harshly and drives him away. Disillusioned with Goneril, Lear goes to stay with Regan who is equally harsh. When Lear realizes that Regan also wishes to drive him away, he leaves, almost alone, in the company only of his

Fool. Then comes the remarkable scene of Lear on "the blasted heath," half mad with misery, on a wild and stormy night.

Throughout all of this, Lear's Fool has been the only one who clearly saw the stupidity of Lear's actions:

Fool: If thou wert my fool, nuncle, I'd have thee beaten for being old before thy time.
Lear: How's that?
Fool: Thou shouldst not have been old 'till thou hadst been wise.

The Fool in *King Lear* is given no name. In all of Shakespeare's other plays that include a fool, the fool has a name. Something remarkably strange occurs in the scene on the blasted heath. Kent and Gloucester appear and so does Edgar, Gloucester's son, in the guise of poor Tom, who is found naked in a hovel and appears to be quite mad.

In this scene, the Fool simply disappears from the play, never mentioned again except in the cryptic comment of Lear later in the play, when he says "And my poor Fool is hanged." (This is possibly a reference to the hanged man of the Tarot.)

Tom gradually loses his apparent madness and becomes the hero of the play. In the end he defeats his half-brother Edmund, the bastard son of Gloucester, in battle. Goneril, Regan and Cordelia, all die. Cordelia is hanged as the result of plotting by Goneril, who poisons her other sister Regan and commits suicide. King Lear finally dies, holding the dead Cordelia, the daughter he truly loved, in his arms.

This is a complex play. None of the action makes much sense as a literal story, but as a psychic drama it is alive with meaning. Central to this is the character of the Fool and the mystery of his disappearance that coincides with the appearance of Poor Tom.

The Fool in *King Lear*, and the fools in other Shakespeare plays are wise, dispensing truth in a comic manner. They represent something within us. *King Lear* itself, we believe, is an allegory about the transformation and evolution of man.

The New Testament

Most of us will be familiar with the English versions of *The Old Testament* and *The New Testament*. These two Holy Books are distinctly different. *The Old Testament* comprises a multitude of different Judaic texts, commencing with *The Torah* (called *The Pentateuch* in Christianity – from the Greek, meaning five books),

Chapter 9: Allegory

which is attributed to Moses, and was written in Ancient Hebrew, a very specialized form of Aramaic.

The New Testament was originally written in Aramaic but was translated almost immediately into Greek. The symbolism of *The New Testament* is notably different from that of either *The Torah* or *The Koran*, just as the central dynamic of Christianity, "love," is not the central dynamic of Judaism or Islam. The allegories of *The New Testament* are, in the main, incidents in the life of Jesus Christ.

If we like, we can think of *The New Testament* as a set of allegorical myths. It could be that Jesus did indeed teach in various ways to his disciples and speak to various crowds of people in the Holy Land, and that some of his words and activities are are recorded faithfully in *The New Testament*. Nevertheless, such events and other events that may not have taken place as described have been "mythologized" to some degree in order to convey an allegorical meaning to the reader.

There is an alternative possibility, which many of us are unable to dismiss. It is this:

Every event recorded in *The New Testament* was actualized by Jesus Christ. In his life, he performed a miraculous, profound and complete allegory of the evolution of man, witnessed by his disciples and followers, and recorded accurately.

The Woman Caught In Adultery

We can consider the following excerpt from *The New Testament, John 8:1-11*, which relates the incident of the woman caught in adultery.

> *Jesus went unto the mount of Olives.*
>
> *And early in the morning he came again into the temple, and all the people came unto him; and he sat down, and taught them.*
>
> *And the scribes and pharisees brought unto him a woman taken in adultery; and when they had set her in the midst, they say unto him, Master, this woman was taken in adultery, in the very act.*
>
> *Now Moses in the law commanded us, that such should be stoned: but what sayest thou?*
>
> *This they said, tempting him, that they might have to accuse him. But Jesus stooped down, and with his finger wrote on the ground, as though he heard them not.*

> *So when they continued asking him, he lifted up himself, and said unto them, He that is without sin among you, let him first cast a stone at her.*
>
> *And again he stooped down, and wrote on the ground.*
>
> *And they which heard it, being convicted by their own conscience, went out one by one, beginning at the eldest, even unto the last: and Jesus was left alone, and the woman standing in the midst.*
>
> *When Jesus had lifted up himself, and saw none but the woman, he said unto her, Woman, where are those thine accusers? Hath no man condemned thee?*
>
> *She said, No man, Lord.*
>
> *And Jesus said unto her, Neither do I condemn thee: go, and sin no more.*

What might the meaning of this be in allegory?

Consider first the sin of adultery. We understand what it means literally, but what might it symbolize?

It is possible that it symbolizes the act of mixing one doctrine with another. This is a common activity among those who are seeking the truth and it can be a mistake. We might take some of the concepts of Taoism or Theosophy or Yoga, and mix them in with the concepts of The Work. The part of us that might initiate it could be our female side, which has become attached to this concept by some association or other.

Other parts of us, our "scribes" (intellectual parts) and "pharisees" (elements of personality), are appalled by this. They consult the Jesus within us. At first this, the highest part of us, ignores the clamor for something to be done. But the clamor persists.

What is the symbolic meaning of "stoning?"

Again the literal meaning of this is obvious, but here, and in other parts of *The New Testament*, the stone can be thought of as symbolizing intellectual rigidity–the blind acceptance of some concepts without any pondering or logical confrontation, the literal interpretation of a teaching–in short, dogma. It is natural for the scribes and pharisees within us to think in this manner. That's what they do.

Jesus simply suggests that any amongst this inner crowd that is "perfect" should cast the first stone. Naturally the crowd fades away,

Chapter 9: Allegory

one by one–the eldest (wisest) first. Jesus is left with the "woman caught in adultery." He simply tells her to go and sin no more.

In *The New Testament*, the word that has been translated from Greek into English as "sin" was originally *hamartia*. It was not a word in common usage, being used mainly in the context of archery or spear throwing. It had the meaning of "missing the target" or "missing the mark." It can be understood in this way: if you have no aim, then you cannot sin. So sin was something of which only those who wished to evolve were capable.

The Passion

The Passion is the central allegory of *The New Testament*. The Jesus within us teaches, acquires disciples, performs psychological transformations (miracles), but in the end, he willingly submits himself to judgement by the religious authorities (the Sanhedrin) and by the secular authorities (the Romans.) He is accused of blasphemy by the religious authorities and fomenting insurrection by the Romans. The Sanhedrin are offended by Jesus' teaching and the Roman authorities are concerned that Jesus represents some challenge to the puppet rule of our inner Herod that they support.

At no time in *The New Testament* is it suggested that Jesus expects not to be put to death. The events of the Passion proceed, culminating with his crucifixion and his resurrection as Christ. He is condemned, humiliated, mocked, reviled, tortured and finally crucified, almost alone. Mary Magdalen stands at the foot of the cross and witnesses his final mortal moments.

A question about the Passion that repeatedly presents itself is: Did this actually happen?

Gurdjieff remarked that, at its root, The Work is Esoteric Christianity. Most people in The Work who study the allegories of *The New Testament* realize that they represent ideas in The Work. The ejection of the moneylenders from the temple, is, psychologically, the rejection of the habit of "keeping accounts." Jesus' curing of the blind man can be interpreted as bringing a man who is stuck in the second state (waking sleep, blindness) into the third state (consciousness). Many incidents described in the Gospels are amenable to such an interpretation. The Passion is the final transformation of the risen man, the final birth (crystallization) of the soul. But did this actually happen?

The New Testament would be an extraordinary work of scripture and art if it were just a collection of well constructed myths. If it is also historically accurate, then it stands as a miraculous Earthly drama that has no precedent.

The Sanhedrin reject, Judas betrays, Peter denies, and Thomas doubts. The multitude condemn and Pontius Pilate washes his hands, but the Magdalen remains faithful and witnesses it all. Jesus is condemned, tortured and crucified and, with the death of his body, an immortal soul is born.

The Tales and The Thousand and One Nights

It appears that Gurdjieff modeled *The Tales*, to some degree, on *The Thousand and One Nights (The Arabian Nights)*. Scheherazade is mentioned several times in *The Tales*. In the introduction to *Meetings with Remarkable Men* he writes:

> I myself have seen how hundreds of illiterate people will gather round one literate man to hear a reading of the sacred writings or of the tales known as the "Thousand and One Nights." You will of course reply that the events described, particularly in these tales, are taken from their own life, and are therefore understandable and interesting to them. But that is not the point. These texts—and I speak particularly of the "Thousand and One Nights" are works of literature in the full sense of the word. Anyone reading or hearing this book feels clearly that everything in it is fantasy, but fantasy corresponding to truth, even though composed of episodes which are quite improbable for the ordinary life of people. The interest of the reader or listener is awakened and, enchanted by the author's fine understanding of the psyche of people of all walks of life round him, he follows with curiosity how, little by little, a whole story is formed out of these small incidents of actual life.

We could say that *The Tales*, in some of its chapters, conforms to such a description: "fantasy corresponding to truth, even though composed of episodes which are quite improbable for the ordinary life of people."

In both *The Tales* and *The Thousand and One Nights* there is an overarching theme. In *The Thousand and One Nights*, the theme concerns a Persian king, Shahryar.

The king discovers that his wife is unfaithful and, in anger, he has her executed. In his bitterness, he decides that all women are the same: untrustworthy and ultimately destined to be unfaithful. So Shahryar

Chapter 9: Allegory

chooses to marry a succession of virgins, only to execute each one the next morning, before she has any chance to dishonor him. Eventually the vizier, whose duty involves finding suitable virgins for his master to wed, runs out of possible candidates to become brides. Surprisingly, the vizier's daughter, Scheherazade, volunteers to be the king's next bride. Her father is horrified, but she is insistent and he reluctantly agrees.

On the night of their marriage, Scheherazade begins to tell the king a story, but does not end it. The king postpones her execution in order to hear the conclusion. The next night, as soon as she finishes the tale she begins a new one, and the king again postpones her execution. Her stories are spellbinding and this goes on for 1,001 nights. In the end he removes the possibility of execution and she remains his now fully-trusted and deeply loved bride.

The "great allegory" of *The Thousand and One Nights* is the slow transformation of Shahryar under the influence of Scheherazade–the personality gradually consumed by the essence (perhaps). Scheherazade understands the language of allegory and uses it to great effect. Her behavior is heroic. It is her stories and the telling of them that provokes the transformation of Shahryar.

The theme of *The Tales* is different, but in some ways it is similar. It is an allegory of transformation. Beelzebub recounts his allegorical tales and Hassein undergoes a gradual transformation. We are Hassein, just as in *The Thousand and One Nights*, we are Shahryar.

The "great allegory" of *The Tales* is the education of Hassein. Our ability to fathom the gist of this book depends to a great extent upon our ability to receive the allegorical meaning, not as a literal collection of words, but as a series of images.

The Great Allegory of The Tales

Our lives play out at the intersection of two universes: the universe within and the universe without. We comprehend the outer universe by virtue of a gradually constructed narrative that is fed to us from the moment that we can absorb information from others. From this we build a representation of the outer universe.

The general details of this constructed narrative varies from age to age and from culture to culture. Currently, for most people in the Western World, a good deal of that narrative is based upon the prevailing dogma of science. Prior to that, the prevailing narrative in the Western World derived from the dogmas approved of by the Christian church, mixed to some degree with the musings of Greek philosophers (mainly Plato and Aristotle).

In our education, and via modern media, it is suggested to us that certain theories are true. For example, we are currently led to believe that the universe was created in a rapid expansion of energy/matter from 'a singularity'—a single point that had an infinite gravitational field. We can easily adhere to such a belief even if we have no well-researched idea as to what energy, matter, gravitation or a singularity actually are.

Thus is constructed our inner model of the outer universe, from unproven ideas and speculative schemes, that we have remembered and stitched together over time.

And yet, the whole of the outer universe that we have any appreciation of at all is within us. The outer universe impinges upon us via our six senses. This information is received and interpreted by us through our inner model of the universe. So, although the planets Mercury, Venus, Mars, Jupiter, Saturn, and Neptune exist in the outer universe, they also exist in our inner universe, through our own observations of the night sky, and through photographs and information we may have been fed about them. This is true of everything that arrives as sensory information from the outer universe, no matter how mundane. It includes all theories that we give credence to. If we accept the existence of a single God, that God exists within us in some way.

The education of Hassein is the remolding or possibly the destruction and recrystallization of our inner models of the outer universe. It is the rewriting of that accidentally constructed narrative. Gurdjieff attempts to achieve this by precise allegory.

The critical point is this: *The Tales* are stories that depict our inner universe using literal descriptions or mythical tales of the outer universe. We can make the most effective use of these allegories by applying them to our inner world.

Metaphors and Symbols

Our earlier discussion of 'The Woman Caught In Adultery' from *The New Testament* was included as an example of the use of metaphorical words (you may prefer to think of them as symbols) to create allegorical meaning. There is a whole series of words that are used in

Chapter 9: Allegory

this way in *The New Testament*. For example, water signifies knowledge and wine signifies understanding, so when Christ turns water into wine, the allegorical meaning is of transforming knowledge into understanding. Maurice Nicoll's two excellent books, *The New Man* and *The Mark*, consider the allegorical meaning of *The New Testament* in depth, so we do not intend to discuss it further here, except to say that Gurdjieff uses some of *The New Testament* symbols in *The Tales*. For that reason we think it a good idea for those who study *The Tales* to read Nicoll's books, and also perhaps, give some time to reading *The New Testament*.

Gurdjieff often used such metaphors in individual teaching. For example, he is quoted as having said, "I have very good leather to sell to those who want to make themselves shoes." Clearly he wasn't speaking literally. We can find many examples of this in written records of people encountering Gurdjieff. He could also be very precise in using such metaphors, as he is in the last chapter of *The Tales*, *Chapter 48, From the Author*, when he describes our three brains as "horse, carriage and driver" in great detail.

Gurdjieff uses metaphors extensively in *The Tales*. In our view, unlocking the meaning of the metaphors he uses is an essential part of accessing the allegorical meaning of *The Tales*. However it is not such a simple task. It is easy enough, for example, to take the story of *Pinocchio* and understand the allegory it embodies. With *The Tales* we are faced with something far more complex.

It is clear that in some parts of the book he wants to be understood literally. One example is when he writes about "keva" as follows:

> *"Thanks to this keva their teeth are also strengthened and the cavities in their mouths too are cleaned from the remains of the first food; the use of keva is very necessary for your favorites, particularly for this second purpose, as these remains, not decomposing owing to the chewing of keva, do not give off that disagreeable 'odor' from their mouths which has already become proper particularly to the contemporary three-brained beings there.*

It may be that such writing has allegorical meaning, or it may not. At other times, especially where the literal meaning seems to make no sense, it is clear that an allegorical meaning is intended. Often his allegories are very precise. Perhaps they are all very precise, but in some instances do not seem precise because we are not capable, when we read the words, of fully appreciating the allegory. Sometimes we cannot appreciate an allegory because he has introduced one or two neologisms and we cannot penetrate the meaning of those words.

To add to the difficulty of the text, we are beset with the problem of "the target of the allegory." We have the important idea of a cosmos: a living thing that embodies in its processes and manifestations the laws of Triamazikamno and Heptaparaparshinokh. The megalocosmos, galaxies, suns, planets and we ourselves, are cosmoses. The whole of the external universe, in theory, corresponds to our inner universe. But there are other cosmoses too: the cosmos of Nature, the cosmos of a nation, the cosmos of a work group, the cosmos of The Work itself.

While we may be able to accept in theory that all of these are, as Gurdjieff says, "the same system," few of us see that clearly. An allegory from *The Tales* may apply to all of these cosmoses, but may be far easier for us to comprehend when applied to just one of these cosmoses.

We are also constrained by our level of being. If an allegory from *The Tales* is only easy to comprehend in terms of our own psyche then, if we have not clearly observed that aspect of our psyche, we will not feel the correspondence between Gurdjieff's words and that part of us. Our level of being becomes the stumbling block.

There are many words Gurdjieff uses that we suspect or are even convinced are used metaphorically or allegorically. Here is a fairly short list:

- Sun
- Planet
- Mars
- Saturn
- Two-brained beings
- One-brained beings
- Transapalnian perturbation
- Ship
- Opium
- Alcohol
- Desert
- Mountain
- Ape
- Woman

Chapter 9: Allegory

It would have been easy to create a far longer list, but it will be better for readers of this book, who see the need, to make and maintain their own list.

The Characters: Beelzebub, Ahoon, Hassein

The great arc of *The Tales* is the education of Hassein by Beelzebub with Ahoon lending assistance occasionally. Beelzebub has been exiled:

> It was just then that, owing to the as yet unformed Reason due to his youth, and owing to his callow and therefore still impetuous mentation with unequally flowing associations – that is, owing to a mentation based, as is natural to beings who have not yet become definitely responsible, on a limited understanding-Beelzebub once saw in the government of the World something which seemed to him "illogical, and having found support among his comrades, beings like himself not yet formed, interfered in what was none of his business.
>
> Thanks to the impetuosity and force of Beelzebub's nature, his intervention together with his comrades then soon captured all minds, and the effect was to bring the central kingdom of the Megalocosmos almost to the edge of revolution.
>
> Having learned of this, HIS ENDLESSNESS, notwithstanding his All-lovingness and All-forgiveness, was constrained to banish Beelzebub with his comrades to one of the remote corners of the Universe, namely, to the solar system "Ors" whose inhabitants call it simply the "Solar System," and to assign as the place of their existence one of the planets of that solar system, namely, Mars, with the privilege of existing on other planets also, though only of the same solar system.

Gurdjieff explains his choice of Beelzebub as "the hero of the book" in *Chapter 1, The Arousing of Thought* – clearly announcing that Beelzebub is taken as a name for the Devil. The name Beelzebub is interpreted etymologically as "Lord of the Flies," from the Hebrew, which is a distortion of the Canaanite Baal-Zebul. Beelzebub was originally the name of a Philistine god and, in Christian demonology, he is one of the seven princes of Hell and regarded as a fallen angel.

Ahoon is described as Beelzebub's "devoted old servant." He accompanies Beelzebub everywhere and when he speaks he speaks entirely in the style of his master, as if Beelzebub himself were speaking. Except that this is not so. There are parts of The Tales where Ahoon does not accompany Beelzebub, and for the attentive reader this provides a clue to the allegorical meaning of Ahoon.

Finally we have Hassein, the eager-to-learn grandchild of Beelzebub, who reveres his grandfather and sits in rapt attention hanging on every word. The etymology of the name "Hassein" is not entirely clear to us. We suspect that it is formed from the Turkish adjective *Has* meaning "pure" or "unmixed," or the English verb "Has," and the German noun *sein*, which can mean "essence" or "being." This seems appropriate because we can view *The Tales* as Gurdjieff (Beelzebub) speaking directly to us (Hassein, our essence). The relationship between Hassein and Beelzebub is curious indeed, since it goes far beyond the normal relationship between grandchild and grandparent. We are told:

> *This was Hassein, the son of Beelzebub's favorite son Tooloof.*
>
> *After his return home from exile, Beelzebub had seen this grandson of his, Hassein, for the first time, and, appreciating his good heart, and also owing to what is called "family attraction," he took an instant liking to him.*
>
> *And as the time happened to coincide with the time when the Reason of little Hassein needed to be developed, Beelzebub, having a great deal of free time there, himself undertook the education of his grandson, and from that time on took Hassein everywhere about with him.*
>
> *That is why Hassein also was accompanying Beelzebub on this long journey and was among the number around him.*
>
> *And Hassein, on his side, so loved his grandfather that he would not stir a step without him, and he eagerly absorbed everything his grandfather either said or taught.*

We are also treated to the following exchange between Ahoon and Hassein:

> *When the captain had gone, Hassein suddenly sprang to his feet and began to dance and clap his hands and shout:*
>
> *"Oh, I'm glad, I'm glad, I'm glad of this."*
>
> *Beelzebub looked with affection on these joyous manifestations of his favorite, but old Ahoon could not restrain himself and, shaking his head reproachfully, called the boy–half to himself–a "growing egoist."*

Chapter 9: Allegory

Hearing what Ahoon called him, Hassein stopped in front of him, and, looking at him mischievously, said:

"Don't be angry with me, old Ahoon. The reason for my joy is not egoism but only the coincidence which chances to be happy for me. You heard, didn't you? My dear grandfather did not decide only just to make a stop, but he also promised the captain to talk with him . . .

"And you know, don't you, that the talks of my dear grandfather always bring out tales of places where he has been, and you know also how delightfully he tells them and how much new and interesting information becomes crystallized in our presences from these tales.

"Where is the egoism? Hasn't he himself, of his own free will, having weighed with his wise reason all the circumstances of this unforeseen event, decided to make a stop which evidently doesn't upset his intended plans very much?

"It seems to me that my dear grandfather has no need to hurry; everything necessary for his rest and comfort is present on the Karnak and here also are many who love him and whom he loves.

"Don't you remember he said recently 'we must not oppose forces higher than our own and added that not only one must not oppose them, but even submit and receive all their results with reverence, at the same time praising and glorifying the wonderful and providential works of Our Lord Creator.'

"I am not glad because of the misadventure but because an unforeseen event issuing from above has occurred, owing to which we shall be able to listen once more to The Tales of my dear grandfather.

This is particularly surprising because the text clearly indicates that Hassein is quite self-aware and also articulate. He is, it could be said, more aware than is Ahoon. In fact as *The Tales* progress it becomes clear that Ahoon is not particularly clever.

So the natural question we might ask is: "What does Ahoon represent within us?"

And we can also ask: "What does Hassein represent within us?"

Indeed, it may well be worth our while to focus in particular on Hassein, the questions he asks and his reactions to the information that Beelzebub provides him with.

Further, we can ask: "What does the 'triple' of Beelzebub, Ahoon and Hassein represent within us?"

A Short Note on Mullah Nassr Eddin

The name "Nassr Eddin" is Arabic and means literally "the triumph of the faith." Mullah Nassr Eddin was a historical figure, who was, according to record, born in the village of Hortu in Sivrihisar, Eskişehir Province, Turkey, around 1208 and died in Akşehir, near Konya, around 1284 or 1285. Some accounts suggest he was an imam (preacher) and a qadi (judge). There is a tomb to him in Akşehir and an annual International Nasreddin Hodja Festival is held there.

We were told by a Turkish national who had visited this tomb that it is a small building with statues of fierce soldiers guarding three sides of it, but the fourth side, where you can enter, is completely unguarded.

In *The Tales*, Mullah Nassr Eddin is analogous to a Shakespearean jester. His sayings, which crop up time and again, constitute a comic but piercing commentary that complements Beelzebub's narrative. From a literary perspective, it is Gurdjieff using a different voice. Curiously, Mullah Nassr Eddin even appears as a character in *The Tales* in *Chapter 34, Russia,* where he meets with Beelzebub near Ispahan and, from a rooftop, while watching a cavalcade pass by, makes comments to Beelzebub about the nature of Persians and Russians.

Do we have a Mullah Nassr Eddin within us?

Three Other Characters in The Tales

Aside from Beelzebub, Ahoon and Hassein, there are many less frequently mentioned characters in *The Tales*. It is possible, in fact likely, that each of these represents some aspect of our psyche. We will consider first the Captain of the Karnak. What does he represent within us?"

The Captain describes himself to Beelzebub in the following way:

"Your Right Reverence, I was destined by my father, as soon as I reached the age of a responsible being, for this career in the service of our ENDLESS CREATOR.

"Starting with the lowest positions on the transspace ships, I ultimately merited to perform the duties of captain, and it is now eight years that I have been captain on the long-distance ships.

"This last post of mine, namely, that of captain of the ship Karnak, I took, strictly speaking, in succession to my father, when after his

Chapter 9: Allegory

long years of blameless service to HIS ENDLESSNESS in the performance of the duties of captain from almost the very beginning of the World-creation, he had become worthy to be promoted to the post of Ruler of the solar system 'Kalman.

"In short" continued the captain, "I began my service just when your Right Reverence was departing for the place of your exile.

"I was still only a 'sweeper' on the long-distance ships of that period.

"Yes... a long, long time has passed by.

"Everything has undergone change and is changed since then; only our LORD AND SOVEREIGN remains unchanged.

The blessings of 'Amenzano" on HIS UNCHANGEABLENESS throughout Eternity!

So, in respect of our common presence, what is the captain, and what is the solar system Kalman, for that matter?

Another fairly prominent character is Gornahoor Harharkh, Beelzebub's essence friend from Saturn. Gornahoor Harharkh is prominent on Saturn, but is not the ruler (the Harahrahroohry) of the planet. He is described in these words:

"Gornahoor Harharkh, who afterwards, as I have already told you, became my essence-friend, was then considered one of the foremost scientists among the ordinary three-brained beings of the whole Universe, and all his constatations as well as the elucidatory apparatuses he had invented were everywhere widespread, and other learned beings on the various planets were using them more and more.

We note that he is considered an important scientist, but only among ordinary three-brained beings. Nevertheless he was exceedingly helpful to Beelzebub, who subsequently says:

"Here it will do no harm to remark that I also, thanks only to his learning, had later in my observatory on the planet Mars that Teskooano which, when it was finally established, enabled my sight to perceive, or as is said, 'approach-the-visibility' of remote cosmic concentrations, 7,000,285 times.

"Strictly speaking, it was owing to just this Teskooano that my observatory was afterwards considered one of the best constructions of its kind in the whole Universe; and, most important of all, it was by means of this Teskooano that I myself thereafter could, even while staying at home on the planet Mars, relatively easily see and observe the processes of the existence occurring on the surfaces of those parts of the other planets of that solar system which, in accordance with what is called the 'common-cosmic Harmonious-Movement,' could be perceived by being-sight at the given moment.

In describing the experiments in which Beelzebub participated with Gornahoor Harharkh, he provides the following detail about him:

"Without this appliance we could not have communicated with each other in any way, chiefly because Gornahoor Harharkh was at that time still a being with a presence perfected only up to the state called the 'Sacred Inkozarno; and a being with such a presence not only cannot manifest himself in an absolutely empty space, but he cannot even exist in it, even though the products of all the three being-foods be artificially introduced into him in such a space.

Beelzebub later makes the following curious comment about Gornahoor Harharkh:

"Let us rather return to the tale I have begun about the Omnipresent-Okidanokh and my essence-friend Gornahoor Harharkh, who was, by the way, at one time considered everywhere among ordinary three-brained beings as a 'great-scientist, and is now, though he still continues to exist, not only considered not 'great, but thanks to his own result, that is to say, to his own son, is what our dear Mullah Nassr Eddin would call a 'has-been' or, as he sometimes says in such cases, 'He-is-already-sitting-in-an-old-American-galosh.'

Here is another detail about Gornahoor Harharkh that Beelzebub provides, en passant:

"The problem was that our route from the planet Saturn to the planet Mars would cross such cosmic spheres as did not correspond to the presence of Gornahoor Harharkh, a being who had as yet the possibilities only for an ordinary planetary existence.

In a later part of *The Tales*, Beelzebub introduces Gornahoor Rakhoorkh with the words:

"And this family solemnity of Gornahoor Harharkh's was that beings like himself around him were to consecrate the first heir produced by him.

Chapter 9: Allegory

"I promised to attend this family solemnity Krik hrak hri in order to under take, regarding his recently arisen heir, what is called the 'Alnatoorornian-being-duty.

"Here it is interesting to remark that this kind of procedure for undertaking this being-duty, took place among the ancient three-brained beings of your planet also, and even reached your contemporary favorites, though these latter, just as in everything else, take only the external form of this serious and important procedure. The beings who undertake, as it were, these duties, are called by your contemporary favorites 'godfathers' and 'godmothers'

"The heir of Gornahoor Harharkh was then called Rakhoorkh."

Relating his attendance at this family solemnity, Beelzebub says:

"In the evening of our arrival there I, by the way, asked this essence-friend of mine during friendly conversation how the existence of his heir proceeded, that is, my dear 'Kesdjanian-result-outside-of-me,' or as your favorites would say my godson, Gornahoor Rakhoorkh.

"He thanked me and said that Rakhoorkh existed quite well, that he had already become his heir in all respects, and that he had made the aim of his existence also the study of the details of the Omnipresent substance Okidanokh which had previously been for himself also the aim of all his responsible existence.

"After having paused a little, he added that in respect of the knowledge attained of the question of the cosmic substance Okidanokh his heir had already, as he expressed himself, 'smelled-out-its-very-essence.'

"He said further that owing to the results of the scientific attainments of his heir, all the data for every conviction that had been previously crystallized in his essence, thanks to persevering labors during long years, had by that time not only been totally decrystallized, but that he had even entirely destroyed all his inventions relating to the investigations of this omnipresent cosmic substance, among which was also his famous 'non-radiating lamp'; and sighing deeply, he ended by saying:

" 'I am now in full agreement with the opinion of the "result-of-my-all," that it was the greatest misfortune for me to have been occupied so long with this, in the objective sense, absolutely "unredeemable sin."

We may be inclined to wonder at this. Gornahoor Harharkh has destroyed all his previous inventions relating to experiments with Okidanokh and has come to accept, under the influence of his heir, that it was a great misfortune to have spent so much time in such experiments. It seems clear that Gornahoor Rakhoorkh, who was Beelzebub's godson superseded his father in some way. Nevertheless we are told in the following extract that these bird-beings:

> ...were only ordinary three-brained beings; my friend probably did not suspect that in most cases concerning these questions, just these ordinary three-brained beings, who acquire information about every kind of genuine cosmic fact exclusively only thanks to their being-Partkdolg-duty, are more competent than any of the Angels or Cherubim with their prepared Being, who, though perfected in Reason to high gradations, yet as regards practical confrontation may appear to be only such Individuals as our always respected Mullah Nassr Eddin defines in the following words:
>
> "Never will he understand the sufferings of another who has not experienced them himself though he may have divine Reason and the nature of a genuine Devil"

The natural question for us to ask is: What do Gornahoor Harharkh and Gornahoor Rakhoorkh represent within us?

The Journey

The various elements of the journey that the Karnak takes throughout *The Tales* are easily lost sight of. We can easily forget them as we become immersed in many of the intervening tales. So here we thread these parts together.

> Through the Universe flew the ship Karnak of the "transspace" communication.
>
> It was flying from the spaces "Assooparatsata," that is, from the spaces of the "Milky Way, from the planet Karatas to the solar system "Pandetznokh," the sun of which is also called the "Pole Star."

The journey that Beelzebub is taking is from his home planet Karatas to a solar system called Pandetznokh.

> He was on his way to the planet Revozvradendr to a special conference in which he had consented to take part, at the request of his friends of long standing.

Chapter 9: Allegory

The first stop on the journey is Revozvradendr. However the journey is soon impeded by the need to pass through the solar system "Vuanik." Unfortunately there is a comet in that system called "Sakoor," also known as "Madcap," and it leaves "Zilnotrago" in its wake, which it is necessary for the space-ship to avoid. The captain decides to stop the ship and wait, which provides Beelzebub with the possibility of educating his grandson. After recommencing the journey the Karnak arrives at Revozvradendr. The arrival is described as follows:

> At this place in Beelzebub's tale the hoofs of all the passengers of the transspace ship Karnak suddenly, as it were, radiated from themselves "something phosphorescent."
>
> This meant that the ship Karnak was nearing the place of her destination, that is the planet Revozvradendr. Hence, a bustling movement began among the passengers preparing to descend from the ship.
>
> Beelzebub, Hassein, and Ahoon ended their conversation and hurriedly began to prepare themselves also.
>
> The phosphorescent gleaming of the hoofs was obtained because, concentrated in a particular proportion, there were directed from the engine room to that part of the ship the holy parts of the sacred Omnipresent Okidanokh.

The description of the departure is brief.

> When after two "Ornakres" the cosmic intersystem ship Karnak had left the spheres of the atmosphere of the planet Revozvradendr and began to fall back in the direction of the solar system 'Pandetznokh' onto the planet Karatas...

At this point in *The Tales*, Beelzebub is about to relate the details of his sixth and last sojourn on the planet Earth. The next interruption on the return journey is a visit to The Holy Planet Purgatory. The Captain of the ship speaks to Beelzebub, saying:

> "Your Reverence, at the beginning of our journey you condescended to let fall a word which hinted that on the return journey you would perhaps decide to stop on the way at the holy planet Purgatory to see the family of your son Tooilan. If this is indeed your intention, then it will be better if you give me the order to do so now, because we shall soon be passing through the solar system Khalmian, and if having passed this system we do not direct

the falling of our ship immediately more to the left, we shall greatly lengthen the path of its falling."

So on the return journey when the planet Khalmian is reached, a decision is taken to stop at the holy planet Purgatory, but when this decision has been made, Beelzebub suddenly says to the Captain:

"Wait, my dear Captain, I want to ask you to accede to yet another of my requests." And when the captain, drawing nearer, had sat down in his appointed place, Beelzebub continued thus:

"My request to you is that you consent after the visit to the holy planet Purgatory, to give our ship Karnak such a course of falling that on the way we may reach the surface of the planet Deskaldino.

"The point is that, in the present period of the flow of time on that planet, the Great Saroonoorishan, my first educator, so to say the fundamental cause of all the spiritualized parts of my genuine common presence, has the place of his permanent existence. "I should like, as at that first time, before going to the sphere on which I arose, to profit by this occasion and fall once more at the feet of the prime creator of my genuine being, the more so, since just now, returning from my perhaps last conference, the entire satisfactoriness of the present functioning of all the separate spiritualized parts of my common presence was revealed not only to me myself, but also to most of the individuals I met, and in consequence, the beingimpulse of gratitude towards that Great Saroonoorishan arose in me and is still inextinguishably maintained.

I very well know, my dear Captain, that I am giving you no easy task, because I have already been a witness of the difficulties in carrying out this same request of mine, when, returning for the first time after my gracious pardon to the place of my arising on the planet Karatas, I desired before descending onto it, to visit the surface of the planet Deskaldino. On that occasion, when the captain of the intersystem ship Omnipresent had agreed to this and directed the falling of the Omnipresent in the direction of the atmosphere of that planet and was indeed able to carry out my request, I was able, before my return to my native land, to reach the surface of the planet Deskaldino and I had the happiness of greeting the Great Saroonoorishan, the creator of my genuine being-existence, and to receive from him his 'creator-benediction, most dear and most precious to me."

Chapter 9: Allegory

To this request of Beelzebub's, the captain of the ship Karnak answered:

"Very good, your Reverence, I will think out how it may be possible to carry out your desire. I do not know just what obstacles there were then for the captain of the ship Omnipresent, but in the present case, on the direct route between the holy planet Purgatory and the planet Deskaldino, there lies the solar system called Salzmanino, in which there are many of those cosmic concentrations which, for purposes of the general cosmic Trogoautoegocratic process, are predetermined for the transformation and radiation of the substances Zilnotrago; and therefore the direct falling of our ship Karnak, unhindered, through this system, will scarcely be possible. In any case, I will try in one way or another to satisfy the desire expressed by your Reverence."

The next point on the journey is when the Karnak stops at the Holy Planet Purgatory.

At this point in Beelzebub's tales, he and all the passengers of the inter-solar-system ship Karnak suddenly sensed in their organ of taste a special sour-bitterish taste.

This signified that their ship was approaching that place of their destination, in the given case the holy planet Purgatory.

They sensed the sour-bitterish taste because a special magnetic current was released from the steering compartment of the ship to inform all the passengers of the approach to the place of destination.

On leaving The Holy Planet Purgatory, the Karnak then falls in the direction of Deskaldino.

At this place of Beelzebub's tale, all the passengers of the transsystem ship Karnak experienced something like a sweet-sour taste in the region of the inner part of their mouths.

This signified that the ship Karnak was now approaching some planet, namely, a place of unforeseen stopping.

And this planet was the planet Deskaldino.

Whereupon Beelzebub ceased his narration and, with Ahoon and Hassein, all three went to their "Kesshahs" to get ready for the descent to the planet Deskaldino.

The Karnak resumes its journey after two "Dionosks." The next description of activity on the Karnak is:

> At this point of Beelzebub's tales, what is called a "crosscurrent" or "agitation" began in the ether which penetrated the whole of the ship Karnak. This signified that the passengers of the ship Karnak were summoned to the "Djamdjampal," that is, that "refectory" of the ship in which all the passengers together periodically fed on the second and first being-foods.
>
> So Beelzebub, Hassein, and Ahoon ceased their conversation and hastily went off to the Djamdjampal.

This occurs just prior to the time when Beelzebub relates his opinion of war. Subsequent to this, just prior to the point where Beelzebub explains the form and sequence of his tales to Hassein, we are told:

> At this point of Beelzebub's tales, there were diffused all along the intersystem ship Karnak artificially produced vibrations which had the property of penetrating into the common presences of all the passengers of the ship and which acted on what are called the "wandering nerves" of the stomach.
>
> This artificially produced manifestation was an announcement to the passengers about their assembling in the common what is called "Djameechoonatra" a kind of terrestrial "monasterial refectory" in which the second being-food is collectively taken.

The next and final event described concerning Beelzebub's return journey to Karatas is introduced as follows:

> Beelzebub intended to say more, but just then everything was suddenly lit up with a "pale blue something." From that moment the falling of the ship Karnak began to diminish perceptibly in speed.

All this meant that one of the great Cosmic Egolionopties was about to come alongside the space-ship Karnak.

It is at this point that the Beatification of Beelzebub proceeds and he is seen to have raised himself to the level of the sacred Podkoolad.

What is the meaning of this long journey?

This is the great arc of the book and hence it is important, in our view, to attempt to fathom its meaning. One possible theory is provided by the two points at which the progress of the journey is arrested. If we regard this journey as an octave then the first interval occurs right at the beginning of the journey when, on leaving Karatas,

Chapter 9: Allegory

the space-ship is forced to stop on the journey to Revozvradendr, as it needs to pass through the system "Vuanik" because of the comet "Sakoor" that leaves "Zilnotrago" in its wake. We could take this to be the "mi-fa interval" the interval in The Work that all those who come to The Work experience, and which is difficult to pass.

The second time that the journey is impeded is between the Holy Planet Purgatory and Deskaldino. The difficulty here is presented by the solar system Salzmanino, which also is pervaded by Zilnotrago. If Revozvradendr represents the note "Fa" and the planet Khalmian represents the note "Sol" then the holy planet Purgatory may represent the note "La," and Deskaldino the note "Si."

This, of course, is nothing more than a theory.

Beelzebub's Sojourns to the Planet Earth

Another major arc of *The Tales* are Beelzebub's visits to Earth. There are six sojourns, which we will describe briefly before discussing them together.

The First Descent of Beelzebub upon the Planet Earth

The first sojourn occurs because one of Beelzebub's tribe, whose name is never given, enters into a foolish wager with King Appolis of Atlantis. The outcome of the wager is that the "wealth" of Beelzebub's tribe is brought into jeopardy and King Appolis' position is also threatened. Beelzebub descends to Earth and moors the Occasion on the shores of Atlantis. He then resolves the situation and returns to Mars.

Beelzebub's Second Descent onto the Planet Earth

The second sojourn occurs because the three-brained beings of planet Earth have adopted the habit of sacrificing two-brained and one-brained beings to their imaginary gods and idols. A group of "Most High Sacred Individuals" arrive on Mars requesting Beelzebub to intervene. The Archangel Looisos says:

> "And it is just about this that I have decided to apply to you, your Reverence, and to request you to consent to undertake in the Name of the UNI-BEING CREATOR, the task of trying to spare us the necessity of resorting to some extreme sacred process, unbecoming for three-centered beings, and to remove this undesirable phenomenon in some ordinary way through the "being-Reason" they have in their presences.

Looisos explains the underlying problem with the following words:

"This custom is at present so widespread there, and the destruction of the existence of beings of various forms for this maleficent purpose has reached such dimensions, that there is already a surplus of the "Sacred Askokin" required from the planet Earth for its former parts, that is to say, a surplus of those vibrations which arise during the sacred process of "Rascooarno" of beings of every exterior form arising and existing on that planet from which the said sacred cosmic arising is required.

"For the normal formation of the atmosphere of the newly arisen planet Moon, the said surplus of the Sacred Askokin has already begun seriously to hinder the correct exchange of matters between the planet Moon itself and its atmosphere, and the apprehension has already arisen that its atmosphere may in consequence be formed incorrectly and later become an obstacle to the harmonious movement of the whole system Ors, and perhaps again give rise to factors menacing a catastrophe on a greater common-cosmic scale.

As a consequence, Beelzebub descends to Earth and moors the Occasion on the Caspian Sea, which then had the name "Kolhidious." He proceeds to Koorkalai, the chief city of Tikliamish. He resolves the problem among the inhabitants of that country by urging a local "priest," Abdil, to preach respect for two-brained beings as God's creatures. Abdil is eventually martyred because of this. Beelzebub ascends to Mars with the body of Abdil and buries him on Mars. The outcome of this is that the custom of "sacrificial offerings" is diminished, but not eliminated.

The Third Flight of Beelzebub to the Planet Earth

Beelzebub then descends to Earth and moors the Occasion on the "Sea of Beneficence." He travels to the "City of Gob" and leverages the fact that the "wise King Konuzion" has, because of the habit among his subjects of chewing poppy seeds, spread a religious doctrine that is based on the ideas of heaven and hell. Beelzebub leverages this doctrine by inventing and spreading the idea, via the proprietor of a large Chaihana, that two-brained beings act as witnesses on behalf of the "Mister God" who determines our fate at our death. This stratagem proves to be very effective.

Chapter 9: Allegory

Beelzebub then travels to Pearl-land. There he leverages local beliefs that had descended from the teachings of Saint Buddha. Part of Saint Buddhas original teaching is explained as follows:

"Further, it seems Saint Buddha also told them:

" 'You, three-centered beings of the planet Earth, having the possibility of acquiring in yourselves both chief fundamental, universal, sacred laws, have the full possibility also of coating yourselves with this most sacred part of the Great All-embracing of everything existing and of perfecting it by the required Divine Reason.

"And this Great All-embracing of all that is embraced, is called "Holy Prana."

"This quite definite explanation of Saint Buddha was well understood by his contemporaries and many of them began, as I have already said, to strive with eagerness, first to absorb and to coat in their presences the particle of this Most Great Greatness and afterwards to 'make-inherent to it Divine objective Reason.

The inhabitants of Pearl-land had come to believe that they already possess "Holy Prana" within themselves – a distortion of Saint Buddha's original teaching. Beelzebub invents the idea that:

"A particle of that fundamental Most Great Great All-embracing, namely, the Most-Sacred-Prana, has already from the very beginning settled in every form of being of every scale, breeding on the surface of the planet, in the water, and also in the atmosphere.

Once this idea has spread, the people of Pearl-land cease to sacrifice beings of other forms – indeed some begin to revere them. At this point, Beelzebub has completed the task that was set for him. Beelzebub returns to the Occasion by way of Tibet and then ascends to Mars.

The Fourth Personal Sojourn of Beelzebub on the Planet Earth

Beelzebub's fourth descent was due to a request from Gornahoor Harharkh. The reason for this is explained as follows:

"Well then, my dear boy, while Gornahoor Harharkh was then staying with me as my guest and we were once together observing the existence of these favorites of yours, a certain fact which we happened to notice was the cause of a very serious exchange of opinions between us concerning the three-centered beings of that peculiar planet of yours.

> "The result of this 'exchange of opinions' of ours was that I undertook to descend onto the surface of that planet and to bring back to the planet Saturn a certain number of the beings called there : 'apes, in order to carry out certain elucidating experiments with them concerning the fact we had noticed and which had then surprised us."

On the fourth flight the ship Occasion is moored on the Red Sea, and Beelzebub visits the continent Grabontzi (Africa). After visiting Egypt, Beelzebub, with "two of our tribe" catches the required ape-beings and returns to Mars.

Beelzebub's Flight to the Planet Earth for the Fifth Time

Beelzebub witnesses over many centuries, using his Teskooano, the peculiarity of the psyche of the three-brained beings of Earth which he describes as the 'periodic-need-to-destroy-the-existence-of-others-like-oneself. He gradually also realizes that the length of the existence of these beings is becoming shorter and shorter.

> "And so, my boy, since, at the time when I suddenly constated such a fact there, I had no special business on the planet Mars and it was quite impossible to try to probe this novel peculiarity by means of the Teskooano, I therefore decided to go there myself in order perhaps to clear up for myself there on the spot the causes of this also.

On this visit the *Occasion* is moored on the "Persian Gulf" and Beelzebub visits Babylon. There is no mention in the book of Beelzebub returning to Mars from this fifth descent. Beelzebub's account of his visit ends with his description of the various activities of the Babylonian Legominists. In *Chapter 45, In the Opinion of Beelzebub, Man's Extraction of Electricity from Nature and Its Destruction During Its Use, Is One of the Chief Causes of the Shortening of the Life of Man*, Beelzebub explains his eventual conclusion that man's use of electricity is the underlying cause.

The Sixth and Last Sojourn of Beelzebub on the Planet Earth

The last sojourn is caused by Beelzebub's curiosity about the use of guns by three-brained beings for their reciprocal destruction. This time, when Beelzebub descends, the *Occasion* is moored at the North Pole. Again, there is no mention of Beelzebub returning to Mars from this visit. The visit concludes with his sailing away from New York after visiting America. In *Chapter 43, Beelzebub's Survey of the Process of* the

Chapter 9: Allegory

Periodic Reciprocal Destruction of Men, or Beelzebub's Opinion of War, Beelzebub explains what he surmises from his sixth visit.

His Six Sojourns

On the first three visits Beelzebub actually does something that interferes with the activity of three-brained beings. On the fourth he simply collects ape-beings. On the fifth and sixth visits he descends to Earth only to gather information.

What are we to try to understand from these visits.

What do these visits represent?

He has a Teskooano and thus can observe Earth from Mars, but chooses to visit Earth only for those stated reasons. He never visits Earth unless he has a specific purpose.

The Genesis of the Moon

The comet Kondoor collides with Earth and Earth is split into the triple bodies of Earth, Moon and Anulios. Anulios is enigmatic:

> "As for the beings there now, not only have they no name at all for this smaller fragment, but they do not even suspect its existence.
>
> "It is interesting to notice here that the beings of a continent on that planet called Atlantis, which afterwards perished, still knew of this second fragment of their planet and also called it 'Anulios, but the beings of the last period of the same continent, in whom the results of the consequences of the properties of that organ called 'Kundabuffer'—about which, it now seems, I shall have to explain to you even in great detail-had begun to be crystallized and to become part of their common presences, called it also 'Kimespai, the meaning of which for them was Never-Allowing-One-toSleep-in-Peace.
>
> "Contemporary three-brained beings of this peculiar planet do not know of this former fragment of their planet, chiefly because its comparatively small size and the remoteness of the place of its movement make it quite invisible to their sight, and also because no 'grandmother' ever told them that once upon a time any such little satellite of their planet was known.
>
> "And if any of them should by chance see it through their good, but nevertheless child's toy of theirs called a telescope, he would pay no attention to it, mistaking it simply for a big aerolite.

> "The contemporary beings will probably never see it again, since it has become quite proper to their nature to see only unreality."

We might naturally ask whether there is, in reality, a small aerolite (a large meteorite or possibly asteroid) that regularly orbits the Earth and has done for millennia?

There are what astronomers call "Trojan Asteroids" in our solar system. Trojan Asteroids occupy 'orbits' quite far from their host planet, kept in position by the gravitational pull of the Sun and the host planet. They neither orbit the host planet nor the Sun, but usually oscillate in an almost chaotic manner around a point between their host planet and Sun, where the gravitational pull between the planet and the Sun cancels out.

Mathematically, these are called Lagrange points and there are several such points for every planet. Trojan asteroids can oscillate in that area rather than mark out an orbit around the host planet. So far, many such Trojan asteroids have been discovered in the solar system. Mars has three such 'orbiting asteroids, and possibly a fourth. Neptune and Jupiter appear to have very many.

Only one such asteroid has been confirmed for Earth. Named 2010 TK7, it was first noticed in 2010 and confirmed as a Trojan asteroid in 2011. It is very small – about 1000 feet (300 meters) in diameter. 2010 TK7 always precedes the Earth in its orbit around the Sun. Its closest approach to the Earth is estimated to be 12.4 million miles and its furthest distance away is estimated to be 49.7 million miles – thus, at times it can be further from the Earth than Venus, which comes within about 26 million miles of the Earth at its closest approach.

It is possible, but very unlikely, that an asteroid could exist in a geostationary orbit around Earth, which is 22,237 miles above the Earth. If such an asteroid existed in that area, it is almost certain that it would have been detected, since satellites are regularly launched into geostationary orbits – and any asteroid in that orbit would be a space hazard.

In any event, the Earth does indeed have at least one Trojan asteroid, although it may not be a fragment of Earth. This Trojan asteroid does not have an elliptical orbit around the Earth. As such, it cannot be Anulios as described in the text. Neither could any other Trojan asteroid. They do not have elliptical orbits around the Earth.

The text states:

Chapter 9: Allegory

" 'The broken-off fragments of the planet Earth had lost the momentum they received from the shock before they had reached the limit of that part of space which is the sphere of this planet, and hence, according to the "Law of Falling," these fragments had begun to fall back towards their fundamental piece.

"'But they could no longer fall upon their fundamental piece, because in the meantime they had come under the cosmic law called "Law-of-Catching-Up" and were entirely subject to its influence, and they would therefore now make regular elliptic orbits around their fundamental piece, just as the fundamental piece, namely, the planet Earth, made and makes its orbit around its sun "Ors."

In summary, there is no physical evidence of any 'Anulios' in an elliptical orbit around the Earth.

We can also ask: "Is the Moon actually a fragment that was thrown off by the Earth?"

Modern scientific opinion is divided on this. There are two theories: either the Moon was captured by the Earth's gravitational field at some time, or there was a collision between Earth and another body a long time ago which resulted in the Moon forming from material thrown out by Earth and material from that other body. The second theory is usually preferred.

According to that second theory, a Mars-sized planet called Theia collided with Earth. Computer models indicate that, for the collision to give the now observed result, at least 40 percent of the Moon's mass would have had to come from Theia. If Theia ever existed, nobody has any clear idea of what happened to its remnants. In any event, this theory suggests that the collision would have resulted in a disk of matter orbiting the Earth which gradually coalesced into and became the Moon. It does not suggest that a whole chunk formed immediately.

Isotopic examination of Moon rocks collected by NASA suggests that the Moon has identical or similar material in its rocks to the Earth. This is why this theory is preferred at the moment, although the alternate theory also has adherents, who argue that the regrouping of fragments to form the Moon could not have happened as described.

So it is feasible, from some of the specimens of Moon rock that scientists have examined and tested, that the Moon is a fragment of the Earth in some way.

Beelzebub's description of "the cause of the genesis of the Moon" is, we have no doubt, an allegory. A final problem with interpreting the story literally is that, even if a very large comet did collide with Earth some time in the past, it is hard to imagine that the comet would survive the collision. And yet Beelzebub definitely states that the comet Kondoor still exists:

> *"It was subsequently learned that in accordance with this said 'General-Cosmic-Harmony-of-Reciprocal-Maintenance-of-All-Cosmic-Concentrations there had also to function in this system a comet of what is called 'vast orbit' still existing and named the comet 'Kondoor.*

This leaves us with the question: "If this tale is a myth, then what does Anulios signify?"

It helps to examine Anulios etymologically. We can break Anulios into the two root words "Anu" and "lios."

- *Anu:* Anu was a Sumerian god, and later, by inheritance, a Babylonian god. In Sumerian mythology, Anu (from Sumerian "An" meaning "sky," or "heaven") was the sky-god: the god of heaven and ruler of all the gods, and also spirits and demons. He was lord of constellations and he dwelt in the highest heavenly regions. He had the power to judge those who had committed crimes and he had created the stars as soldiers to destroy the wicked. He was, as far as we can ascertain, more elevated than any Sun god or leader of the gods in any other pantheon.
- *Lios:* We may automatically associate from Anulios to Helios, because of the identical suffix, *lios*. Helios was the Greek Sun god. *Lios* in Greek means "smooth" or "level" It may suggest a place or a center. *Ilios* was Greek for Troy. The only other possibility we can suggest is that *lios* could also be derived from the French *lieu*, meaning "place," transposed into a Greek format. The suffix or root word *lios* is also found in *The Tales* in Samlios, the capital city of Atlantis.

So, we ask the question: "What does Anulios represent within us?" We may be inclined to conclude that it represents the highest part of us.

CHAPTER 9: ALLEGORY

The Italians

Finally, for the sake of example, we take a specific extract from *The Tales* and analyze it, in the hope that this will prove useful to the reader. The extract appears to be about the Italians:

"And as for the descendants of the famous Romans, although they too continue to arise and exist, they no longer even bear the name of their ancestors, though they still call the chief place of their community by the name 'Rome?'

"The contemporary beings of the community formed by the descendants of those former shepherds, afterwards the great Romans, are called by the other beings there 'Italians.'

"Except for that specific being-impulse which the ancient Roman beings were the first on that planet to crystallize in their presences, and which subsequently spread gradually to all the other three-brained beings of that planet, scarcely anything else has passed by inheritance from their ancestors to these beings called Italians.

"The beings of that contemporary community Italy exist at the present time very quietly and peacefully, doing nothing more than unostentatiously inventing ever new forms of their harmless and very innocent what is called 'macaroni.'

"Nevertheless, there had passed to certain beings of that contemporary Italy, by heredity from their ancestors, one special and very peculiar 'property' called 'giving-pleasure-to-others'

"Only they manifest this inherited need, that is to say this giving-pleasure, not towards beings there like themselves, but to beings of other forms.

"It must in fairness be stated that the said special property passed to beings of various parts of contemporary Italy not from the great Romans alone; this inherited property became more 'naturalized' by their ancestors of considerably later epochs, namely, at the time when they began spreading, among other beings both of their own community and of the neighboring weaker communities, the doctrines, already changed for their egoistic purposes, of a certain genuine 'sacred-Messenger-from-Above.

"At the present time the beings of various parts of contemporary Italy actualize this property of giving-pleasure-to-others in the following way:

> "The existence of the quadruped beings called 'sheep' and 'goats', whose planetary bodies they also use for their first food, they do not destroy all at once; but in order to give this 'pleasure they do it 'slowly' and 'gently over a period of many days; that is to say, one day they take off one leg, then a few days later, a second leg, and so on, for as long as the sheep or goat still breathes. And sheep and goats can breathe without the said parts of their common presence for a very long time because, in the main functions of the taking in of cosmic substances for the possibility of existing, these parts do not participate, though they do participate in the functions which actualize those impulses giving self-sensations.

The passage first states that the present day Italians inherited very little from the Romans, except that "specific being impulse" which the ancient Romans were first to crystallize in their presences and which gradually affected all the other three-brained beings on that planet. This probably refers to the abuse of sexuality and sexual energy. It then says:

> "Nevertheless, there had passed to certain beings of that contemporary Italy, by heredity from their ancestors, one special and very peculiar 'property' called 'giving-pleasure-to-others.

The description of 'giving pleasure to others' that then follows does not, in any way indicate 'giving pleasure.' However the idea that an ironic meaning is intended also seems unlikely, because the behavior described is brutal:

> "The existence of the quadruped beings called sheep' and 'goats, whose planetary bodies they also use for their first food, they do not destroy all at once; but in order to give this pleasure they do it 'slowly' and 'gently over a period of many days; that is to say, one day they take off one leg, then a few days later, a second leg, and so on, for as long as the sheep or goat still breathes.

As far as we are aware, this is not an invention of Gurdjieff's. Long before we read *The Tales* we talked to a British soldier who had spent time in North Africa, in Abyssinia and Eritrea, during the Second World War. He related that in some areas the local inhabitants would, for the sake of keeping meat fresh, kill an animal bit by bit, removing one limb at a time. He witnessed such a treatment being given to an old camel. Since the Italians had colonized North Africa years before they were driven from there by the British, the North Africans may have learned this unpleasant procedure from the Italians of the time.

Chapter 9: Allegory

> "It must in fairness be stated that the said special property passed to beings of various parts of contemporary Italy not from the great Romans alone; this inherited property became more 'naturalized' by their ancestors of considerably later epochs, namely, at the time when they began spreading, among other beings both of their own community and of the neighboring weaker communities, the doctrines, already changed for their egoistic purposes, of a certain genuine 'sacred-Messenger-from-Above.'

Here Gurdjieff is speaking of the Roman Catholic Church, which eventually became secular in its goals 'propagating' Christianity both within Italy and to weaker neighboring communities. At one point the Church was propagating its "teaching" via political means and at times by warfare. There are many examples: The interference in monarchic politics in various European countries and within the Holy Roman Empire, The Albigensian Crusade, The Crusades to Jerusalem, Papal wars and so on. We could also include the Inquisition.

For most readers of *The Tales*, the allegorical meaning of this passage will not leap off the page. However, it may emerge after pondering its meaning. Allegorically, two-brained beings can be taken to signify the emotional center. It is possible that Beelzebub is describing a specific outcome of Catholicism in a symbolic manner. It is, after all, a strange anomaly that Catholicism has, in recent times, so badly maimed the emotions of some of its adherents. For some it became an eternal circle of "sin" and "guilt" and "confession" and "absolution," devoid of any inner meaning. And yet, at the outset, according to Gurdjieff, Catholicism was pure and Christianity itself was, beyond dispute, the religion that emphasized love.

> And 'sheep' and 'goats' can breathe for a long time without these parts of their common presence, because although these parts do not participate in the main functions of the taking in of cosmic substances required for existence, they do participate in those functions that engender in all beings the impulses giving self-sensations.

The final paragraph suggests a particular consequence of this activity. It points out that this giving pleasure to others, results in the gradual loss of the function of self-sensation.

For us to proceed any further with this, we may now need to start applying this allegory to ourselves. What do we do that 'gives pleasure to others?' Perhaps we have seen at times that in the presence of others we subvert our behavior to conform with our inner belief of what another individual wants our behavior to be.

When we do this, what happens to the essential part of us? In order to please others we may notice that we suppress our natural emotional responses and instead manifest in a manner more pleasing to the other individual – a manner that is distinctly less genuine?

If we observe such behavior in ourselves are we able at that particular moment to self-sense, or is it the case that we have established barriers for such a situation that preclude self-sensing?

Consider the idea of a domineering inner religion that has taken over much of the behavior of our psyche "by force." Do we have such an inner religion? How did we acquire that inner religion and, more to the point, what are its gods?

Does not the supreme inner god of this religion bear the name "Self-calming?" Were we co-opted into this religion as children when we were taught specific behaviors to enact in the presence of adults, and even to other children? Were we at that time a "neighboring weak community" that was unable to resist a crusading religion? And does that crusading religion still hold sway over inner parts of ourselves?

Do we now maim some of our emotional responses to support our hypocrisy to the point of slowly destroying them, and do we also numb our bodies for the sake of "giving pleasure to others?"

Chapter 10: The Oskiano Of "Man In Quotation Marks"

"The difference between knowledge and understanding becomes clear when we realize that knowledge may be the function of one center. Understanding, however, is the function of three centers. Thus the thinking apparatus may know something. But understanding appears only when a man feels and senses what is connected with it.
Gurdjieff to Ouspensky ~ *In Search of the Miraculous*

The Tales embodies a treasure hunt of a kind. But if we take the above quotation from Gurdjieff seriously, we will not pursue this naively as an "armchair treasure hunt" to be conducted by leisurely skipping from one page of *The Tales* to another, hoping to stumble upon jewels that are hidden beneath the words.

In our view *The Tales* is a map, perhaps a very precise map. And if there are jewels to be discovered, the jewels are within ourselves, not in the book. The book tells us where to look and where to dig.

If we review our natures honestly in the light of its "objectively impartial criticism," what do we see?

Do we manifest vanity and self-love?

Are we not prone to self-calming when the least trifling event disturbs our composure?

Do we wiseacre?

Are we not gullible and prone to believe any old tale as long as it is delivered to us in a pleasing and authoritative manner?

Are we not trapped and burdened by the consequences of our history? If we can at times be as sensitive as young Hassein, are we not also capable of entertaining the vainglorious philosophy of Lentrohamsanin?

Are not our inner angels and archangels remarkably fallible?

Do we not sacrifice our inner two-brained beings to primitive inner idols? Are we not ape-beings of a kind?

We begin as "man in quotation marks" in search of Man. *The Tales* is the map and we are the territory.

Analysis

While "fathoming the gist" may involve a kind of intellectual literary analysis of *The Tales* carried out by you the reader, such an analysis is, in our view, just a useful preparation. In this book we have described many activities that might be characterized as "intellectual" and we have described them mainly from the perspective of the intellectual center. We do not conceive of such activities as purely intellectual.

Consider the meaning of "Iransamkeep" explained in the following excerpt from *The Tales*:

> *"In the common presence of every being existing merely on the basis of Itoklanoz, 'something' similar to the regulator in a mechanical watch is present and is called Iransamkeep; this 'something' means: 'not-to-give-oneself-up-to-those-of-one's-associations-resulting-from-the-functioning-of-only-one-or-another-of-one's-brains.'*
>
> *"But even if they should understand such a simple secret it will be all just the same; they still would not make the necessary being-effort, quite accessible even to the contemporary beings and thanks to which, by the foresight of Nature, beings in general acquire the possibility of what is called 'harmonious association, by virtue of which alone energy is created for active being-existence in the presence of every three-brained being and consequently in them themselves. But at the present time, this energy can be elaborated in the presences of your favorites only during their quite unconscious state, that is to say during what they call 'sleep.'*

Are we capable of "harmonious association?"

Perhaps we have never experienced any inner activity that we could honestly describe as "harmonious association." It will be useful, we believe, for those who wish to pursue any of the techniques suggested in this book, to bear this in mind.

Most of the analytical activity we have suggested will be driven by the intellectual center, but we believe it will bear the greatest fruit if it is pursued with the active participation of the emotional center, and also with the presence of the moving-instinctive center. We conceive of this as a kind of dance.

CHAPTER 10: OSKIANO OF "MAN"

Attention

Gurdjieff explains the following to Ouspensky in *In Search of the Miraculous*:

> "Moving center working for thinking center produces, for example, mechanical reading or mechanical listening, as when a man reads or listens to nothing but words and is utterly unconscious of what he is reading or hearing. This generally happens when attention, that is, the direction of the thinking center's activity, is occupied with something else and when the moving center is trying to replace the absent thinking center; but this very easily becomes a habit, because the thinking center is generally distracted not by useful work, by thought, or by contemplation, but simply by daydreaming or by imagination.

Most of us will recognize what Gurdjieff describes here, and most of us will at times lapse into such inner behavior when reading *The Tales*. It may thus be useful if we make a specific effort when reading *The Tales* for "the third time" to marshal our attention and keep it focused on the effort to read. But our attention will additionally need to be occupied with analyzing what we are reading.

We need to try to absorb and weigh every detail of the text, noticing not just every word, but the typography and the rhythm of the words. We may need to read through sections of the text several times. In doing so we will discover, perhaps, words or phrases or ideas that we need to research. We will thus either need to make a note or embark on such research directly. Our experience suggests that the profound realizations and revelations that *The Tales* can provoke rarely occur while carrying out this activity. They occur later when pondering the meaning of a particular tale. For us, the reading and analysis is a preparation for that, but it may not be so for everyone – and it may not always be so anyway.

The Oskiano of the Intellectual Center

What is the current state of our intellectual center? In *The Tales*, Gurdjieff includes in *Chapter 48, From The Author*, a lecture entitled: THE VARIETY, ACCORDING TO LAW, OF THE MANIFESTATIONS OF HUMAN INDIVIDUALITY. Part of the lecture includes a description of the analogy of horse, carriage and driver. About the driver, who represents the intellect of man, Gurdjieff writes:

Like all hired coachmen in general, he is a type called "cabby." He is not entirely illiterate because, owing to the regulations existing in his country for the "general compulsory teaching of the three R's," he was obliged in his childhood to put in an occasional attendance at what is called the "parish church school." Although he himself is from the country and has remained as ignorant as his fellow rustics, yet rubbing shoulders, owing to his profession, with people of various positions and education, picking up from them, by bits here and bits there, a variety of expressions embodying various notions, he has now come to regard everything smacking of the country with superiority and contempt, indignantly dismissing it all as "ignorance."

In short, this is a type to whom applies perfectly the definition, "The crows he raced but by peacocks outpaced."

He considers himself competent even in questions of religion, politics, and sociology; with his equals he likes to argue; those whom he regards as his inferiors, he likes to teach; his superiors he flatters, with them he is servile; before them, as is said, "he stands cap in hand."

One of his chief weaknesses is to dangle after the neighboring cooks and housemaids, but, best of all, he likes a good hearty tuck-in, and to gulp down another glass or two, and then, fully satiated, drowsily to daydream.

To gratify these weaknesses of his, he always steals a part of the money given him by his employer to buy fodder for the horse.

Like every "cabby" he works as is said always "under the lash," and if occasionally he does a job without being made, it is only in the hope of receiving tips.

The desire for tips has gradually taught him to be aware of certain weaknesses in the people with whom he has dealings, and to profit himself by them; he has automatically learned to be cunning, to flatter, so to say, to stroke people the right way, and, in general, to lie.

On every convenient occasion and at every free moment he slips into a saloon or to a bar, where over a glass of beer he daydreams for hours at a time, or talks with a type like himself, or just reads the paper.

He tries to appear imposing, wears a beard, and if he is thin pads himself out to appear more important.

Chapter 10: Oskiano of "man"

Does this analogy provide a fair representation of our intellect? If we are honest, then we will have to confess that some aspects of it are, at least, distressingly accurate. We daydream, we flirt, we can be deceptive and cunning. Our intellectual education may well be deficient. If we are part of The Work, then it is likely that our intellect may have been repaired to some degree. Nevertheless, it is unlikely that it has approached its full potential.

We have intellectual habits. Some may be useful, others not so useful. On the negative side, if we observe ourselves we probably notice that many of our intellectual responses to situations or people are governed by the first association that the monkey mind comes up with. We often repeat opinions we encountered elsewhere as if we had formulated them ourselves. We easily accept assertions that are unproven just because someone delivered them confidently.

On the positive side, maybe we keep our mind relatively fit, exercising it by doing crosswords or playing bridge. Perhaps we pursue intellectual interests, reading books on science or the arts, or learning a new language or studying history. In this book we have discussed a number of intellectual postures and processes. How many do we actually use?

Let us ask ourselves a few questions about this:

- Do we know what logical confrontation is? When did we ever do that? What was the circumstance?
- Do we know how to ponder? What did we ever ponder? How often do we ponder?
- Do we ever think by analogy? When did we do that?
- Do we know how to treat a theory as if we are holding a dove?

Another useful question to ask is: What does my intellectual vocabulary consist of?

Indeed, which words do I frequently depend on?

This final question is, we believe, particularly important. Gurdjieff uses many unfamiliar English words with which we have few or even no associations. In doing so, he may provoke us to extend our inner vocabulary, by employing these words ourselves. Gurdjieff also invented wholly new words that we had never seen before and with which we had no associations. In important areas of thought he has provided us with a new vocabulary to use.

Gurdjieff describes the intellectual state of the average man with the following words *(Chapter 48, From The Author)*:

> *Owing to the loss of the capacity to ponder and reflect, whenever the contemporary average man hears or employs in conversation any word with which he is familiar only by its consonance, he does not pause to think, nor does there even arise in him any question as to what exactly is meant by this word, he having already decided, once and for all, both that he knows it and that others know it too.*
>
> *A question, perhaps, does sometimes arise in him when he hears an entirely unfamiliar word the first time; but in this case he is content merely to substitute for the unfamiliar word another suitable word of familiar consonance and then to imagine that he has understood it.*

In our view we need to observe our inner intellectual laziness with words that Gurdjieff describes. In connection with this, we may also profit from pondering the following paragraph from *Chapter 1, Introduction, Meetings with Remarkable Men*.

> *'As one who has now become to some degree a "linguist," I consider it necessary to remark here, by the way, that it is never possible to think in a foreign language, even though knowing it to perfection, if one continues to speak one's native language or some other language in which one is accustomed to thinking.*

The point is that we probably need to make a genuine effort to absorb Gurdjieff's version of the English language, including all his neologisms into our inner vocabulary and "think" in that manner.

The Tales provides education for the intellect. Gurdjieff suggests that we have two modes of mentation: mentation by words and mentation by form. His use of language can help us to improve our mentation by words. Perhaps we will then have appropriate words that we can apply accurately to many of our inner states and inner activities.

The Oskiano of the Emotional Center

The Tales intends to bring a much more profound change to our emotional center than to our thinking center. Consider now the description of the "horse" of Gurdjieff's hackney carriage:

> *The totality of the manifestations of the feeling-localization in a man and the whole system of its functioning correspond perfectly to the horse of the hackney carriage in our analogy.*

Chapter 10: Oskiano of "Man"

Incidentally, this comparison of the horse with the organization of human feeling will serve to show up particularly clearly the error and one-sidedness of the contemporary education of the rising generation.

The horse as a whole, owing to the negligence of those around it during its early years, and to its constant solitude, is as if locked up within itself; that is to say, its so to say "inner life" is driven inside, and for external manifestations it has nothing but inertia.

Thanks to the abnormal conditions around it, the horse has never received any special education, but has been molded exclusively under the influence of constant thrashings and vile abuse.

It has always been kept tied up; and for food, instead of oats and hay, there is given to it merely straw which is utterly worthless for its real needs.

Never having seen in any of the manifestations towards it even the least love or friendliness, the horse is now ready to surrender itself completely to anybody who gives it the slightest caress.

The consequence of all this is that all the inclinations of the horse, deprived of all interests and aspirations, must inevitably be concentrated on food, drink, and the automatic yearning towards the opposite sex; hence it invariably veers in the direction where it can obtain any of these. If, for example, it catches sight of a place where even once or twice it gratified one of the enumerated needs, it waits for the chance to run off in that direction.

This description depicts our emotional life as sorry indeed. Our emotional center has received little education of any kind and has largely been mistreated or ignored throughout our lives. Again, if we have worked on ourselves to some degree, our situation may not be as dire as this suggests, but neither are we likely to have fulfilled our emotional potential. In Chapter 3 of this book, Intellectual Postures and Processes, we mentioned Gurdjieff's description of the principle of Itoklanoz, the seventh actualization of which is:

> The quality of what are called the being-egoplastikoori of the given being himself, that is his being-efforts for the transubstantiation in himself of all the data for obtaining objective Reason.

We noted that for three-brained beings like ourselves, who have reached the age of responsibility, the first six of these actualizations are already part of the past, allowing little possibility for change. The seventh actualization of the principle of Itoklanoz is extremely important and, in our view, *The Tales* makes a direct effort to improve the quality of our being-egoplastikoori. Egoplastikoori is a word that we need to genuinely understand.

Gurdjieff explains the meaning of being-egoplastikoori in *The Tales* in *Chapter 24, Beelzebub's Flight to the Planet Earth for the Fifth Time* with reference to our normal conception of The Tower of Babel:

> *"Now I wish to explain to you about the expression I just used, namely, the 'Building-of-the-Tower-of-Babel.' This expression is very often used on your planet by the contemporary three-brained beings there also.*
>
> *"I wish to touch upon this expression frequently used there and to elucidate it to you chiefly because firstly I chanced to be a witness at that time of all the events which gave rise to it, and secondly because the history of the arising of this expression and its transubstantiation in the understanding of your contemporary favorites can very clearly and instructively elucidate to you that, thanks as always to the same abnormally established conditions of ordinary being-existence, no precise information of events there which have indeed occurred to beings of former epochs ever reaches beings of later generations. And if, by chance, something like this expression does reach them, then the fantastic Reason of your favorites constructs a whole theory on the basis of just one expression such as this, with the result that those illusory being-egoplastikoori, or what they call 'psychic-picturings' increase and multiply in their presences owing to which there has arisen in the Universe the strange 'unique-psyche' of three-brained beings which every one of your favorites has.*

Our usual "picturing" of The Tower of Babel comes from *The Bible* in *The Book of Genesis*, where the generations following the Great Flood, who settled in Babylon, built a tower which attempted to reach up to heaven. The Old Testament God, displeased by this act, decides to punish these presumptuous men and causes them to speak different languages. As a consequence they stop building the tower.

In *The Tales* Gurdjieff suggests that the concept of The Tower of Babel came directly from a speech delivered by Hamolinadir at a "general-learned-conference" that discusses the question of whether man has a soul. He spoke thus:

Chapter 10: Oskiano of "Man"

" 'During this time, I have very attentively and seriously followed all the old and new theories about the "soul" and there is not a single theory with the author of which I do not inwardly agree, since all of them are very logically and plausibly expounded, and such Reason as I have cannot but agree with their logic and plausibility.

" 'During this time I have even myself written a very lengthy work on this "question-of-the-beyond"; and many of those present here have surely become acquainted with my logical mentation and most probably there is not one of you here who does not envy this logical mentation of mine.

" 'Yet at the same time I now honestly declare to you all, that concerning this "question-of-the-beyond" I myself, with the whole of the knowledge that has been accumulated in me, am neither more nor less than just an "idiot-cubed."

" 'There is now proceeding among us in the city of Babylon the general public "building-of-a-tower" by means of which to ascend to "Heaven" and there to see with our own eyes what goes on there.

" 'This tower is being built of bricks which outwardly all look alike, but which are made of quite different materials.

" 'Among these bricks are bricks of iron and wood and also of "dough" and even of "eider down."

" 'Well then, at the present time, a stupendously enormous tower is being built of such bricks right in the center of Babylon, and every more or less conscious person must bear in mind that sooner or later this tower will certainly fall and crush not only all the people of Babylon, but also everything else that is there.

" 'As I personally still wish to live and have no desire to be crushed by this Babylonian tower, I shall therefore now immediately go away from here, and all of you, do as you please.'

So Gurdjieff depicts the Tower of Babel symbolically, as an intellectual tower of groundless speculation, which did nothing but sow confusion. In doing so he confers meaning upon an allegory that previously had little or no meaning for most of us, adding the nuance of bricks made of iron, wood, "dough" and "eider down." He provides us with a more useful "psychic picturing" for this symbol.

In our opinion, Gurdjieff, our Oskianotsner, provides us with a multitude of such egoplastikoori through his tales, and in doing so provides material for the education of our emotional center. For our part, we need to be able to readily accept and absorb them. We need to sit at his feet like Hassein.

The Twin Princes

The general malaise of our emotional center is also described in a different way by Gurdjieff in *Chapter 1, Introduction, Meetings with Remarkable Men:*

> 'For any impartial man this viewpoint of mine can be conclusively confirmed by observing the difference between the degree of development of feeling in people who are born and spend their whole lives on the continent of Asia, and in people born and educated in the conditions of contemporary civilization on the continent of Europe.
>
> 'It is a fact, noted by a great many people, that among all the present day inhabitants of the continent of Asia who, owing to geographical and other conditions, are isolated from the effects of modern civilization, feeling has reached a much higher level of development than among any of the inhabitants of Europe. And since feeling is the foundation of common sense, these Asiatic people, in spite of having less general knowledge, have a more correct notion of any object they observe than those belonging to the very tzimuss of contemporary civilization.

Gurdjieff's statement that "feeling is the foundation of common sense" is, we believe, particularly important. In this book we have discussed intellectual postures in a way that may have given the impression that the intellect is an independent force that acts alone.

It can certainly behave in that manner and, when it does so, experience suggests that we are far more likely to find ourselves on the road to confusion or the road to Hell than the road to enlightenment. In *Chapter 22, Beelzebub for the First Time in Tibet,* Gurdjieff describes the Buddhist sect of "Self-tamers." Buddha has stated that:

> " 'One of the best means of rendering ineffective the predisposition present in your nature of the crystallization of the consequences of the properties of the organ Kundabuffer is "intentional-suffering"; and the greatest intentional-suffering can be obtained in your presences if you compel yourselves to be able to endure the "displeasing-manifestations-of-others-towards-yourselves."

Chapter 10: Oskiano of "man"

The Self-tamers, in their desire to eliminate the consequences of the properties of the organ Kundabuffer, invent what they believe to be an appropriate organized form of suffering. The monastery that the Self-tamers eventually establish is described as follows:

"*Around the outside wall, on its inner side, stood a row of small, strongly built, closely adjoining compartments, like cells.*

"*It was just these same 'cells' that represented the difference between this monastery and other monasteries in general on the planet Earth.*

"*These sentry-box structures were entirely walled in on all sides, except that near the bottom they had a small aperture through which, with great difficulty, a hand could be thrust.*

"*These strong sentry-box structures were for the perpetual immurement of the already 'deserving' beings of that sect-and they were to occupy themselves with their famous manipulation of what they call their 'emotions' and 'thoughts'—until the total destruction of their planetary existence.*

"*And so, it was when the wives of these 'self-tamer-sectarians' learned of just this that they made the said great outcry.*

"*In the fundamental religious teaching of this sect there was a full explanation of just what manipulations and for how long a time it is necessary to produce them upon oneself in order to merit being immured in one of the strongly built cells, there to receive every twenty-four hours a piece of bread and a small jug of water.*

"*At that time when we came within the walls of that terrible monastery, all these monstrous cells were already occupied; and the care of the immured, that is, giving them once in twenty-four hours, through the aforementioned tiny apertures, a piece of bread and a small jug of water, was carried out with great reverence by those sectarians who were candidates for that immurement, and who, while waiting their turn, existed in the said large building that stood in the monastery square.*

"*Your immured favorites did indeed exist in the said monastery sepulchres until their existence, so full of deprivations, half-starved and motionless, came quite to an end.*

This is almost laughable. Simple common sense suggests that enduring the "displeasing-manifestations-of-others-towards-oneself" is not something one can do in isolation. The Self-tamers may have "logically invented" a cure for the pernicious influence of Kundabuffer, but they never constated anything.

The allegorical meaning of this section of *The Tales* is very powerful indeed, depicting as it does the intellect acting from an absurd conviction and the outcry of the emotional center against it.

In Brief Summary...

The Tales assists in the Oskiano of both our intellectual and emotional centers. We can picture the properly educated intellectual center and emotional center as twin princes, who are not only capable of working together, but are also inclined to work together, and can work together joyfully.

In Chapter 3 of this book we described a gamut of intellectual postures and processes that we can usefully deploy in our attempt to fathom the gist of *The Tales*. In our view, each of these intellectual activities requires complementary emotional participation to assist it.

At its finest, this will manifest as mentation by words in full harmony with mentation by form; the power of the intellect twinned with the fine discrimination of the emotions.

The Appendices

These appendices provide brief summaries of Chapters 3 to 9.

Appendix A: Notes on Intellectual Postures And Processes

Appendix B: Notes on Research

Appendix C: Notes on Objective Science

Appendix D: Notes on Language and Style

Appendix E: Notes on Etymology and Neologisms

Appendix F: Notes on Intentional Inexactitudes

Appendix G: Notes on Allegorical Meaning

Appendix A: Notes On Intellectual Postures And Processes

In the last chapter of this book we expressed the opinion that our work to fathom the gist of *The Tales* is not a "lone intellectual endeavor" but an activity that requires both the intellectual and the emotional center to work together. In our view it will also help a great deal if you can participate in work-group activities that focus on Gurdjieff's writings.

For those who choose to actively use these postures, we recommend that you do not confine practice in this area to reading *The Tales*, but attempt to strengthen the use of these postures in every appropriate area of your normal life.

The following are summary notes on each posture or process we have written about:

The Monkey Mind

Associative mentation is undisciplined and distracting and hence needs to be kept under control. Nevertheless, when studying *The Tales*, the associative mind is capable of unearthing useful associations.

Aim

Without an aim there can be no destination. "Aim" is hierarchical. A big aim ultimately consists of an aggregation of small aims, which form a progression.

Concentration

Every octave has intervals. Concentration or focus helps in overcoming lesser intervals. Group study of *The Tales* may help overcome intervals. Realization and revelation help to overcome other intervals. Concentration has a brother whose name is patience.

Analysis

The Tales contains many ideas, statements, images, subtleties and cross-references. We do not necessarily take it all in during the first two modes of reading it. In the third mode of reading we need to pay attention to every typographical feature, every word, every sentence, every paragraph. We need to absorb it all from its lowest level of detail up to its major themes. This is an analytical activity that gathers data for later use.

Representation

Our natural mentation in words can be complemented by a mentation in images. We prefer to call this representation rather than imagination.

Materializing Thought

To materialize thought, write it down or draw pictures. This helps to fix data in our memory. We articulate the thought as if to someone else.

The Quest for Questions

Asking questions is necessary. We need to cultivate the habit and we need to realize that there is quality in this. Some questions are more useful than others. A question can be a prayer.

Pattern Matching

This is a natural capability. Intentionally seeking to find patterns helps us to grasp the meaning of allegories.

Thinking By Analogy

The primary analogy to focus on, we believe, is the concept of a cosmos. God, sun, planet, man and microbe are, Gurdjieff suggests, "the same system." There are parallels.

Words

We need to be mindful of the words we employ in our mentation by words. We may need to be more precise in our use of words.

Pondering

After formulating a worthwhile question, we need to ponder. We need to "walk around the question."

Impartiality No matter how unpalatable or inconvenient an objective truth may be to us personally, it is still objective truth. We need to remove the personal.

Appendix A: Intellectual Postures And Processes

Holding The Dove

A theory held too firmly becomes dogma; held too lightly it becomes a source of confusion. We need to learn how to "hold the dove."

Logical confrontation–common sense

Logic is the servant of Reason, not its master. It is precise only with the well-behaved variables of mathematics. When the emotional side provides discrimination, logic becomes a dutiful servant.

Constatation

To constate is to assemble everything known in a given area together and to consider it all.

Egoplastikoori

These are psychic picturings; the means by which the intellect can communicate with our emotional side. We need to cultivate the ability to form such pictures. Gurdjieff describes this as "mentation by form."

Reading Material

We can think of no specific books to recommend as background reading that deal specifically with the topic of intellectual postures. Nevertheless, there are references to most of these postures in many books that have been written about The Work, and throughout Gurdjieff's writings.

Appendix B: Notes On Research

Most, if not all, readers will have gaps in their background knowledge of the various factual and historical references that appear in *The Tales*. Our advice is that the reader should do their own research into every such reference they notice. Sometimes such research will yield useful information that improves one's understanding of the text.

As regards the various versions of *The Tales*, our view is that:

Study of the 1931 Version can be useful, partly because segments of it are different to the 1950 Version and partly because it can provide insight into the etymology of some of the neologisms

- The 1950 Version is the authentic version
- The 1992 version is, in our view, of little or no value at all

Currently there are few books we are aware of that directly aim to improve background knowledge of The Tales. We believe the following two may be of value:

- *A. R. Orage's commentaries on G. I. Gurdjieff's All and Everything: Beelzebub's Tales to His Grandson*, by A. Orage and edited by C. S. Nott or *The Teachings of Gurdjieff*, by C. S. Nott
- *Guide and Index to G. I. Gurdjieff's Beelzebub's Tales to His Grandson*, edited by Louise Welch and published by Traditional Studies Press in Toronto.

Appendix C: Notes On Objective Science

People in The Work often give credence to the theories and assertions of modern science. Gurdjieff clearly did not, and, in our view, wished to arrest our habit of simply accepting the validity of modern science. As we are, we may not know whether Gurdjieff's statements and explanations of Objective Science are any more valid. However, we believe students of The Work need to be aware of the distinct differences between the two views.

Objective Science	Modern Science
There is an ether.	There is no ether, but space is permeated by a "Higgs Field."
Time is subjective, but the flow of time is objective in a given location as experienced by a single observer.	Time is a fundamental dimension of the universe equivalent to the three dimensions of length in every respect.
The whole megalocosmos operates according to two laws: heptaparaparshinokh and triamazikamno, assisted by theomertmalogos (the will of the Absolute).	There are quite a few immutable Physical Laws including the Three/Four Laws of Thermodynamics, Law of Gravity etc.
The creation is a consequence of a change to these two laws stated above, which was initiated by the Absolute.	The creation is a consequence of the emergence of a vast amount of energy from a single point in the universe.
Elements are defined to be substances that have different properties. The atom of an element is the smallest quantity of that element which retains all its properties including its cosmic properties.	Elements are defined by the number of protons in the nucleus of an atom of that specific element. Elements can have isotopes.

Objective Science	Modern Science
The Sun grows of its own accord and is not running down. This does not preclude nuclear fusion being involved in the Sun's behavior.	The Sun is powered entirely by nuclear fusion and is slowly running down.
The planets grow of their own accord, from within.	Planets grow only as a result of collision with other solar system bodies (comets and meteors).
The Moon is a "child" of the Earth and it is growing/evolving.	The Moon may be a child of the Earth, thrown out after planetary collision. But it is not evolving. It is an inanimate aggregation of rocks.
Life on Earth formed because of the need to fill the interval in the Ray of Creation, and also to feed the moon.	Life on Earth formed accidentally via chemical reaction.
The evolution of life on Earth is governed by the influence of the planets. Great Nature, in her entirety, transmits the influence of other planets directly to the Earth itself.	Evolution of life occurred by "Natural Selection."
There is a God.	There may or may not be a God.

Modern Science

In making a critical assessment of modern science it is vitally important to distinguish between the data of modern science and the theories that various scientists promote. In our view, because of the intellectual discipline that pervades science, there is little reason to doubt the observational measurements and scientific experiments that scientists carry out. We simply need to ensure that we make a separation between data and theoretic explanations and speculations.

Reading Material

Aside from the references to Objective Science in *The Tales*, the only other book we are aware of that contains Gurdjieff's definitive

Appendix C: Notes On Objective Science

statements about Objective Science is *In Search of the Miraculous*, by Peter Ouspensky.

In our view it will also be worthwhile for those who wish to study the ideas of Objective Science to read the books:

- *The Theory of Celestial Influence,* by Rodney Collin
- *Perspectives on Beelzebub's Tales,* by Keith A. Buzzell

In our opinion, readers who wish to investigate an approach to physics and astrophysics that is fairly closely aligned to the statements of Objective Science will profit from reading the following books:

- *A Beginner's View of Our Electric Universe* by Tom Findlay
- *The Electric Universe* by Wallace Thornhill and David Talbott
- *The Electric Sky* by Donald E. Scott
- *Thunderbolts of the Gods* by David Talbott and Wallace Thornhill

Appendix D: Notes On Language And Style

The writing style and techniques that Gurdjieff employed in composing *The Tales* are unique. It employs a broad variety of literary techniques, but as every reader of *The Tales* will surely agree, this does not make it easy to read. Here we list distinct features of the book that drew our attention and which we discussed in Chapter 5:

- Gurdjieff was meticulous and exact in his choice of English words. On many occasions he chooses English words that other authors rarely use, possibly because we will have few associations with these words.
- Gurdjieff was a skilled philologist and spoke many languages fluently. He occasionally uses English "loan words" and foreign words, presumably to convey meaning more effectively. His neologisms also reflect his extensive language capabilities.
- Gurdjieff uses quotation marks around many words, indicating that we should not just accept the normal meaning of the word. Sometimes this is metaphor, sometimes satire, sometimes just emphasis. We need to consider the context to know for sure.
- Gurdjieff frequently employs capitalization (capitalizing the first letter of a word) and full capitalization (writing the whole word in capitals). This normally indicates that we consider the "highest" meaning of the word
- Aside from when using the names of spaceships, Gurdjieff uses italics only once, when he refers to the "after-dinner *Cheshma*" of Sheherazade.
- Hyphens that concatenate words seem to suggest that we should consider the collection of words as a single concept.
- Gurdjieff's use of footnotes to explain the meaning of some words is mystifying, since he usually explains the meaning of unfamiliar words directly in the text. We presume that the use of footnotes indicates that the word is particularly important.
- Gurdjieff uses several forms of indirect reference: e.g. "what they call," "what is called," and "something like." He is indicating that there is no appropriate English word for him to use.

Appendix D: Notes On Language And Style

- When repeatedly mentioning something, as he does in many instances, he adopts two different approaches. On the one hand he simply repeats the same expression (e.g., the consequences of the properties of the organ Kundabuffer) in what we think of as a hypnotic manner. On the other hand he provides a great deal of variety, continually broadening the way we might conceive of what he is referring to.
- He uses some adjectives repeatedly in many contexts. Two examples are "being" and "essence."
- At times he includes lists of words to define a concept. Sometimes these lists contain an unexpected word.
- His long sentences can be viewed almost as musical compositions, with repeating themes and surprising variations.

We are not aware of any other books you might read that discuss the writing styles that Gurdjieff employed in writing *The Tales*.

Appendix E: Notes On Etymology and Neologisms

There are three methods of word construction that we regard as important in attempting to discern the intended meaning of Gurdjieff's neologisms. They are:

- Agglutination: This is the process of gluing root words or morphemes together to make a new word. Many of the languages of the Caucasus that Gurdjieff spoke are agglutinative.
- Blending: Blending occurs when letters are dropped in the process of agglutination, sometimes making it difficult to know what the original morphemes of a neologism were.
- Compounding: This process is similar to agglutination, where words are concatenated to form a new word. The difference is slight, in that the concatenated words are not necessarily morphemes.

It is our experience that Gurdjieff has used morphemes or words from a multitude of languages in creating his many neologisms. We have (we believe) found morphemes or whole words included in his neologisms that derive from the following languages: Arabic, Armenian, Dutch, English, French, German, Persian, Russian, Slovenian, Turkish, and Yiddish.

We believe it is a worthwhile effort to categorize Gurdjieff's neologisms under specific headings. We suggest the following categories: Names of characters, tribes and peoples, festivals, animals, plants, substances, physical objects, devices, astronomical objects (comets, planets, suns, systems), places (cities, countries, continents), concepts and processes, laws, octaves, opium derivatives, Saturnian words, Martian words, foreign words, loanwords, and miscellaneous.

Internet Resources

We have found the following Internet resources useful in trying to discover the meaning of some of Gurdjieff's neologisms:

- Wikipedia: en.wikipedia.org.
- Google Search.

Appendix E: Notes On Etymology And Neologisms

- Dictionaries: we can recommend both www.oxforddictionaries.com and www.merriamwebster.com.
- OneLook Dictionary Search (www.onelook.com) offers a useful wildcard search capability.
- Etymology Online (www.etymonline.com) and Dictionary.com are useful for etymological research.
- Google Translate (translate.google.com) is a useful tool for translation.

Morphemes and Neologisms

The following section comprises a list of Gurdjieff's neologisms and a list of morphemes and the neologisms in which they occur.

Many of these words are proper names that may have been constructed by Gurdjieff to have specific meaning. It is also possible that some of the words in *The Tales* that we have not listed here are of Gurdjieff's "invention." We have tried to be thorough in this list of words. Also, please note that words are capitalized if they appear in *The Tales* with a capital letter. Some of the neologisms Gurdjieff introduced were not capitalized, but most of them were.

Neologisms and Names

A

Abaranian

abdest	Aiesakhaldan
Abdil	Aiessirittoorassnian
Abrustdonis	Aimnophnian
Absoizomosa	Aisorian
Actavus	Akhaldan
Adashsikra	Akhaldanfokhsovors
Adashtanas	Akhaldangezpoodjnisovors
Adiat	Akhaldanharnosovors
Adossia	Akhaldanmetrosovors
Afalkalna	Akhaldanmistessovors
Again-Tarnotoltoor	Akhaldanpsychosovors
Agoorokhrostiny	Akhaldansovors
Ahoon	Akhaldanstrassovors
Aieioiuoa	Aklonoatistitchian

To Fathom The Gist: Vol I

Aksharpanziar
Algamatant
Alla Ek Linakh
Aliamizoornakalu
Alil
Alillonofarab
Aliman
alisarine
Alla-attapan
Almacornian
Almznoshinoo
Alnatoorornian
Alnepoosian
Alnokhoorian
Alstoozori
Amambakhlootr
Amarhoodan
Amarloos
Amenzano
Amersamarskanapa
Amskomoutator
Androperasty
Anklad
Anodnatious
Anoklinism
Anoroparionikima
Ansanbaluiazar
Ansapalnian
Antkooano
Anulios
Appolis
Arachiaplnish
Aravians
Arax
Arguenia
Arhoonilo
Arkhatozine

Armanatoora
Arostodesokh
Ashagiprotoëhary
Ashhana
Ashhark
Ashiata Shiemash
Asiman
Askalnooazar
Asklay (also Asklaian)
Askokin
Asoochilon
Assadulla Ibrahim Ogly
Assooparatsata
Astralnomonian
Astroluolucizoin
Astrosovors
Atarnakh
Ateshkain
Autoegocrat
Autokolizikners
Avazlin

B

bagooshis
Balakhanira
Baleaooto
Bambini
Beelzebub
Being-Impulsakri
Being-Nerhitrogool
Being-obligolnian-strivings
Being-Partkdolg-duty
Belcultassi
Berdichev
Blagonoorarirnian
Blastegoklornian
Bliss-stokirno

Appendix E: Notes On Etymology And Neologisms

Bobbin-kandelnosts
Boolmarshano
Boordook
Brade

C
Caironana
Canineson
Cathodnatious
centrotino
Cevorksikra
Chai-Yoo
Chaihana
Chainonizironness
Chakla
Chaltandr
chambardakh
Chamianian
Champarnakh
Chatterlitz
Cheshma
Chiklaral
Chiltoonakh
chinkrooaries
Chirniano
Chirnooanovo
Chiromants
Choon
Choon-Kil-Tez
Choon-Tro-Pel
choongary
Choortetev
Choot-God-Litanical
Choozna
Chorortdiapan
Chrkhrta-Zoorrt
Cinchona

D
Daivibrizkar
Darthelhlustnian
Davlaksherian
Defterocosmos
Defteroëhary
Degindad
Demisakhsakhsa
Dephteropine
Desagroanskrad
Deskaldino
Devd'el Kascho
Dezonakooasanz
Dezsoopsentoziroso
Dgloz
Dglozidzi
dianosk
Diapharon
Diardookin
Dimtzoneero
dionosk
Disputekrialnian
Djamdjampal
Djameechoonatra
Djamtesternokhi
Djartklom
Djedjims
Djerymetly
Djoolfapal
Dooczako
Doonyasha
Doosico
Dynamoumzoin
Dzedzatzshoon
Dzendvokh
Dzi

To Fathom The Gist: Vol I

E
Egoaitoorassian
Egokoolnatsnarnian-sensation
Egolionopty
egoplastikoori
Ekbarzerbazia
Eknokh
El Koona Nassa
Elekilpomagtistzen
Elmooarno
Elnapara
Emptykralnian
Ephrosinia
Epodrenekhs
Epsi-Noora-Chaka
Epsi-Pikan-On
Erkrordiapan
Erordiapan
Erti-Noora-Chaka
Erti-Pikan-On
Essoaieritoorassnian
etherogram
Etherokrilno
Etzikolnianakhnian
Evosikra
Evotanas
Exioëhary

F
Fal-Fe-Foof
Ferghanian
Filnooanzi
Foolon
Foos
foscalia
Frianktzanarali
Ftofoo

Fulasnitamnian

G
Gaidoropoolo
Gasometronoltooriko
Gemchania
Geneotriamazikamnian
Gnoskopine
Gob
Goblandia
Goolgoolian
Goorban
Gornahoor
Govorktanis
Grabontzi
Gromwell
Gulgulian
Gynekokhrostiny

H
Hachi
Hadii-Asvatz-Troov
Hadji-Zephir-Bogga-Eddin
Haidia
Hamilodox
Hamolinadir
Hanbledzoin
Hanja
Hanziano
Haoorma
Harahrahroohry
Harharkh
Harhoory
Harhrinhrarh
Hariton
Harnahoom
Harnatoolkpararana

Appendix E: Notes On Etymology And Neologisms

Harnel-Aoot
Harnelmiatznel
Hasnamuss
Hassein
Havatvernoni
Heechtvori
Helkdonis
Helkgematios
Hellenaki
Hentralispana
Heptaparaparshinokh
Herailaz
Herkission
Hernasdjensa
Heropass
Hertoonano
Heteratogetar
Hikhdjnapar
Hirr-Hirr
Hivintzes
Hlodistomaticules
Hoodazbabognari
Hooltanpanas
Hrahaharhtzaha
Hraprkhabeekhrokhnian
Hre-Hree-Hra
Hrhaharhtzaha
Hrkh-hr-hoo
Hydro-oomiak
Hydrokatarnine

I
Iabolioonosar
Ibrkh
Ikriltazkakra
Ilnosoparno
Impulsakri

Inkiranoodel
Inkliazanikshanas
Inkozarno
Insapalnian
Instincto-terebelnian
Instruarian
intelligentsics
Iranan
Iraniranumange
Irankipaekh
Iransamkeep
Irodohahoon
Ischmetch
Ishmetch
Isklolunitsinernly
Iskoloonizinernly
Isoliazsokhlanness
Issi-Noora
Itoklanoz

K
Kafirian
Kafiristan
Kahketeenian
Kaialana
Kaimon
Kal-da-zakh-tee
Kalianjesh
Kalkali
Being Kalkali
Kalkians
Kalman
Kalmanuior
Kalnokranonis
Kaltaan(i)
Kaltusara
Kalunom

Kalyan
Kalzanooarnian
Kanil-El-Norkel
Karabaghian.
Karakoom
Karapet
Karatas
Karatsiag
Karnak
karoona
Kartotakhnian
Kashiman
Kashireitleer
Kashmanoon
Kasnik
Kasoaadjy
Katarnine
Katoshkihydooraki
kazi
Kaznookizkernian
Keesookesschoor
Keeziak
Kefal
Kelli-E-Ofoo
Kelnuanian
Kelnuk
Kerbalai-Azis-Nuaran
Keria-chi
Kerkoolnonarnian
Kesbaadji
Keschapmartnian
Kesdjan
Keskestasantnian
Kesshah
keva
Kezmaral
Khaboor-Chooboor

Khaivansanansaks
Khaivatine
Khaizarian
Khalmian
Khenionian
Khevsoory
Khlarfogo
Khooti-Noora-Chaka
Khooti-Pikan-On
Khorassanian
Khrh
Khritofalmonofarab
Kilmantooshian
Kilpreno
Kimespai
King-Too-Toz
Kirkistcheri
Kirmankshana
Kirmininasha
Kishmenhof
Klananoizufarab
Kldazacht (also kladtzacht)
Klian-of-the-mountains,
Klians
Klintrana
Kmalkanatonashachermacher
Knaneomeny
Kodomine
Kofensharnian
Koilononine
Kolbana
Kolenian(Kolenian Loots)
Kolhidious
Kolhidshissi
Kolomonine
Kolotine
Kondoor

Appendix E: Notes On Etymology And Neologisms

Konuzion
Koorfooristanian
Koorkalai
Koritesnokhnian
Korkaptilnian
Korkolans
Kreemboolazoomara
Krentonalnian-revolution
Krhrrhihirhi
Krik hrak hri
Krilnomolnifarab
Krintonine
Krishnatkharna
kroahn
Kronbernkzion
Kronbookhon
Ksheltarna
Ksherknara
kshtatsavacht
(also kshtatzavacht)
Ksvaznell
Ktulnotz
Kulnabo
Kundabuffer
Kundalina
Kupaitarian
Kurlandtech

L
Labolioonosar
Lanthopine
Latinaki
Laudanine
Laudanosine
Lav-Merz-Nokh
Legominism
Leitoochanbros

Lentrohamsanin
Lifechakan
Liktonozine
Litsvrtsi
Logicnestarian
London-Phu-Phu-Kle
Looisos
Lookosikra
Lookotanas
Loonderperzo
Loonias
Loosochepana

M
Maikitanis
Maikosikra
Makanidine
Makar
Makary
Kronbernkzion
Makhokh
Makkar
Mal-el-Lel
Malmanash
Mamzolin
Maralpleicie
Margelan
Martaadamlik
Martfotai
Martna
Mdnel-in
Mdnel-outian
mechanogentsia
Megalocosmos
Mekonoiozine
Melik
Menitkel

Mentekithzoin
Messaine
Metamorphine
Microparaine
Microtebaine
Midosikra
Midotanis
Mindari
Mirozinoo
Modiktheo
Momonodooar
Mongolplanzura
monkism
Monoenithits
Moordoorten
Morkrokh
Mosulopolis
Moyasul
Mungull

N
Naloo-osnian
Nammus
Nammuslik
Naoolan
Naoolan El Aool
Nar-Khra-Noora
Narcotine
Naria-chi
Nartzeine
Nerhitrogool
Neomothists
Nievia
Nilia
Nipilhooatchi
Nirioonossian
Nokhan

Nolniolnian
Noorfooftafaf
Nooxhomists
Noughtounichtono

O
Oblekioonerish
obligolnian
Oduristelnian
Oilopine
Okaniaki
Okhtapanatsakhnian
Okhtatralnian
Okhterordiapan
Okhti-Noora-Chaka
Okhti-Pikan-On
Okiartaaitokhsa
Okidanokh
Okipkhalevnian
Okrualno
Oksoseria
Olbogmek
Olmantaboor
Olooessultratesnokhnian
Olooestesnokhnian
Onandjiki
Onanson
Ooamonvanosinian
Ooissapagaoomnian
Ookazemotra
Oonastralnian
Ooretstaknilkaroolni
Oornel
Opianine
Ori-Noora-Chaka
Ori-Pikan-On
Ornakres (also Ornakras)

Appendix E: Notes On Etymology And Neologisms

Orpheist
Ors
Orthodoxhydooraki
Oskiano
Oskianotsner
Oskianotznel
Oskolnikoo
Osmooalnian
Otkalooparnian

P
paischakir
Paleomothists
Palnassoorian
Pandetznokh
Pantemeasurability
Papaverine
Papaveroon
Paramorphine
Parijrahatnatioose
Partkdolg-duty
Passavus
Patetook
Pedrini
Perambarrsasidaan
Peshtvogner
Pestolnootiarly
Petrkarmak
Phormine
Photoinzoin
Phykhtonozine
Piandjiapan
Piandjoëhary
Pianje
Pirinjiel
Pirmaral
Pirotine

Pispascana
Pistotorine
Planekurab
Plef-Perf-Noof
Plitazoorali
Podkoolad
Podobnisirnian
Podotorine
Poisonioonoskirian
Pokhdalissdjancha
Polorishboorda
Polormedekhtian
(Also Polormedekhtic)
Polorotheoparl
Pooloodjistius
Porphiroksine
Poundolero
Prokhpaioch
prosphora
Protopine
Prtzathalavr
Pseudocodeine
Pseudophormine

R
Rakhoorkh
Rascooarno
Rastropoonilo
restorial
Resulzarion
Revozvradendr
Rhaharahr
Riank-Pokhortarz
Rimala
Rimk
Rirkh
Rkhee

S

Sakaki
Sakookinoltooriko
Sakoor
Sakronakari
Sakrooalnian
Sakrooalnian
Sakroopiaks
Saliakooriap
Salkamourskian
Salnichizinooarnian
Salounilovian
Salzmanino
Sami-Noora-Chakoo
Sami-Pikan-On
Samlios
Samoniks
Samonoltooriko
Samookoorooazar
Samos
Sandoor
Sarnuonino
Saroonoorishan
Sarpitimnian
Satkaine
Seccruano
Sekronoolanzaknian
Selchans
Selneh-eh-Avaz
Selnoano
Selos
Selzelnualno
Semooniranoos
Semzekionally
Senkoo-ori
Sensimiriniko
Serooazar
Setrenotzinarco
Sevohtartra
Sevrodox
Shachermacher
Shamai
Shat-Chai-Mernis
Sherakhoorian
Shila-Plav
Shmana
Shooroomooroomnian
Shooshoonian
Shuenists
Shvidi-Noora-Chakoo
Shvidi-Pikan-On
Sianoorinam
Siapora
Sikharenenian
Sikitians
Sikt ner chorn
Silkoornano
Silnooyegordpana
Similnisirnian
Simkalash
Sincratorza
Sinkrpoosarams
Sinndraga
Sinokooloopianian
Sinonoums
Sinooa
Sirioonorifarab
Sirkliniamen
Sitrik
Skernalitsionniks
Skinikoonartzino
Skoohiatchiny
Sobrionolian

Appendix E: Notes On Etymology And Neologisms

Solianka
Soldjinoha
Solioonensius
Solni
Soloohnorahoona
Soniasikra
Sonitanis
Sooanso-Toorabizo
sooniat
Sooptaninalnian
Soorptakalknian
Soort
Spetsitooalitivian
Spirna
Spipsychoonalian
Stopinder
Stumpsinschmausen
Surp-Athanotos
Surp-Otheos
Surp-Skiros
Svolibroonolnian

T
Tadjik
tainolair
Tak-tschan-nan
Talaialtnikoom
Talkoprafarab
Tambak
Tanguori
Taranooranura
Tastartoonarian
Tatakh
Tazaloorinono
Tchaftantouri
Tchai-kanas
Tchaikanas

Techgekdnel
Teleoghinooras
Teleokrimalnichnian
Tempo-Davlaksherian
Tenikdoa
Terasakhaboora
Terbelnian
Terebelnian
Ternoonald
Teskooano
Tetartocosmoses
Tetartoëhary
Tetetos
Tetetzender
Thebaine
Tikliamish
Tiklunia
Tiktoutine
Tirdiank
Tiriakrkomnian
Tirzikiano
Tokitozine
Toof-Nef-Tef
Toogoortski
Tooilan
Took-soo-kef
Tookha
Tes Nalool Pan
Tookloonian
Toolkhtotino
Tooloof
Toolookhterzinek
Toorinoorino
Toosidji
Toosook
Toosooly
Toospooshokh

Toosy
Tralalaooalalalala
Transapalnian
Trentroodianos
Triakrkomnian
Triamazikamno
Trioshka
Tritocosmos
Tritoëhary
Trnlva
Troemedekhfe
Trogoautoegocratic
Trotopine
Tsirikooakhtz
Tzel putz kann
Tzimus

U
Uneano
Urdekhplifata
Urmia

V
Vallikrin
Veggendiadi
Venoma
Vermassan-Zeroonan-Alaram
Veroonk
Vetserordiapan

Veziniama
Vibroechonitanko
vibrosho
Vietro-yretznel
Viloyer
Vojiano
Vuanik
Vznooshlitzval

Y
Yagliyemmish
Yenikishlak
Ypsylodox

Z
Zadik
Zalnakatar
Zapoopoonchik
Zarooary
Zernakoor
Zernofookalnian
Zevrocrats
Zilnotrago
Zirlikner
Zoostat
Zoutine

Appendix E: Notes On Etymology And Neologisms

The Morphemes of the Neologisms

A

Adash: Adashsikra, Adashtanas

Aie: Aieioiuoa, Aiesakhaldan, Aiessirittoorassnian, Essoaieritoorassnian

Akhaldan: Aiesakhaldan, Akhaldan, Akhaldanfokhsovors, Akhaldangezpoodjnisovors, Akhaldanharnosovors, Akhaldanmetrosovors, Akhaldanmistessovors, Akhaldanpsychosovors, Akhaldansovors, Akhaldanstrassovors

Alil: Alil, Alillonofarab

Amar: Amarhoodan, Amarloos, Amersamarskanapa

Ank: Anklad, Frianktzanarali, Irankipaekh, Kirmankshana, Riank-Pokhortarz, Solianka, Tirdiank, Vibroechonitanko

Ano: Antkooano, Boolmarshano, Chirniano, Chirnooanovo, Hanziano, Hertoonano, Itoklanoz, Klananoizufarab, Laudanosine, mechanogentsia, Okidanokh, Coamonvanosinian, Oskiano, Oskianotsner, Oskianotznel, Seccruano, Selnoano, Silkoornano, Teskooano, Tirzikiano, Trentroodianos, Unean, Vojiano

Anoo: Inkiranoodel, Kalzanooarnian, Kashmanoon, Semooniranoos, Sianoorinam, Taranooranura

Ant: Antkooano, Keskestasantnian, Kilmantooshian, Olmantaboor, Tchaftantouri

Apan: Alla-attapan, Chorortdiapan, Erkrordiapan, Erordiapan, Okhtapanatsakhnian, Okhterordiapan, Piandjiapan, Vetserordiapan

Ass: Akhaldanstrassovors, Aiessirittoorassnian, Assadulla Ibrahim Ogly, Assooparatsata, Belcultassi, Egoaitoorassian, El Koona Nassa, Essoaieritoorassnian, Hassein, Heropass, Khorassanian, Mullah Nassr Eddin, palnassoorian, Passavus, Vermassan-Zeroonan-Alaram

B

Bool: Boolmarshano, Kreemboolazoomara

Bog: Hadji-Zephir-Bogga-Eddin, Hoodazbabognari, Olbogmek

C

Chan: Gemchania, Leitoochanbros, Selchans, Tak-tschan-nan

Chir: Chirman, Chirniano, Chirnooanovo

To Fathom The Gist: Vol I

Choon: Choon, Choon-Kil-Tez, Choon-Tro-Pel, Choongary, Djameechoonatra, Spipsychoonalian

D

Djam: Djamdjampal, Djameechoonatra, Djamtesternokhi

Dji: Djedjims, Hadji-Asvatz-Troov, Hadji-Zephir-Bogga-Eddin, Kesbaadji, Onandjiki, Pooloodjistius, Soldjinoha, Tadjiks, Toosidji, Piandjiapan

Donis: Abrustdonis, Helkdonis

Doo: Boordook, Diardookin, Dooczako, Doonyasha, Doosico, Momonodooar

Door: Katoshkihydooraki, Kondoor, Moordoorten, Orthodoxhydooraki, Tandoor

Eę

Ego: Egoaitoorassian, Egokoolnatsnarnian-sensation, Egolionopty, Egoplastikoori, Silëooyegordpana, Trogoautoegocratic

Ehary: Ashagiprotëhary, Defteroëhary, Exioëhary, Piandjoëhary, Protoëhary, Tetartoëhary, Tritoëhary

Ek: Alla Ek Linakh, Disputekrialnian, Ekbarzerbazia, Eknokh, Elekilpomagtistzen, Gynekokhrostiny, mekonine, Mekonoiozine, Mentekithzoin, Oblekioonerish, Olbogmek, Sekronoolanzaknian, Semzekionally, Techgekdnel, Toolookhterzinek, Zehbek

Ekh: Epodrenekhs, Hraprkhabeekhrokhnian, Irankipaekh, Polormedekhtian, Troemedekhfe, Urdekhplifata

El: El Koona Nassa, Elekilpomagtistzen, Elmooarno, Elnapara, HarnelAoot, Harnelmiatznel, Inkiranoodel, instincto-terebelnian, Kanil-ElNorkel, Ksvaznell, Mal-el-Lel, Margelan, Mdnel-in, Mdnel-outian, Menitkel, Techgekdnel, Choon-Tro-Pel, Pirinjiel

F

Fal: Afalkalna, Fal-Fe-Foof, Kefal, Khritofalmonofarab

Farab: Alillonofarab, Krilnomolnifarab, Khritofalmonofarab, Klananoizufarab, Sirioonorifarab, Talkoprafarab

Foo: Fal-Fe-Foof, Foolon, Foos, Ftofoo, Kelli-E-Ofoo, Koorfooristanian, Noorfooftafaf, Zernofookalnian

APPENDIX E: NOTES ON ETYMOLOGY AND NEOLOGISMS

G
Goor: Agoorokhrostiny, Goorban, Toogoortski

H
Ham: Hamilodox, hammams, Hamolinadir, Lentrohamsanin

Han: Ankliazanikshanas, Hanbledzoin, Hanja, Hanziano, Kirmankshana, Saroonoorishan

Harn: Akhaldanharnosovors, Harnahoom, Harnatoolkpararana, Harnel-Aoot, Harnelmiatznel, Kofensharnian, Krishnatkharna

Hood: Amarhoodan, Hoodazbabognari Hoon: Ahoon, Arhoonilo, Dzedzatzshoon, Irodohahoon, Shooshoonian, Soloohnorahoona

Hoor: Harhoory, Keesookesschoor, Rakhoorkh, Sherakhoorian, Shooroomooroomnian

Har: Harahrahroohry, Harhrinhrarh

Hr: Hrahaharhtzaha, Hraprkhabeekhrokhnian, Hre-Hree-Hra, Hrhaharhtzaha, Hrkh-hrhoo, Khrh, Krhrrhihirhi, Krik hrak hri, Rhaharahr

I
Ilo: Arhoonilo, Asoochilon, Hamilodox, Rastropoonilo, Salounilovian

Ink: chinkrooaries, Inkiranoodel, Inkliazanikshanas, Inkozarno, Sinkrpoosarams

Iran: Inkiranoodel, Iranan, Iraniranumange, Irankipaekh, Iransamkeep, Semooniranoos

Ish: Arachiaplnish, Ishias, Ishmetch, Krishnatkharna, Oblekioonerish, Saroonoorishan, Tikliamish, Yagliyemmish, Yenikishlak, Polorishboorda

K
Kai: Kaialana, Kaimon, Ateshkain

Kal: Afalkalna, Aliamizoornakalu, Askalnooazar, Deskaldino, Kalda-zakh-tee, Kalianjesh, Kalkali, Kalkians, Kalman, Kalmanuior, Kalnokranonis, Kaltaan (i), Kaltusara, Kalunom, Kalyan, Kalzanooarnian, Koorkalai, Otkalooparnian, Simkalash, Soorptakalknian, Zernofookalnian

Kar: Karabaghian, Karabakh, Karakoom, Karapet, Karatas, Karatsiag, Kardec, Karnak, karoona, Kartotakhnian, Makar,

Makary Kronbernkzion, Makkar, Ooretstaknilkaroolni, Petrkarmak, Sakronakari

Kas: Devd'el Kascho, Kashiman, Kashireitleer, Kashmanoon, Kasnik, Kasoaadjy

Kana: Tchaikanas, Kmalkanatonashachermacher, Amersamarskanapa

Kat: Katarnine, Katoshkihydooraki, Hydrokatarnine, Zalnakatar

Kaz: kazi, Kaznookizkernian, Ookazemotra

Kee: Keesookesschoor, Keeziak

Ker: Kaznookizkernian, Kerbalai-Azis-Nuaran, Keria-chi, Kerkoolnonarnian

Kes: Keesookesschoor, Kesbaadji, Keschapmartnian, Kesdjan, Keskestasantnian, Kesshah

Khai: Khaivansanansaks, Khaivatine, Khaizarian

Kil: Elekilpomagtistzen, Kilmantooshian, Kilpreno, Choon-Kil-Tez

Kim: Anoroparionikima, Kimespai

Kir: Kirkistcheri, Kirmankshana, Kirmininasha, paischakir, Poisonioonoskirian, Surp-Skiros

Kol: Autokolizikners, Etzikolnianakhnian, Iskoloonizinernly, Kolbana, Kolenian, Kolhidious, Kolhidshissi, Korkolans, Oskolnikoo, Kolotine

Kon: Kondoor, Konuzion, mekonine, Mekonoiozine

Koor: Egoplastikoori, Koorfooristanian, Koorkalai, Sakoor, Saliakooriap, Saliakooriapa, Saliakooriapnian, Zernakoor

Kor: Koritesnokhnian, Korkaptilnian, Korkolans Kril: Etherokrilno, Ikriltazkakra, Krilnomolnifarab

Kron: Kronbernkzion, Kronbookhon, Sakronakari, Sekronoolanzaknian

Kshe: Davlaksherian, Ksheltarna, Ksherknara

L

Lad: Anklad, kladtzacht, Podkoolad

Lak: Balakhanira, Davlaksherian, Yenikishlak

Appendix E: Notes On Etymology And Neologisms

Lin: Alla Ek Linakh, Aniline, Anoklinism, Avazlin, Bartholinian, Hamolinadir, Klintrana, Kundalina, Mamzolin, Sirkliniamen, Unter den Linden

Lono: Aklonoatistitchian, Alillonofarab, Koilononine

Loon: Loonderperzo, Loonias, Tookloonian, Iskoloonizinernly

Loos: Amarloos, Loosochepana

M

Mak: Makar, Makary Kronbernkzion, Makhokh, Makhokhitchne, Makkar, Petrkarmak, Makanidine

Mal: Mal-el-Lel, Malmanash, Rimala, Teleokrimalnichnian, Theomertmalogos Mam: Mamzolin, Amambakhlootr

Maral: Kezmaral, Pirmaral, Maralpleicie

Mart: Keschapmartnian, Martaadamlik, Martfotai, Martna

Men: Amenzano, Barmen, Kishmenhof, Knaneomeny, Mendelejeff, Menitkel, Mentekithzoin, Sirkliniamen

Mono: Momonodooar, Monoenithits, Samonoltooriko, Khritofalmonofarab

Moor: Moordoorten, Shooroomooroomnian

N

Nak: Alla Ek Linakh Aliamizoornakalu, Atarnakh, Champarnakh, Chiltoonakh, Dezonakooasanz, Etzikolnianakhnian, Hellenaki, Karnak, Latinaki, Ornakres, Sakronakari, Zalnakatar, Zernakoor

Nal: Krentonalnian, Naloo-osnian, Semzekionally, Skernalitsionniks, Sooptaninalnian, Spipsychoonalian, Ternoonald, Tookha Tes Nalool Pan

Nam: Dynamoumzoin, Hasnamuss, Nammus, Nammuslik, Sianoorinam Nir: Semooniranoos, Nirioonossian, Balakhanira

Nokh: Alnokhoorian, Djamtesternokhi, Eknokh, Heptaparaparshinokh, Koritesnokhnian, Lav-Merz-Nokh, Nokhan, Okidanokh, Olooessultratesnokhnian, Olooestesnokhnian, Pandetznokh, Prnokhpaioch

Nol: Gasometronoltooriko, Nolniolnian, Sakookinoltooriko, Samonoltooriko, Sobrionolian, Svolibroonolnian, Tainolair

Noora: Blagonoorarirnian, Erti-Noora-Chaka, Issi-Noora, KhootiNoora-Chaka, Nar-Khra-Noora, Ori-Noora-Chaka, Sami-

To Fathom The Gist: Vol I

NooraChakoo, Shvidi-Noora-Chakoo, Taranooranura Teleoghinooras

O

Okht: Okhtapanatsakhnian, Okhtatralnian, Okhterordiapan, OkhtiPikan-On, Okhti-Noora-Chaka, Toolookhterzinek

Oki: Askokin, Bliss-stokirno, Diardookin, Kaznookizkernian, Okiartaaitokhsa, Okidanokh, Okina, Okipkhalevnian, Sakookinoltooriko, Tokitozine

Ol: Olbogmek, Olmantaboor, Olooessultratesnokhnian, Olooestesnokhnian, Olooestesnokhnian, Oskolnikoo, Pestolnootiarly, Poundolero, Sakookinoltooriko, Samonoltooriko, Sekronoolanzaknian, Sinokooloopianian, Sobrionolian, Svolibroonolnian

Osk: Gnoskopine. Oskiano, Oskianotsner, Oskianotznel, Oskolnikoo, Poisonioonoskirian

P

Pal: Ansapalnian, Djamdjampal, Djoolfapal, Insapalnian, palnassoorian, Transapalnian

Pan: Aksharpanziar, Alla-attapan, Chorortdiapan, Erkrordiapan, Erordiapan, Hentralispana, Hooltanpanas, Loosochepana, Okhtapanatsakhnian, Okhterordiapan, Pandetznokh, Pantemeasurability, Piandjiapan, Silnooyegordpana, Tookha Tes Nalool Pan, Vetserordiapan

Pana: Hentralispana, Hooltanpanas, Loosochepana, Okhtapanatsakhnian, Silnooyegordpana

Par: Anoroparionikima, Assooparatsata, Champarnakh, Elnapara, Harnatoolkpararana, Heptaparaparshinokh, Hikhdjnapar, IInosoparno, Otkalooparnian, Parijrahatnatioose, Parsis, Paramorphine, Microparaine

Per: Androperasty, Loonderperzo, Pera, Perambarrsasidaan, Plef-PerfNoof

Pian: Piandjoehary, Pianje, Piandjiapan, Opianine, Sinokooloopianian

Pikan: Epsi-Pikan-On, Erti-Pikan-On, Khooti-Pikan-On, OkhtiPikan-On, Ori-Pikan-On, Sami-Pikan-On, Shvidi-Pikan-On

Polor: Polorotheoparl, Polormedekhtian, Polorishboorda

Appendix E: Notes On Etymology And Neologisms

Poo: Akhaldangezpoodjnisovors, Alnepoosian, Gaidoropoolo, Pooloodjistius, Rastropoonilo, Sinkrpoosarams, Toospooshokh, Zapoopoonchik

Proto: Ashagiprotoehary, Protocosmos, Protoehary, Protoplasts, Protopine

S

Sak: Demisakhsakhsa, Impulsakri, Khaivansanansaks, Okhtapanatsakhnian, Sakaki, Sakookinoltooriko, Sakoor, Sakronakari, Sakrooalnian, Sakroopiaks, Terasakhaboora

Sal: Salzmanino, Salounilovian, Salnichizinooarnian, Salkamourskian, Saliakooriap, saliakooriapa, Saliakooriapnian

Sel: Selchans, Selneh-eh-Avaz, Selnoano, Selos, Selzelnualno

Sem: Semooniranoos, Semzekionally

Shar: Aksharpanziar, Kofensharnian,

Sikra: Adashsikra, Evosikra, Cevorksikra, Midosikra, Maikosikra, Lookosikra, Soniasikra

Sim: Sensimiriniko, Similnisirnian, Simkalash

Sin: Ephrosinia, Isklolunitsinernly, Ooamonvanosinian, Stumpsinschmausen, Sincratorza, Sinkrpoosarams, Sinndraga, Sinokooloopianian, Sinonoums, Sinooa

Sol: Isoliazsokhlanness, Solianka, Soldjinoha, Solioonensius, Solni, Soloohnorahoona

Sul: Mosulopolis, Moyasul, Olooessultratesnokhnian, Resulzarion

Surp: Surp-Athanotos, Surp-Otheos, Surp-Skiros

T

Tan: Algamatant, Adashtanas, Hooltanpanas Koorfooristanian, Lookotanas, Maikitanis, Midotanis, Sonitanis, Tanguori, Sooptaninalnian, Tchaftantouri, Vibroechonitanko

Teleo: Teleoghinooras, Teleokrimalnichnian

Ter: Djamtesternokhi, Heteratogetar, Terasakhaboora, Terbelnian, Terebelnian, Ternoonald, Toolookhterzinek, Unter den Linden, Dephteropine Tetarto: Tetartocosmoses, Tetartoehary

Tik: Tikliamish, Tiklunia, Tiktoutine

Tir: Tirdiank, Tiriakrkomnian, Tirzikiano

Tok: Itoklanoz, Okiartaaitokhsa, Tokitozine

Too: Alstoozori, Hertoonano, Kilmantooshian, King-Too-Toz, Leitoochanbros, Spetsitooalitivian, Toof-Nef-Tef, Toogoortski, Tooilan, Took-soo-kef, Tookha Tes Nalool Pan, Tookloonian, Toolkhtotino, Tooloof, Toolookhterzinek, Toorinoorino, Toosidji, Toosook, Toosooly, Toospooshokh, Toosy

Toon: Chiltoonakh, Hertoonano, Tastartoonarian

Toor: Again-Tarnotoltoor, Aiessirittoorassnian, Alnatoorornian, Armanatoora, Egoaitoorassian, Essoaieritoorassnian, Gasometronoltooriko, Sakookinoltooriko, Samonoltooriko, SooansToorabizo, Toorinoorino

Tri: Geneotriamazikamnian, Sitrik, Triakrkomnian, Triamazikamno, Trioshka, Tritocosmos, Tritoehary

Z

Zern: Zernakoor, Zernofookalnian Zoin: Astroluolucizoin, Dynamoumzoin, Hanbledzoin, Mentekithzoin, Photoinzoin

Appendix F: Notes On Intentional Inexactitudes

We take the view that every anomaly of any kind in *The Tales* is an intentional inexactitude deliberately created by Gurdjieff to attract our attention that we might ponder its meaning.

For example, the assertion on the first page of Beelzebub's Tales that there are ten books in three series, when clearly there are not. There are many such inexactitudes which must clearly be intentional.

There are some anomalies that may simply be typographical errors. We pointed out all those we have noticed in Chapter 7, but there may be others.

We are not aware of any books that focus specifically on this topic, but it is referred to, en passant, in *Commentaries on G. I. Gurdjieff's All and Everything: Beelzebub's Tales to His Grandson*, by A. Orage and edited by C. S. Nott, and *The Teachings of Gurdjieff*, by C. S. Nott.

Appendix G: Notes On Allegorical Meaning

It is our view that, to fathom the gist of *The Tales*, the reader needs to experience the meaning of the allegories that the book embodies. The intellect can assist in preparing for that experience. That is its contribution, and it is an important one. Nevertheless, ultimately it is the emotional side of the reader that experiences the meaning of the allegories and may, at times, be brought to tears by it.

Gurdjieff uses many words in a metaphorical way. We believe it will help the reader if they make a list of words that seem to have or clearly do have an allegorical meaning. We have provided a short list of such words: Sun, Planet, Mars, Saturn, Two-brained being, One-brained being, Transapalnian perturbation, Ship, Opium, Alcohol, Desert, Mountain, Ape and Woman. There are many more.

Easily the most important book that touches on the allegorical nature of *The Tales* is:

- *Commentaries on G. I. Gurdjieff's All and Everything: Beelzebub's Tales to His Grandson*, by A. Orage and edited by C. S. Nott. *The Teachings of Gurdjieff*, by C. S. Nott also contains Orage's commentaries.

We believe it is important for readers of *The Tales* to have an understanding of the allegorical meaning of *The New Testament*. For this we can recommend the following two books:

- *The New Man,* by Maurice Nicoll
- *The Mark,* by Maurice Nicoll

Readers of *The Tales* may also profit from studying the allegorical meanings of Shakespeare's plays. For this we can recommend the following book:

- *In The East My Pleasure Lies,* by Beryl Pogson

There are several other books that deal with *The Tales* directly, which may have value for some readers. They are:

- *The Enneagram in the Writings of Gurdjieff,* by Richard J. Defouw. This approaches the meaning of *The Tales* from the perspective of the enneagram.

- *Gurdjieff, Astrology and Beelzebub's Tales,* by Sophia Wellbeloved. This approaches the meaning of *The Tales* from the perspective of astrology.
- *Gurdjieff and the Arch-Preposterous – An Hermetic Descent Into The Mind,* by Joy Lonsdale. This approaches the meaning of *The Tales* from the perspective of Hermeticism.
- *Talks on Beelzebub's Tales,* by John G. Bennett. This offers a general discussion on aspects of *The Tales*.

To Fathom The Gist: Vol I

Bibliography

This is the full list of books consulted by the author in producing this book:

- *Talks on Beelzebub's Tales,* by John G. Bennett
- *Gurdjieff: Making A New World,* by John G. Bennett
- *Idiots in Paris: Diaries of J. G. Bennett and Elizabeth Bennett, 1949,* by John G. and Elizabeth Bennett
- *Perspectives on Beelzebub's Tales,* by Keith A. Buzzell
- *Explorations in Active Mentation,* by Keith A. Buzzell
- *Man, A Three Brained Being,* by Keith A. Buzzell
- *Gurdjieff's Whim,* by Keith A. Buzzell
- *The Theory of Celestial Influence,* by Rodney Collin
- *Our Life with Mr. Gurdjieff,* by Thomas and Olga de Hartmann
- *The Reality of Being: The Fourth Way of Gurdjieff,* by Jeanne de Salzmann
- *Beelzebub's Tales to His Grandson: All and Everything: 1st Series,* by G. I. Gurdjieff
- *Life Is Real Only Then, When 'I Am',* by G. I. Gurdjieff
- *Meetings with Remarkable Men,* by G. I. Gurdjieff
- *The Herald of Coming Good,* by G. I. Gurdjieff
- *Transcripts of Gurdjieff's Meetings: 1941-1946,* published by Book Studio, London
- *Views from the Real World: Early Talks,* by G. I. Gurdjieff
- *Diary of Madam Egout Pour Sweet,* by Rina Hands
- *A Beginner's View of Our Electric Universe* by Tom Findlay
- *The Electric Universe* by Wallace Thornhill and David Talbott
- *The Electric Sky* by Donald E. Scott
- *Thunderbolts of the Gods* by David Talbott and Wallace Thornhill
- *Beyond the Big Bang,* by Paul A. La Violette
- *Gurdjieff and the Arch-Preposterous – An Hermetic Descent into the Mind,* by Joy Lonsdale
- *The New Man,* by Maurice Nicoll

To Fathom The Gist: Vol I

- *The Mark,* by Maurice Nicoll
- *The Teachings of Gurdjieff,* by C. S. Nott
- *Further Teachings of Gurdjieff: Journey Through This World,* by C. S. Nott
- *A. R. Orage's commentaries on G. I. Gurdjieff's All and Everything: Beelzebub's Tales to His Grandson,* by A. Orage and edited by C. S. Nott
- *Index and Study Guide,* by Willem Nyland
- *In Search of the Miraculous,* by Peter Ouspensky
- *In The East My Pleasure Lies,* by Beryl Pogson
- *Cosmic Secrets,* by Russell Smith
- *Memories of Gurdjieff,* by A. L. Staveley
- *Mister Gurdjieff's Hapax Legomena,* by Nicolas Tereschenko
- *Guide and Index to G. I. Gurdjieff's Beelzebub's Tales to His Grandson,* edited by Louise Welch and published by Traditional Studies Press in Toronto.
- *Gurdjieff, Astrology and Beelzebub's Tales,* by Sophia Wellbeloved

The only publicly available books we have found useful in our effort to identify the meaning of Gurdjieff's neologisms are:

- *Guide and Index to G. I. Gurdjieff's Beelzebub's Tales to His Grandson,* edited by Louise Welch and published by Traditional Studies Press in Toronto
- *Mister Gurdjieff's Hapax Legomena,* by Nicolas Tereschenko

Author's Autobiographical Notes

Robin Bloor was born in 1951 in Liverpool, UK. He obtained a BSc in Mathematics at Nottingham University and took up a career in the computer industry, initially writing software. From 1989 onwards, he became a technology analyst and consultant. He has thus been a writer of a kind ever since. In 2002, he was awarded an honorary Ph.D. in Computer Science by Wolverhampton University in the UK. He currently resides in and works from Austin, Texas in the USA.

In 1988, after drifting through several work groups, Bloor met and became a pupil of Rina Hands. Rina was a one-time associate of J. G. Bennett, a student of Peter Ouspensky's, and later, a pupil of George Gurdjieff. Following Gurdjieff's death, she remained part of J. G. Bennett's group for a while. Subsequently, she formed groups both in London, where she lived, and in Bradford in the North of England – initially in conjunction with Madame Nott. She was both an accomplished movements teacher and an inspirational group leader. She died in 1994 and is buried next to Jane Heap in a cemetery in North London.

The author acknowledges the following individuals, who – whether they realize it or not – were of assistance in writing and publishing this book, and to whom he is grateful: Rina Hands, Jim Foster, Paul Beekman Taylor, Derek Sinko, Clare Mingins, Paula Schmidt, Stephen Aronson, Harry Bennett, Ron Jennings, Mark Thomasson, Marcel Lopez, and Judith Ryser.

www.ingramcontent.com/pod-product-compliance
Lightning Source LLC
Chambersburg PA
CBHW032335300426
44109CB00041B/926